The Seven Swabians, and Other German Folktales

World Folklore Advisory Board

The Seven Swabians, and Other German Folktales

Anna E. Altmann

World Folklore Series

LIBRARIES

U N L I M I T E D

A Member of the Greenwood Publishing Group

Westport, Connecticut • London

Library of Congress Cataloging-in-Publication Data

Altmann, Anna E.
    The seven Swabians, and other German folktales / by Anna E. Altmann.
        p. cm. — (World folklore series)
    Includes bibliographical references and index.
    ISBN 1-56308-967-X (alk. paper)
    1. Tales—Germany. 2. Fairy tales—Germany. I. Title. II. Series.
    GR166.A58   2006
    398.20943—dc22   2005028601

British Library Cataloguing in Publication Data is available.

Library of Congress Catalog Card Number: 2005028601
ISBN: 1-56308-967-X

First published in 2006

Libraries Unlimited, 88 Post Road West, Westport, CT 06881
A Member of the Greenwood Publishing Group, Inc.
www.lu.com

Printed in the United States of America

The paper used in this book complies with the
Permanent Paper Standard issued by the National
Information Standards Organization (Z39.48–1984).

10   9   8   7   6   5   4   3   2   1

The publisher has done its best to make sure the instructions
and/or recipes in this book are correct. However, users should
apply judgment and experience when preparing recipes, especially
parents and teachers working with young people. The publisher
accepts no responsibility for the outcome of any recipe included in this volume.

For David, himself a tale spinner and story weaver,
who said I should and knew I would.

And for my family's children, who have enriched my life
and are the future: Danny, Steve, Justin, Leo, Amos,
Talia, Neil, Theo, Jackson, Lucas, and Mika.

Contents

Zaubermärchen (*Fairy Tales*)

Sagen (*Local Legends*)

Acknowledgments

My thanks go first to Barbara Ittner of Libraries Unlimited for giving me the opportunity to write this book and for her guidance and patience. The University of Alberta helped the work with a travel grant and a sabbatical leave, and the University of Alberta Libraries provided astonishing riches by way of source materials: a good research library is a joy forever! Artur Bohnet told me the story of the Brezel and led me to www.ingeb.org, a Web site of German folksongs. Heiko Schlieper, iconographer and Renaissance man, drew the black-and-white title pages for the four sections of stories in nineteenth-century German style and the most delightful of the decorative vignettes. My friend Karen Braun answered many questions about spinning and weaving and let me take photographs of the tools of her craft.

My family contributed generously to this book. Hans and Birgit Welcker showed us their Kannbruch Revier and allowed us to take pictures of Gebrauchsjäger in an ancient forest. Elisabeth and Klaus Schöning gave us hospitality, laughter, photographs, recipes, and the *Erinnerungen* of my great-grandfather Rudolph Welcker. My mother, Anne Welcker Altmann, and my father of beloved memory, Hans Altmann, gave me the traditions from which this book is drawn. My mother also contributed recipes, proverbs, and advice. My deepest gratitude goes to my husband, David Goa, for his scholarship and knowledge of folk tradition, for his unfailing interest in and support for this project, for his confidence that I could do it and do it well, for taking most of the photographs for the book and documenting them magnificently, and for his fearless driving on the Autobahn!

Introduction

When I was a child, my mother told us folktales whenever one of us was sick. They were stories from the Grimms's *Kinder- und Hausmärchen* and, although we had brought a copy of that collection with us when we emigrated to Canada from Germany, the stories were always told, never read, and always in German. The Seven Swabians, Rapunzel, Snow White, Cinderella, Rumpelstiltskin, Briar Rose, Hans in Luck, and the Hare and the Hedgehog were early familiars of mine in the world of enchantment offered by fictional narrative. They belonged to the landscape we had left not only because their language was German, but also because my grandmother in Lübeck kept two spinning wheels in the attic, where round apple slices and mushrooms were hung to dry, and fed hens in a green garden enclosed by rosy brick walls that might have belonged to the sorceress who took Rapunzel. And my grandfather and uncles were huntsmen, with green hats and long boots, who brought rabbits, wild boar, and venison home for dinner. My father, who brought us and the stories to a different, emptier country, embodied the truth of the tales for me. Like many a fairy-tale hero, he was the youngest of three sons and set out penniless to meet adventure with blithe courage and a generous heart, always ready to share what little he had, always open to wonder and good fortune. And he was a storyteller, too. He could make you believe that he had been the emperor of China's shoe polisher unless you noticed that his nose was twitching.

When I was ten or eleven years old, I discovered that there were other versions of these tales. I spent a week at a United Church camp, and after lights-out in our cabin, I told the story of Cinderella as my contribution to the mildly illicit entertainment. My bunkmates were enthralled. They all knew the story, of course, but had never heard about the tree on Cinderella's mother's grave, the stepsisters cutting off their heel or toe, the blood in the shoe, the doves pecking out the stepsisters' eyes at the wedding. I became a minor celebrity for the week, and every night told another of the grim/Grimm tales. With childish chauvinism I assumed I had the real, original stories and that they were better than the watered-down, prettied-up Disney versions my friends knew. In a sense I was right. German folktales are more robust and earthy than the North American versions, more folk-like, because the hugely influential nineteenth-century German collections were made by scholars and writers who were pioneers in the study of folklore.

The German Folktale Tradition

In the countries of western Europe, folktales have been in print since Gutenberg invented moveable type. We're inclined to think of oral traditions as clearly divided from literary traditions, but in Italy, England, France, and Germany, oral narrative traditions and literature coexisted in a state of symbiosis from the beginning of the sixteenth century. Printers published anonymous poems, songs, and stories from the oral tradition in small, inexpensive chapbooks that circulated widely, and wherever they were read the stories were undoubtedly told again. Writers retold folktales in collections of stories such as Giovan Francesco Straparola's *The Pleasant Nights,* published in 1550, Giambattista Basile's *Pentamerone,* published in 1634, and Charles Perrault's *Histoires, ou contes du temps passé* published in 1697. When the published versions were memorable, as these three collections were, they made their way back into the oral tradition, not only in their countries of origin but all across Europe, including Germany. *The 1001 Nights* were translated from a fourteenth-century Arabic manuscript into French and published in ten volumes between the years 1704 and 1717, and they, too, became part of the European folk tradition.

In Germany the *Volksbuch* (folk book), traceable first in fifteenth-century manuscripts and from the beginning of the sixteenth century in print, bridged the oral and literary traditions. Published for a broad audience, *Volksbücher* were made up of epic verse, courtly prose romances, *chansons de geste*, saints' legends, literary story cycles like that of Till Eulenspiegel (ca. 1510), and collections of stories from the oral tradition, like the legends about Dr. Faustus (1587). Some of the literary inventions such as the Till Eulenspiegel cycle were taken into the oral tradition and flourished there, and some of the stories from the oral tradition became the basis of major literary works like Christopher Marlowe's *Tragical History of Dr. Faustus* (1605) and Goethe's *Faust* (begun in 1773).

There is a notion that true folktales must be free of literary influence. This notion is reinforced by the use of the word "contamination" as a technical folklore term for mixing sources. But that sort of purity could be expected only in entirely aliterate and extremely isolated societies. Nor can folk traditions be culturally pure, except in isolation. Certainly in the European countries folktales have traveled back and forth across linguistic and national borders. Variants of a tale can be identified as German, or Russian, or French, or English, but seldom the tale itself. The durability of folk traditions is based on memorability, not on purity. Regardless of sources, if a story is remembered and told often enough, it becomes a traditional tale.

The study of folklore began with field research into German folksongs and folktales early in the nineteenth century. The Romantic movement, with its focus on medievalism and nature as antidotes to the rationalism of the Enlightenment, looked to folk traditions to find the truly German roots of German culture. Jakob and Wilhelm Grimm were among the first scholars to record, compile, and publish German folktales. They were part of a network of collectors, professional and amateur, all consciously engaged in the same task. The first edition of the Grimms's *Kinder- und Hausmärchen* (Children's and Household Tales) was published in 1812–14. It contained 156 stories. A second edition, enlarged and revised, with 177 stories came out in 1819, and a collection of fifty stories selected for children from the second edition was published in 1825, the *Kleine Ausgabe* (Small Edition). Further full editions, each extended and revised primarily by Wilhelm Grimm, came out in 1837, 1840, 1843, 1850, and finally in 1857. The 1857 edition is the one always referred to as the complete edition of the *Kinder- und Hausmärchen* (KHM). It contains 210 tales: 200 *Märchen*, commonly called fairy tales in English, and a section of ten separately numbered *Kinderlegenden,* children's legends, which are largely unknown in popular culture today.

Over time the 1857 edition of the KHM became and still is the definitive collection of German folktales, but the Grimms had a rough start. The first volume of the first edition (1812) met with severe criticism, and most of the print run of the second volume (1814) remained unsold when the second edition was published in 1819. The criticism focused on two points: first, that the selection and narrative tone of the stories made them unsuitable for children; and second, that the narrative style was insufficiently literary. The fact that the Grimms explicitly intended to publish stories recorded from the oral tradition in a style as close to an oral telling style as possible and that their work was intended primarily for other scholars was apparently not taken into account. The KHM only became popular with the publication of the *Kleine Ausgabe* for children in 1825. (This selection of fifty stories went through ten editions between 1825 and 1858.)

Since the 1980s the Grimms have been attacked by some literary critics for exactly the opposite reasons. These critics basically accuse the Brothers Grimm of deliberately perpetrating a fraud when they claimed to be publishing in something close to their original form folktales collected from the oral tradition. When the rediscovery of the Grimms's manuscript notes from 1810 revealed that their most important informants were not simple peasants but two or three well-educated middle-class women, the critics, particularly U.S. academics, took serious umbrage. They did not stop to consider from whom these women learned the stories and whether they might not have collected them from servants and other sources that would count as "folk" in order to pass them on to the Grimms (Rölleke, *Die Märchen,* p. 84). They also point to all the editing the Grimms, particularly Wilhelm, did from the manuscript notes to the first edition and then in the succeeding editions. These revisions, claim the critics, changed the folktales into literary stories consciously shaped for children by a patriarchal nineteenth-century bourgeois ideology. There is some truth in these accusations, but they should not be accepted entirely and without question. The analysis these critics make is itself obviously driven by an ideological program. And the Grimms were a good deal more conscious of the difficulties inherent in the task they had set for themselves than their accusers would have us believe. In 1812 Jakob Grimm wrote to his colleague Achim von Arnim that to reproduce an oral tale in print without falsifying is as impossible as breaking an egg without having egg white stick to the shell (Rölleke, *Die Märchen,* p. 55). It is in the nature of folktale to be filtered. Only secular literalists, never having experienced the vitality of telling and retelling in a traditional culture, could imagine that there is a pure or neutral telling of a folktale that is the genuine version.

In any case, for the purpose of this book it doesn't actually matter whether the Grimms got hold of and published genuine German folktales from oral sources or not. Their tales *are* the German folktales now. The Grimm versions moved back into the oral *Märchen* tradition, capturing it almost entirely, and if you ask Germans about folktales today, they will say, "Ah, yes, the Brothers Grimm."

The effect of the KHM outside of Germany has been enormous. Selections were translated into Danish in 1816, Dutch in 1820, and English in 1826—and that was only the beginning. According to the article on the KHM in the *Enzyklopädie des Märchens*, the Grimms's collection has influenced, and in some cased even superseded, the native folktale traditions in a hundred languages (Rölleke, "Kinder- und Hausmärchen"). Within Germany, the KHM became the definitive collection of German folktales. There certainly were other collectors of German folktales who published their work at roughly the same time as the Grimms and into the early twentieth century. The most widely known of them, Ludwig Bechstein, was actually more popular than the Grimms until the 1890s. His complete works as well as selections of his fairy tales published as children's books are still in print. I expected to use Bechstein as one of my major sources, but when I compared the Bechstein version of a tale with the Grimm version, the Grimm version was always simpler and more memorable. Bechstein's stories are extremely literary in style, full of ornamentation and details. He borrowed many of his stories from the Grimms's collection but introduced changes that suited educated, middle-class readers of his time: he added irony, caricature, and satire; he took out the wicked stepmothers; the good mothers survived; and families were reunited. The result was that his tales lost the memorable quality of folktales and were tied down to a particular time and place. "[Wilhelm] Grimm, on the other hand, smoothed his fairy tales' vocabulary until it achieved a transcendent timelessness" ("Bechstein," p. 49). Other collections made by German folklorists are primarily of historical or scholarly interest now. The Grimms alone seized the popular imagination to the point where their stories have given rise to a huge body of adaptations, parodies, quotations, and allusions.

The KHM is the definitive collection of German folktales, both inside Germany and in other countries, for good reason: Wilhelm Grimm was a better storyteller than any of the others, a storyteller of genius. But the unparalleled influence of the KHM also owes something to timing. The Industrial Revolution, which hit Germany around 1840, brought about rapid changes in the structure of the family, in the ways in which people earned their livings, and in lifestyle. At the same time, the introduction of universal education resulted in widespread literacy. Taken together, these changes deprived the oral folktale tradition of its place in the life of the community. The development of the nuclear family, the disappearance of the workshops of master craftsmen, and the increasing availability of newspapers and books in even modest households reduced both the opportunity and the need for storytelling. By the turn of the century, the places and times for storytelling had almost disappeared (Rölleke, *Die Märchen*, p. 24). But the KHM made the familiar folktales available in print, so that they did not disappear from memory. Parents could read them to their children. And the Grimms's versions of the tales were so memorable that those children never forgot them, read them to their children in turn, and were able to tell them even when the book wasn't handy.

Folktale Genres

The word *Märchen* is a catchall term that includes magic tales, animal stories, and comic stories. It is a diminutive of the old word *Mär*, meaning "news" or "story," and has been in use since the fifteenth century for little stories, often in verse form. Its present meaning was essentially established by the use of the word by the Brothers Grimm. The Grimms drew a distinction between *Märchen*, roughly the equivalent of the English term "fairy tales" in its broadest sense, and *Sagen*, or local legends. They put together a collection of *Sagen* themselves, *Deutsche Sagen*, published in 1816–18, and in their introduction they characterized the fairy tale (*Märchen*) as more poetic, and the legend as more historical. The fairy tale is grounded only in itself, complete in its perfection. The legend is less developed as a story, but it is special because it is always attached to something familiar, something known, such as a place, a landscape, or a name from history. In the preface to the second edition of his *Deutsche Mythologie*, published in 1844, Jakob Grimm wrote that while the fairy tale flies, the legend walks and knocks at your door. Because of the nature of legends, the Grimms's *Deutsche Sagen* never became as definitive as the KHM, and it wasn't translated into English until 1981, but it is frequently cited as a source in the twentieth-century collections of German legends on which I drew.

I have divided the folktales in this book into four genres: the *Tiergeschichten*, or animal stories; the *Schwänke*, or comic stories; the *Zaubermärchen*, or magic tales; and the *Sagen*, or local legends.

The *Tiergeschichten,* animal stories, have no magic in them. The fact that the animals talk and behave like people doesn't count as magic. Animal stories make up the smallest group of folktales and have usually been told as children's stories (Dégh, p. 68). We tend to think of animal stories as didactic tales with explicit morals, like the literary Aesop's fables. But within the folk tradition, many stories with animals as the principal characters have entertainment as their primary purpose. The animals in "The Bremen Town Musicians" have all been betrayed by their human owners, but that is just the initial motivating situation: the story doesn't teach kindness to animals. Absurdity is the point of "The Kinglet and the Bear." In "A Cat and a Mouse Keep House," greed goes unpunished. And to suggest that "The Wolf and the Seven Little Kids" is a moral tale would be a real stretch. Often an animal story is just a good story.

Schwänke are funny stories without magic or fantastic motifs. They are didactic in the sense that they exploit human stupidity or bad conduct as the source of their humor. "The target of the *Schwank* is human frailty" (Dégh, p. 70). All categories leak, and there are some humorous fairy tales that I was inclined to put in with the *Schwänke* rather than the *Zaubermärchen.* For example, "The Brave Little Tailor" would be a *Schwank* if it weren't for the giants and the unicorn in it, and the only fantastical or magic elements in the "The Three Spinners" are the extraordinary physical features of the three old women and their ability to spin faster than any human could. But I decided to stick with "no magic" as the second criterion.

Zaubermärchen, fairy tales with magic in them, are the fairy tales proper. All the classic fairy tales belong to this genre, but it also includes many that are not widely known. Many of them are tragic except for the happy ending, but some are very funny. I've included two fairy tales that are related to legends in the *Sagen* section: "Frau Holle" has the same title for both the fairy tale and the legend, and the fairy tale called "The Shoemaker and the Elves" has a link with two short legends under the title "The Elves." If you compare the fairy tales with the legends, the difference between the two genres is made reasonably clear. There is one folktale always placed with *Zaubermärchen* that doesn't actually fit the definition: the story of the little girl with the red cap or hood and the wicked wolf ("Little Red Cap," or "Little Red Ridinghood"). There is no magic in it, but, for reasons no one has been able to explain, it has such a strong affinity with the fairy tales proper that it is always included with them.

Sagen, local legends, speak of one's own world, the end of the garden, the wood across the way, the familiar stream, the bridge on the way to town, as an enchanted world. The enchantment is in the familiar rather than in the strange and exotic. It makes the back of your neck prickle because it lives right next to you. Legends are told to be believed, even when they deal with the uncanny, and especially when they deal with local history. There are a few legends in the KHM, and

I've included three of them in the *Sagen* chapter. I've also put the two *Kinderlegenden* I chose from the KHM here. But most of the stories in this section come from sources other than the Grimms.

Finally, there is a very small genre called the *Vexiermärchen*, the folktale intended to vex. I've used *Vexiermärchen* as the Opening Tale and the Closing Tale to bracket the story sections of the book. My Opening Tale, "The Golden Key," was always number 200 in the KHM, the last *Märchen* before the ten *Kinderlegenden* at the end, the Grimms's point being that no story is ever really over. The opening of the treasure box seems to me a very suitable metaphor for the beginning of a collection of tales. My Closing Tale, "The Narrow Bridge," from a source other than the KHM, suggests that there are many more stories outside the covers of this book.

The Selection of Stories

The purpose of this book is to bring together in one convenient volume a representative collection of German folktales and to place them in their cultural context. I've chosen "The Seven Swabians" as the title story to reflect that purpose. Because it names a particular region in Germany, the title locates this collection geographically. And because the tale is a *Schwank* rather than one of the more familiar *Zaubermärchen*—and almost unknown in English, although it is a classic in Germany—it suggests that this collection offers something new.

Because the Brothers Grimm had such international success, there is no shortage of stories from the KHM in English. There are two English translations of the complete KHM currently in print. They are both very thick volumes: the Manheim translation is 656 pages long, and the Zipes translation runs to 784 pages. There are also retellings of some of the most popular Grimms's tales as picture books or in small collections. However, I have not come across a collection in English that contains examples of the full range of German folktales. This book is intended to fill that gap. Like the other volumes in the World Folklore series, it offers stories for readers of all ages and is meant for the use of storytellers, librarians, and teachers as well as for children, teenagers, and adults who are reading for their own pleasure.

Because this book is intended to be a representative collection of German folktales, I have chosen stories from the four main genres defined earlier and looked for variety within each genre.

The *Zaubermärchen* section is by far the longest because there are more memorable fairy tales than there are animal stories, legends, or comic tales. I have included many of the most popular stories, and some of the ones that are less well know or almost unknown. There are long stories, stories of medium length, and some very short ones. I made a point of choosing stories that have strong female characters either as heroes or as helpers. (For example, the gormless Snow White is balanced out by Aschenputtel, the Goose Girl, and the nameless heroine of "Spindle, Shuttle, and Needle" who have magic of their own and use it.) And certainly my selection was guided by my memory of the tales I loved as a child.

The *Zaubermärchen* section begins with "Hansel and Gretel" because this is generally held to be the most German of fairy tales. "Aschenputtel" comes next because it is the German variant of the most famous of all fairy tales. "The Fisherman and His Wife" is a wonderful story, but I've included it for another reason as well: the Grimms considered it a model of what a folktale should be. It was recorded by Otto Runge, a well-known painter, who heard it in Pomerania and wrote it down in Plattdeutsch, Low German, as it had been told to him. "Rumpelstiltskin" has to be included as the most famous spinning story of them all, and "The Three Spinners" follows it as counterpoint. The Grimms gave "Starsilver" special significance by making it the last story in their selection of stories for children, the *Kleine Ausgabe,* and it has always been one of my favorites, so it is the last story in the fairy-tale section.

One of my considerations in choosing legends was to represent many different regions of Germany. Germany was the last of the western European nations to take shape. The many principalities and kingdoms and free cities making up the territory that was culturally German didn't come together under an effective federal government until 1871, and some of that territory is now part of other nations. So Bohemia, now in the Czech Republic, and parts of Austria, Poland, and Italy, are all represented. The geographic source is given at the end of each legend, in the German form. (I have no location for four of the stories.) Hamburg and Lübeck, which as free cities are independent states in themselves and owed allegiance only to the Holy Roman Emperor, are named independently, not as part of the region in which they are located. Hitler and Mussolini are there as a reminder that legends spring up in modern times, too.

In our secular age readers may be surprised to find four religious legends here. "The Twelve Apostles," "The Little Old Woman," and "The Two Mothers" are Christian, and "The Golem" is a Jewish legend. There are also a few stories with biblical characters, although the themes are not religious: Saint Peter plays a role in "The Moon," "Clever Folk," and "Hitler and Mussolini," and Noah and Mrs. Noah appears in "The Tailor and the Flood." Religion was an integral part of daily life and politics in Germany for centuries, as it was in the rest of Europe. (Indeed, the Lutheran Church and the Roman Catholic Church are still state churches in Germany, which means they are supported by taxes and the clergy are civil servants.) Church steeples mark the center of every village, town, and city, defining the horizon.

There are far fewer animal stories available than either fairy tales or legends. The most famous is "The Bremen Town Musicians." "The Hare and the Hedgehog" and "A Cat and a Mouse Keep House" are also favorites in Germany. I've put "The Hare and the Hedgehog" first because it is so much more than a fable, in spite of the two morals at the end. There are three fables, too, the seventh, eighth and ninth stories. "The Wolf and the Seven Little Kids," another familiar tale, rounds off this section.

The first of the *Schwänke,* "Hans in Luck," was first published by Friedrich Wernicke in 1818 and picked up by the Grimms for their second (1819) edition of the KHM. It is suspected that Wernicke's story was actually an original composition of his own rather than an oral tale that he recorded, as he claims. But here again we see the contra-dance of the literary and the oral in German folktale tradition: "Hans in Luck" has become the definitive German version of this very common folktale motif. The last stories in the *Schwänke* section come from the Till Eulenspiegel cycle. Paul Oppenheimer calls him "Europe's most famous jester" and says that Till "occupies a position of secret happiness in the German soul" (pp. xxi, xxii). Till Eulenspiegel is known in many countries. He first appeared in English as Howleglass some time between 1548 and 1556 in a translation probably made by the publisher and printer William Copeland (Lappenberg, p. 309). Till has been many things to many people: jester, prankster, rogue, social commentator, freedom fighter, revolutionary, spokesman for the oppressed, and, for Oppenheimer, "a protean and original linguistic philosopher" (p. lx). In children's versions, in both German and English, he is a merry scamp. They smooth over what is sometimes a very nasty edge to his pranks and leave out the coarse and scatological parts. I've left in the nasty edge and the coarseness where they occur in the stories I have chosen, and I had resolved not to baulk at the scatological bits but include them for the sake of authenticity. However, after reading through the stories several times, I decided that the episodes in which Eulenspiegel expresses his opinion with human excrement weren't better or more interesting or more characteristic than those that didn't pose this challenge to publishers, teachers, librarians, and parents who feel obliged to uphold standards of public decency. (Children, of course, would not be at all offended, just enjoyably scandalized at seeing in print a most familiar subject that, while it was much discussed during the process of toilet training, was marked as unmentionable soon afterward.) So, in the end, I left them out.

Retelling and Translation

Generally I stayed close to the German texts of the sources I used. However, for some stories from the KHM I followed the example set by the Grimms themselves and edited more substantially. The diminutives, the Christian piety, the pathos, and the bloodiness increased with every edition of the KHM, making the stories more sentimental. Where these seemed to me to be an editorial overlay that motivated nothing in the tale, I left them out. I compared the versions of the stories I chose in four editions of the KHM: the first edition from 1812–14, the second edition from 1819, the third edition from 1837, and the seventh edition from 1857. Where there were choices, I preferred the stronger, shorter forms. In some cases, I also combined elements from different versions. Let me give two examples.

In "Aschenputtel" I took watching from the dovecote, the dying mother's instructions rather than the father's hazel twig, the tree rather than the birds in the tree giving the dresses, and other people besides Aschenputtel and her stepsisters trying on the slipper from the 1812 edition. I took some of the simpler phrasing and stronger repetition from 1819 edition, which in most respects is close to the seventh edition, but I left out the weeping and praying that was added by the Grimms after the first edition. For "Rapunzel," I used the 1812 version, in which Rapunzel unwittingly betrays the prince to the fairy by asking why her clothes are becoming so tight. The question is naive but understandable coming from a girl who has been completely isolated from the world since childhood. In the second edition (1819), the Grimms removed this reference to pregnancy, undoubtedly with complaining parents in mind, and instead Rapunzel asks the fairy why she (the fairy) is so much heavier to pull up than the prince is. This question turns Rapunzel into a witless ninny. By way of compensation, perhaps, in the 1857 edition Rapunzel gets the prince to bring silk rope with him each time he comes so she can braid a ladder with which to escape, and I've included this element from the last edition because it makes Rapunzel a stronger character. From the second edition on, the fairy was a *Zauberin,* sorceress, which a number of English translations give as witch. I've stayed with the fairy of the first edition to counteract the idea that the magic being who hides Rapunzel away is necessarily wicked.

For the sake of the storytellers who may make use of this book, I have named my primary source at the end of every story, and in the case of the KHM the edition or editions I used. In two instances I combined the KHM version with a version from a different collection and indicated both sources at the end of the story.

Some of the stories have well-known English titles and names for the protagonist that I chose not to use. Instead of using "The Pied Piper," I translated the German *Rattenfänger* as "Ratcatcher," which has a much rougher sound and emphasizes the rats rather than the piping. I kept the German title and name "Aschenputtel" because "Cinderella" immediately brings to mind the Perrault and Disney versions of the tale, which are very different from the German one. Interestingly, "Aschenputtel" has no gender: it is used for boys as well as girls. A *Rotkäppchen,* a little red cap, is a type of headgear different from a "Little Red Ridinghood." "Frau Holle" has been translated by others as Mother Holle, which is cozier than it should be. "Frau" could be translated as "Mistress," but that sounds more archaic than it ought to. "Frau" is easy enough to pronounce, so I have left it. *Dornröschen,* thorn-rose, is known in English as "Brier Rose," so it's not really a problem. But the effect of a title is so well illustrated by the more common "Sleeping Beauty," taken from Perrault, that it is worth mentioning here. A brier rose is a thorny wild flower, and the thorns come first. The name "Sleeping Beauty" begins with a passive state—sleeping—and emphasizes appearance, the whole having, at least to my ear, a sense of languid elegance. (It should be noted that in Perrault's title, *La belle au bois dormant,* it is the forest, and not the beauty, that is sleeping: "The Beauty in the Sleeping Forest.")

I worked directly from the German sources and generally did not compare my versions with English translations. However, for the Till Eulenspiegel stories, I did consult Oppenheimer's translation in places where the early-sixteenth-century German gave me difficulty. Oppenheimer's work is very good, but it is not entirely reliable. Anyone wanting a close scholarly translation of the complete Eulenspiegel cycle will have to use Oppenheimer and should be aware that there are some inaccuracies.* Of the translations of the complete KHM currently in print, I recommend Ralph Manheim's *Grimms' Tales for Young and Old.*

---

*I found mistranslations in stories 1, 3, 7, and 27. Only the two errors in number 27 affected the story in any significant way: translating *Herkummen* as "arrival" rather than "lineage" or "ancestry," and *Columneser* as a "pillar of Rome" rather than a member of the legendary Colonna family, makes Eulenspiegel's farrago of nonsense impossible to follow.

A Note for Storytellers and Readers

Storytellers and people reading aloud are very welcome to use my versions of these tales if they acknowledge their source. They are also welcome to make changes as long as they make it clear that the changes are theirs. The violence in some of the stories is going to surprise some North American readers and may seem problematic to them. But these stories are widely known and published as children's stories in Germany today, and American and English picture-book versions, such as Paul Heins's and Trina Schart Hyman's *Snow White* and Anthony Browne's *Hansel and Gretel*, don't leave out the red-hot iron shoes or the miserable death of the witch in her own oven. Folktales are tough as well as wondrous or funny. That's what makes them so durable. And anyone who has watched three-year-olds killing imaginary monsters and bad guys with imaginary swords or superpowers knows that children are more robust, and more concerned with the fundamental dangers of life like death and injustice, than we as adults like to think. Scholars and experts like Norma Livo have pointed out that the abstract violence of folktales gives children a chance to play out their fears. Whatever tellers and readers may chose to edit or skip for small children, most North American children old enough to read these stories for themselves have seen a lot more violence and malevolence in computer games, movies, and on television, even if they only watch the news, than these stories hold. Furthermore, the pictures on the screen are inescapable, but when a story is told in words alone, the listeners or readers can choose how concrete and detailed to make the images in their imagination. These stories won't put any bad ideas into a reader's head that aren't there already, but as with all stories, educators and parents are encouraged to read the story for themselves before asking an audience of any age to listen.

German fairy tales mostly start with "There was . . ." or "There once was . . .," and I've used those openings because they are the ones that to my ear fit the stories. But if tellers or readers-aloud want to begin with "Once upon a time . . .," they should feel free to do so.

A Note on Spinning

Folktales are full of spinning. Before the invention of spinning machines, producing the linen and woolen thread needed for clothing and bedding was an endless task in every household. The women did the spinning, whenever they didn't have their hands full with other work, and the women with the most time to spin were unmarried women, young and old, who weren't in charge of family households. Spinsters are people who spin, and spinning was so constant an occupation for unmarried women that the word came to be used to define their marital status. The distaff, the stick on which flax fiber was arranged for spinning, is an old symbol for women's work. In medieval manuscripts, the image of a woman with a distaff in her hand was used to represent the feminine part of the domestic sphere, and the English expression "the distaff side" refers to the female branch of a family.

Much of the spinning in folktales would have been done with hand spindles rather than with spinning wheels because they were portable, inexpensive, and didn't take up space in a one-room cottage. (The earliest spinning wheel in Europe, the great wheel, called the walking wheel in North America because the spinner has to walk to perform her task, was very big. The wheel itself was around fifty inches in diameter.) When the girls in the fairy tale "Frau Holle" are sent to the well by the road to spin, they would have taken a spindle with them, not a wheel, and they would probably have been spinning flax for linen. Flax must be moistened as it is spun to make a smooth yarn, so the well would have been a convenient place to work. However, saliva is even better than water for dampening flax because saliva contains an enzyme that softens the fiber, so a spinster would moisten her thumb on her lower lip. That's why one of the women in "The Three Spinners" has a bottom lip so large that it hangs down over her chin. Once the flax is spun, the linen yarn is boiled and rinsed up to four times to get rid of the plant matter. That's why the stepmother in "The Three Little Men in the Woods" boils the yarn that she makes her stepdaughter rinse in the frozen river. With each boiling, the color lightens and becomes more variegated and the thread becomes softer and more pliable.

In German, spinning wheels and cats make the same sound: *schnurren*. So spinning wheels purr, and cats spin when they're sitting in the warmest corner of the room behind the stove. There's a spinning song called "Dreh dich, dreh dich Rädchen" ("turn, turn, little wheel") that has the rhythm of treadling a spinning wheel and lists all the reasons why the wheel has to keep turning and turning without rest. (You can hear this song on a Web site devoted to German folksongs at www.ingeb.org. The URL is a play on the name Ingeborg.) A solitary spinner could sing to pass the time, but spinning could also be a social occasion. Girls would gather together with their spindles on an evening, and their young men might drop in, too. While their skilled fingers spun wool and flax, they would chat and sing and spin tales for their amusement.

The Folktale Presence
in Germany Today

Folktales are present everywhere in Germany. There's a "German Fairy-tale Route" for tourists that has Bremen, where a statue commemorates the Bremen Town Musicians, at one end and Hanau, the home of the Brothers Grimm, at the other. Hameln, the Ratcatcher town, is on that road, and Sababurg, where Brier-Rose's castle is, and Polle, where there is an Aschenputtel pageant every year, and Alsfeld, where the regional folk costume includes the kind of cap the Grimms are supposed to have had in mind for Little Red Cap. There are fairy-tale museums and fairy-tale theme parks. Much of this showcasing of fairy tales is a product of the tourist industry. But the folktales are also there naturally, in everyday places. All over Germany there are ancient marketplaces surrounded by fifteenth- and sixteenth-century buildings that are still in full use. The walls and towers that once protected fortified towns now stand in the middle of big cities. The places and buildings named in the local legends are part of daily life. You can go to a church service in the Marienkirche in Lübeck, see the Wartburg high on its mountain as you drive into Eisenach, or walk across the Executioner's Bridge in Schwäbisch Hall where the ghost of a saltboiler drowned a watchman, or stand in Hameln and look across the river at the very hill where the Ratcatcher vanished with the town's children.

And all those fairy-tale forests where children got lost and woodcutters cut wood and hunters saved little girls' lives are there even now. They are cared for as part of the common wealth of the local community, and the hunting rights are leased to hunters who are responsible for the wildlife and the woods themselves all year round. Hunting in Germany is a craft and an avocation, governed by a strong tradition. You can't just buy a gun, a license, and a red shirt and go out into the bush to bag a moose or deer. New hunters have to apprentice themselves to a qualified hunter to learn the necessary skills and rituals. They carefully watch the animals in their hunting preserve, the roe deer, wild boar, badgers, foxes, rabbits, game birds, and song birds. They shoot primarily the old or sick ones or enough to keep the population in balance with its environment. When they have shot something, they blow a ceremonial call on a hunting horn over the kill to show their regard. They wear traditional clothing: green jackets and coats and green hats with a badger's brush in the hat band and long boots. You can drive ten minutes out of Lübeck and be in a forest that has been tended since the thirteenth century.

All over Germany the subjects and settings of folktales are part of the landscape. However, the fact is inescapable that our experience of folktales in Western industrialized countries now depends almost entirely on the literary tradition (Scherf). In Germany today, the minor forms of prose narrative—jokes, family stories, anecdotes about local events—are still passed on by word of mouth. But the comic tale, the legend, and the fairy tale are preserved not by retelling but in books. "Little attempt is made to remember stories because they are available in printed collections and can, if desired, be reproduced orally from these sources" (Neumann, p. 235). The fairy tale has a privileged position in German popular culture: it is actively "cared for." The Europische Märchengesellschaft (European Fairy Tale Society) is dedicated to this purpose. "Its task is to motivate storytellers, hobbyists, field researchers, well-known persons in the fairy tale arena, and scholars from all faculties, as well as artists, to all sorts of fairy tale-related activities" (Wienker-Piepho, p. 239). Storytelling is taught in workshops and courses, and there are storytelling performances at festivals and conferences. This same professionalization of storytelling has occurred in North America, too, but there is an interesting difference in the tellers' attitude to their material:

> Problems arise frequently among circles of storytellers when original material is told in different ways and made to go along with real and local happenings of the present. This debate appears to be specific to Germany. Although German people usually recite word-for-word and in an exceedingly conscientious manner when following the "Grimm type" or the German language edition of international fairy tales, only a few presenters in other countries stress in the same sense an authentic rendition that is true to the written source. (Wienker Piepho, p. 214)

Whether this adherence to the text by German storytellers is a cultural trait or due to the reverence accorded to the Grimms's KHM is open to speculation.

This conscious "caring for" seems artificial. But it is important to realize that when people read or tell traditional tales in Germany today, however self-consciously, they are part of a living story tradition because their language and landscape continue to echo the world of the folktales.

The German World of the Folktales

Except for local legends, folktales are set in an unspecified "Once" and an unspecified "there." But they are full of common folk and common things: millers, tailors, peasants, and simpletons; spindles, featherbeds, hearth fires, and bread ovens. Millers and spinning wheels have for us the romance of the past, but in the early nineteenth century when the Brothers Grimm and their fellow folklorists were writing down folktales in Germany, they were part of daily life, especially in the rural villages and little towns. Even the unlikely sounding kings and queens and earls in their castles were near neighbors of goose girls, and they owned most of the forests where woodcutters earned their meager livings. At the end of the nineteenth century, Germany was still a patchwork of small kingdoms and duchies and earldoms, and a peasant woman on her doorstep might well curtsey to a countess. Country life hadn't changed much for generations.

My great-grandfather, Rudolph Welcker, was born in a small country village called Eckartshausen in the Grand Duchy of Hessen in 1864. His father was the Lutheran pastor, and his grandfather had been the pastor there before him. The presentation of the living was in the gift of the Graf zu Meerholz, and the first mention of a pastor there comes in the record of a purchase of property in the year

1316 witnessed by Sifrid the pastor in Ekkerczhausen and Johann Lochmann and his sons Wernher and Johann. There were still Lochmanns living in Eckartshausen six hundred years later when Rudolph wrote his memoirs.

Rudolph Welcker's childhood was a happy one, and he wrote down his vivid memories of life in Eckartshausen for his children when they were grown. He describes a way of life in which the Grimms's *Märchen,* first published more than fifty years before his birth, are entirely at home, a lived world that could easily be the "once" and the "there" of the folktales. Let me tell you a little about that world.

The parsonage where he grew up was built in 1484 by the abbess of Marienborn because the old one had been burned down in a feud. Like the others in the village, it was a timber-framed house with a red tile roof. The house had been extended on the east side early in the nineteenth century, but the original part was still in full use. The big kitchen was part of it, and the large room next to the kitchen was now the servants' hall where the maidservant slept and the hired help had their meals. The big dinners for the potato harvest, the grain harvest, the butchering, and the twice-yearly wash days when professional washerwomen came to launder the heavy sheets and blankets were held in that room, too. These occasions were treated as festivals and were celebrated with a feast. There were two small bedrooms on the ground floor of the original house as well, and, on the second floor, a large room that was used as the study, a bedroom, and a north-facing room where food was stored.

A yard next to the old part of the house was enclosed by the house on one side, by outbuildings across the back and on the side opposite the house, and at the front by a wall with a wide double door onto the village street big enough to drive a wagon through it. The outbuildings included a stable for one or two horses and two cows, a hay loft, and a woodshed and workshop. There was a coach house that had a harness room and a small bedroom for the hired man and accommodated two wagons, a light carriage, a pony cart, and, up in the loft, a green sleigh with long runners for winter days when snow lay thick on the ground. There was a rabbit stall, a henhouse for twenty chickens, and a pig pen to house the two or three piglets bought in the spring and fattened over the summer. In the fall the butcher would come by appointment to kill them and cut them up, and the whole household would be busy with sausage making and pickling and smoking. Finally there was a sheep pen where the family's five or six sheep spent the winter. For the rest of the year, they were out in the fields and meadows with the village shepherd.

There were no shops in the village. Sugar and salt, tea and coffee, and chocolate had to be bought on infrequent trips to a larger town. The daily necessities of life people grew and made and preserved for themselves. Outside the village the pastor's family had a field for wheat, rye, and flax and a large vegetable garden for potatoes, cabbages, beans, and peas. Part of the pastor's salary was paid in firewood from the Graf zu Meerholz's forests and barley and oats from his estates.

Keeping house in those days required a great many skills and endless work. Even with a maidservant to help in the house, Rudolph's mother was as busy as the day was long. The big kitchen was her workshop. In it was the great wood-fired brick stove topped with an iron plate with numerous holes for cooking. It also heated the hot-water tank next to it and kept the big kettles full of mash for the cows and pigs simmering behind it. In an alcove stood large crocks of mixed grain for the chickens, and next to them the big washtubs for laundry. Opposite the stove, under a window that looked out through the green shade of a grapevine onto the red currant bushes and fruit trees in the kitchen garden, was the ancient stone sink. Water from the sink drained into a channel in the floor underneath it that ran out into the garden. (In the story "The Three Little Men in the Woods," the enchanted duck swims into the castle kitchen up a drainage channel like this one.) Beside the sink was a double trap door that opened onto the cellar stairs.

Down in the cellar were the wine racks, storage shelves for apples, and potato bins. Hanging by chains from the ceiling was the bread shelf, where the fourteen loaves of rye bread baked weekly in the communal bread oven were kept. (All the households in the village drew lots once a week for their baking time in the bake house and brought their bread dough, made at home, in big wooden tubs. The village miser always tried to get the last slot of the day because he could use the accumulated heat of the oven and save a little on firewood.) Arranged along the stone cellar stairs were homemade cheeses ripening in stoneware crocks. And there were lots of mousetraps, baited with bits of fried bacon, that had to be sterilized in boiling water every so often to get rid of the strong smell of mice. A magic Ratcatcher would have been much more convenient!

Behind the kitchen was the north-facing pantry, built out of brick for coolness. In it stood barrels and crocks full of meat preserved in brine and all the other food stores that didn't need to be kept absolutely dry. Upstairs in the old part of the house was a cool, north-facing room called the bacon and sausage room. There sausages of different kinds and flitches of bacon and collared pork hung from horizontal rods suspended from the ceiling. They were smoked hard and would keep indefinitely. (Beef was bought fresh from the Jewish cattle dealer when it was needed.) Sacks of dried peas, beans, corn, and vetch hung on the walls, and among them bunches of dried herbs. On the floor stood open casks full of dried plums, pears, and apples from their own fruit trees. There was a tall cone of sugar, almost two feet high (sugar didn't come in convenient bags), wrapped in blue paper, and a hatchet for hacking off chunks of it that then had to be pounded to bits. And there was a big block of chocolate.

Up another flight of stairs in the attic was the big wooden flour bin with two compartments, one for wheat flour, the other for rye. The grain they grew themselves was taken to the mill, and the flour was brought back to be stored in the bin. When the supply got low, the pastor would take more grain to the mill. The grain was stored in the attic too, in big heaps that had to be turned now and then with a long beech-wood shovel to guard against insects and damp. Where there was grain, there were mice, so the two house cats spent a lot of time in the attic. As a result, the person turning the grain heaps would turn up little rolls of grain-coated cat excrement, too! These were simply tossed out the window into the hen yard, where the hens would deal with the matter.

Next to the flour bin in the attic was the wool room. Sacks and sacks of wool hung there, all of it from their own sheep. At the end of May or early in June, the village shepherd would drive the whole flock into a pond between the schoolhouse and the bake house. The householders would catch and wash their own sheep and then take them home to a sheep pen filled with new straw so that they would stay clean until the shepherd came to shear them. After the shearing, the fleeces were spread out on the ladder-like sides of the hay wagon to air out, and then they would be stored in the wool room. Then one day the wool carder, a Waldensian from Waldenberg, would arrive to card the raw fleeces, and the wool would go back to the wool room ready for spinning, separated into white, brown, and mixed grey. In the time of Rudolph's grandparents, the wool was still spun at home over the winter when there was less outside work. But Rudolph's mother was the only woman of the family living in the house—his grandfather lived with them, but his grandmother was dead, there were no single great aunts or aunts at hand, and he had no sisters. His mother had her hands full with running the household, and keeping up with mending and knitting took up her evenings. So the wool was sent out to spinners who spun for a living, and the skeins came back and were kept in the wool room. In the winter when the evenings were longer, Rudolph's mother, like all the women and girls in the village, and even some of the men and boys, knit stockings and socks and vests and caps and mufflers and gloves and mittens and spencers and shawls.

Next to the wool room in the attic was the "black laundry" room, "black" meaning dirty, needing to be washed. The heavy household linens that needed washing piled up there until professional washerwomen came to the house once in the spring and once in the fall, washed these cumbersome items with home-made lye and curd soap, and hung them out to bleach and dry. (In those days you couldn't get away with two sets of sheets for each bed, one on the bed and one in the dryer.) Also stored in this room were the bolts of linen cloth used to make bedding and clothing, and the bundles of homegrown flax retted and hackled and ready to give to the spinners. In the winter the skeins of linen thread went to the weavers in the village, men who would weave it on their big looms.

And finally, a ladder went up from the attic to the dovecot, or pigeon loft, on the roof. Roast pigeon was an occasional item on the menu.

I want to say a little more about the village shepherd, who was an almost magical figure to young Rudolph. In the evenings and on rainy days when everyone stayed indoors, Rudolph's father would tell him stories about shepherds—shepherds in fables and folktales, the shepherds keeping their flocks by night near Bethlehem who went to find Joseph and Mary and the baby lying in the manger, the village shepherd who looked after everyone's sheep from spring until fall, alone with his dog out in the fields and pastures of the parish. The shepherd slept in the fields next to his flock in a curious little hut on two wheels. It was painted red and looked like a big coffin with a pointed roof. There was a small door at the wider end, and inside it was filled with straw to keep the shepherd warm at night. Underneath it, a flat box, also filled with straw, hung by four chains from the axle-tree, and this was the sheepdog's bed.

The sheepfold was set up next to the shepherd's hut. The shepherd drove four rows of posts into the ground with a big wooden mallet, two long ones and two short ones, to make a large rectangle. Between the posts he hung lattice hurdles, loosely fastened to the post on either side with rings made of willow wands. Every night the sheep were driven into the fold, and every morning when the sheep were out, the fold was moved forward by its own length in a leapfrogging sort of way so that the short wall at the front end became the short wall at the back end. Day by day the sheepfold advanced down the length of the field, which was thoroughly fertilized by sheep manure as a result. When the fold reached the end of the field, the village clerk would announce, "The sheepfold will be auctioned today," and people without manure, or without enough manure from their own stables, could bid to have the fold moved to their land next. The owner of the next field had to transport the sheepfold to its new location on his wagon, and the shepherd's hut would be hitched behind it.

This moving about of the fold meant that gradually the whole parish was grazed over, and no one part overgrazed. In those days before chemical fertilizers, farmers practiced a three-field rotation. In any given year, one field would be in crop, one would be left in stubble from the year before, and one would lie fallow after the stubble had been plowed under. The sheep were pastured on stubble land and fallow land, keeping the weeds down and fertilizing it. They also grazed down the banks of the many hollow ways that crisscrossed the countryside, narrow unpaved roads that had been used for so many centuries that their surfaces were worn down well below the level of the land on either side. (There's a hollow way in the story of "The Post-horn.") In the evening the shepherd would gradually move the flock back to the fold, shut the sheep in safely for the night, and crawl into his hut to sleep. Occasionally, if things were very quiet and none of the sheep was sick or wounded, he might go home for a night to sleep in real bed, leaving his dog on guard.

The Eckartshausen shepherd wore the traditional garb of his craft. From his shoulders hung a long, heavy cloak that started out blue but faded over the years to the colors of the fields: yellowish dun and brown and bottle green. It was fastened at the neck with a brass chain and hook, and the collar was often trimmed with fur. Sun and rain had given his broad-brimmed hat, black to begin with, a foxy, tindery hue. It was proper to decorate the wide hatband with a big brass or mother-of-pearl buckle. Over his shoulder and across his chest the shepherd wore a broad leather bandolier with brass buckles and the dog leash. In his hand he held a long, straight, knobbly blackthorn staff. It was crowned by a polished metal scoop, a little smaller than a cupped hand, with a hook projecting from the side of it. The hook could be used to pull a sheep out of the flock or to hold onto other things. The scoop served as a weapon, especially as a catapult. Thrust into the ground, it would bring up a clod of earth that was launched with a swift swing of the staff and never missed its mark.

The shepherd knew each and every sheep in his flock. He tended their hurts and illnesses with a medicinal decoction that he carried with him in a finely carved and decorated cow's horn. The ingredients of this mixture were a craft secret that was always passed on to his apprentice and to no one else. Shepherds had arcane knowledge about the powers of healing herbs and roots and about wind and weather. They were generally silent, thoughtful men, different from other folk. No wonder Rudolph loved to hear his father's stories about shepherds.

Years later, Rudolph's father was transferred to a parish in Frankfurt, where people had never known a real shepherd. He found his work as pastor much more difficult there, especially with the children, because they were lacking this bridge to link their everyday lives to the many shepherd stories in the Bible, from Abraham leaving Ur of the Chaldees to become the father of Israel, to Jesus, welcomed into the world by the shepherds of the nativity story, who called himself a shepherd and said that a good shepherd would lay down his life for his sheep.

There was another storyteller in Rudoph's life besides his father. The forester in charge of the Graf von Ysenburg-Meerholz's woodlands was a frequent visitor at the Eckartshausen parsonage. Often he brought fried deer liver wrapped in vine leaves as a treat to share with the pastor. He was a gruff, self-important, bullying sort of man, but he was a wonderful storyteller. When he came in the evening after supper, he would settle down on the sofa and tell stories about forestry and hunting and bloodthirsty tales about robbers and highwaymen and murders and executions. They were grisly stories, but fascinating. In his memoirs, written in the 1930s and '40s, Rudolph laments the loss of storytelling, replaced by newspapers and radio broadcasts that jumble events together in a kaleidoscopic way: one turn and the pattern is changed; details heard today are forgotten tomorrow. When he was a child, it was different. People knew how to tell stories then, and how to listen. The men would sit and smoke their pipes, the women would spin or knit or darn socks, while they absorbed the stories. And some other evening they might retell those tales themselves.

Rudoph Welcker made his memories into stories for his children and grandchildren because the world in which he had been a child had disappeared. He wrote about his childhood as if he were speaking to his readers, weaving descriptions, anecdotes, history, and reflections into a narrative so immediate and engaging that it's hard to put the book down. Fifty-one years after his death in 1949, his grandson-in-law, Klaus Schöning, gathered the manuscripts of his memoirs together, transcribed and edited them with the help of his wife Elisabeth, and published them privately for the Welcker family. And now, 140 years after Rudolph Welcker was born in Eckartshausen, I have retold some of his stories here to set the scene for much older tales.

The word "tradition" is made from two Latin words: *trans,* meaning across or beyond, and *dare,* meaning to give. Tradition gives gifts forward across the years, from the past through the present to the future. And tradition allows us to reach back across generations and centuries to a time that tradition makes always now.

The village of Eckartshawson.

Opening Tale

The Golden Key ❧ Der goldene Schlüssel

One winter's day when deep snow covered field and forest a poor boy had to go out to gather firewood. When he had found enough and tied it on his sled, he was so cold that he decided to make a fire and warm up a bit before he went home. He scraped the snow away from the ground in a sheltered corner, and on the bare earth he found a small golden key. He thought that where there was a key, there must also be a lock, so he dug in the earth and found a small iron box. "There must be precious things in the box," he thought. "If only the key fits!" He looked for a keyhole, but there didn't seem to be one. Finally he discovered it, but it was so small that it was almost invisible. He tried the key, and it fit. Then he turned the key once—and now we will have to wait until he finishes unlocking the box and lifts the lid. Then we'll find out what wonderful things were in the box.

Source: Grimm # 200, 1857

Tier~ Geschichten

(Animal Tales)

HCS '03

The Hare and the Hedgehog
Der Hase und der Igel

You're going to tell me this story sounds like a lie, but I got it from my grand-father, and whenever he told it he always said, "It has to be true, girl, because if it isn't, there'd be nothing to tell!" So listen carefully, the story goes like this.

It was a Sunday morning at harvest time, just when the buckwheat is in bloom. The sun shone high in the sky, the morning wind blew warm over the fields, the larks were singing in the air, the bees were humming in the buckwheat, the people dressed in their Sunday best were going to church, and all of creation was happy, including the hedgehog.

The hedgehog stood at his open door with his arms crossed, looking out into the morning wind and singing a little song to himself, just about as well as a hedgehog is likely to sing on a sunny summer Sunday morning. And as he stood there singing and humming a bit, it occurred to him that while his wife was wash-ing and dressing the children he could take a little walk to see how his turnips were doing. The turnips grew in the field right next to his house, and since he and his family ate a lot of those turnips, he looked on them as his own. No sooner said than done. The hedgehog closed the door behind him and strolled toward the tur-nip field. He'd gone no farther than the wild plum tree that grew at the edge of the field when he noticed the hare from up the road out and about on similar business, which was to have a look at his cabbages. The hedgehog said a friendly "Good morning," but the hare was a very distinguished gentleman, and stuck-up on top of that, so the hedgehog got no greeting back.

Instead, the hare asked him in a snooty way, "How does it come about that you are running around in the fields on such merry Sunday morning?"

The hedgehog answered, "I'm taking a walk."

"A walk?" sneered the hare, "Can't you find something better to do with your legs than that?" This comment seriously annoyed the hedgehog because all hedgehogs' legs are crooked. Hedgehogs aren't sensitive about much, but they won't put up with any remarks about their legs.

"You probably think your legs are more useful, eh?" said the hedgehog.

"I do think exactly that," answered the hare.

"Well," said the hedgehog, "you'd have to prove it to me. I'll bet that if you raced me I'd run your legs off."

"That's ridiculous!" laughed the hare. "You'd beat me with your crooked legs? But all right, if you're so eager, we'll run a race. What's the bet?"

"A goldpiece and a bottle of brandywine," said the hedgehog.

"You're on!" said the hare. "Shake on it, and lets get started."

But the hedgehog said, "Not so fast—I haven't had my breakfast yet. I'll go home for a bite to eat and meet you back here in half-an-hour."

So the hedgehog went home, and as he went he thought to himself, "That hare's a fool, for all that he's a fancy gentleman. His long legs won't win him this race—he'll have to pay up."

When he got home, he said to his wife, "Wife, get dressed as quick as you can, you have to come out to the field with me."

"Why, what's the matter?" asked his wife.

"I've bet the hare a goldpiece and a bottle of brandywine that I can beat him in a race, and you have to be there."

"You what?" shrieked his wife. "Are you out of your senses? Have you completely lost your mind? How on earth can you expect to outrun the hare?"

"Oh, button your lip, woman!" answered the hedgehog. "That's my business and I'll thank you to leave it to me. You just get yourself dressed and come along." And that's what she did.

Once they were on their way, the hedgehog said to his wife, "Listen now. See that field? That's where we're going to race. The hare will run in one furrow, and I'll run in another, and we'll start at the top there. All you have to do is stay down here in the furrow I'm going to run in and when the hare gets close you jump up and yell, 'I won!'"

The hedgehog showed his wife where she was to stand and went on up the field to meet the hare.

"Can we start now?" asked the hare.

"Yup!" answered the Hedgehog.

"Then let's get on with it!"

So each got into his furrow, the hare counted "one, two, three," and they were off. The hare ran like a storm wind, but the hedgehog only took about three steps before he stopped and calmly sat down in his furrow.

And when the hare, racing at full speed, got toward the bottom of the field, the hedgehog's wife popped up and yelled, "I won!" The hare stopped short and was considerably astonished; he really thought it was the hedgehog, because as everybody knows, a hedgehog's wife looks just like a hedgehog husband.

The hare thought to himself, "This can't be right," and shouted, "Run again, back the other way!" He took off again like a storm wind, running so fast that his ears streamed out behind him, while the hedgehog's wife calmly stayed where she was.

And when the hare got back to the top of the field, the hedgehog jumped up and yelled, "I won!" The hare was beside himself with rage.

"Run again," he screamed, "back the other way!"

"That's fine with me," answered the hedgehog, "as often as you like." So the hare ran another seventy-three times, and each time he came to the end of the field the hedgehog or his wife would jump up and yell, "I won!"

The seventy-fourth time, the hare didn't get to the end. In the middle of the field, he fell to the ground, dead as a doornail. The hedgehog took the gold piece and the bottle of brandywine, called his wife out of the furrow, and the two of them went home together very pleased with themselves. And if they haven't died, they're still alive today.

So, that's how it happened that the hedgehog ran the hare to death on the Buxtehude Heath. And since then, no hare has ever tried to race the Buxtehude hedgehog again.

Now, there are two morals to this story. First, nobody, no matter how distinguished he thinks he is, should make fun of another person, even if that person is a hedgehog. And second, it's advisable, if you get married, to marry someone who has the same social standing as yourself and looks just like you. So, somebody who's a hedgehog should take care to marry another hedgehog, and so on.

Source: Grimm KHM #187, 1857

The Mouse, the Bird, and the Sausage ❧ Von dem Mäuschen, Vögelchen, und der Bratwurst

Once there were a mouse, a bird, and a sausage who kept house together. They had lived together prosperously, in peace and comfort, for a long time. The bird's job was to fly to the forest every day and bring back firewood. The mouse carried water, made the fire, and set the table. The sausage did the cooking.

But people who are too comfortable become dissatisfied! One day when the bird was out getting firewood, he met another bird and told him about the exceptionally good life he led. The other bird called him a poor sap for doing all the hard work while his two housemates took it easy at home. After all, when the mouse had lit the fire and carried in the water, she could nap in her room until it was time to set the table. As for the sausage, it kept an eye on the pot to make sure it was boiling, and just before mealtime it only had to slide through the porridge or the vegetables once or twice to give them fat and flavor, and dinner was ready. By the time the bird came home and put down his burden, they would already be sitting at the table and after the meal they went to bed and slept like logs until the next morning. It was a glorious life those two lived.

The next day the bird refused to go to the forest. Stirred up by what the other bird had said, he declared that he had been their servant long enough, that they took him for a fool, that it was time to trade jobs and do things a different way. The mouse and the sausage argued vigorously against the idea, but the bird refused to change his mind. So they drew straws and the sausage got the short one—it would have to get the firewood. That meant the mouse became the cook, and the bird would light the fire and carry water.

So what happened? The sausage went out to get wood, the bird lit the fire, the mouse put the pot on, and they waited for the sausage to come home with firewood for the next day. After the sausage had been gone a long time they began to worry, and the bird flew off to look for it. Not far along the road he found a dog that had seen the poor sausage as fair game, attacked it, and eaten it. Sadly, the bird picked up the firewood and flew home. He told the mouse what he had seen and heard. They were both grief stricken but agreed that the best thing to do was to stay together and carry on. So the bird set the table and the mouse cooked dinner. And when the vegetables were ready, she jumped into the pot to flavor them the way the sausage had always done. But she wasn't a sausage: before she had slid half way through she was cooked dead.

When the bird came to put the food on the table, the cook had vanished. The bird was dismayed. He looked everywhere, for the mouse, and even pulled apart the woodpile. Some of the wood landed too close to the hearth and caught fire. The bird hurried to get water, but the pail fell into the well and pulled the bird down with it, and the bird couldn't save himself. So he drowned. That's the end of the story of the mouse, the bird, and the sausage. It's a wise bird that knows when it's well off.

Source: Grimm KHM #23, 1857

The Bremen Town Musicians 🎵
Die Bremer Stadtmusikanten

A man had a donkey that had willingly carried sacks to the mill for many years. But now the donkey was old, his strength was failing, and the farmer was thinking of getting rid of him because he wasn't worth his feed. The donkey noticed which way the wind was blowing and ran away. He decided to go to Bremen, where he thought he could get a job as a town musician.

After he had walked a fair way he found a hunting dog lying in the road, panting as if he had run until he could run no more.

"Now why are you panting like that, old run-and-fetch-it?" asked the donkey.

"Oh," sighed the dog, "Because I'm old and getting weaker every day and not much use for hunting any more my master wanted to shoot me, so I ran away as fast as I could. But how am I going to earn my living now?"

"You know what?" said the donkey, "I'm going to Bremen to be a town musician. Come with me and be a musician, too. I'll play the lute, and you can beat the kettle-drum."

The dog thought this was a good idea and the two of them went on together. Not much farther along they met a cat sitting by the road and looking as dismal as three days of rainy weather.

"What's got you looking so miserable, you old whisker-licker?" asked the donkey.

"It's hard to be cheerful when you're staring death in the face," answered the cat. "Because I'm getting on in years and my teeth are wearing out, and I'd rather sit behind the stove and spin than chase around after mice, my mistress wanted to drown me. I got away, but that was easy. The hard question is, where do I go now?"

"Come with us to Bremen. You've made a lot of night music in you time, you can be a town musician like us."

The cat thought that was good advice, and the three runaways went on together until they came to a farmyard where a rooster sat on the gate crowing his lungs out.

"Your shrieking could break my eardrums," said the donkey. "Why are you crowing?"

"I'm predicting good weather because today is Lady Day, but tomorrow is Sunday and guests are coming for dinner. The woman of the house has no pity: she told the cook to make soup out of me, and I'm supposed to let her cut off my head tonight. So I'm crowing as loud as I can while I still have a throat to crow with."

"Come along with us, redhead," said the donkey. "We're going to Bremen, and anywhere is better than dead. You have a good voice, you could be a town musician like us. We'd make beautiful music together." The rooster thought that was a good idea, and the four of them went on together.

But Bremen was more than one day's journey away, and when evening came the travelers found themselves in a forest, where they decided to spend the night. The donkey and the dog lay down under a big tree, the cat climbed up into its branches, and the rooster flew to the very top of the tree because he felt safer there. Before he went to sleep he took a last look around in all four directions, and he thought he saw a little spark of light glowing in the distance. He called down to his companions that there must be a house near by: he could see a light shining.

Said the donkey, "Then we should get up again and go there, because the accommodations here are less than comfortable." The dog agreed. He thought a couple of bones with some meat still on them would do him a lot of good. So they started off toward the light the rooster had seen, and it wasn't long before they came to a house. It was a robbers' house, and the robbers were at home. The donkey, as the tallest of the four, snuck up to a window and looked in. "What do you see, grayback?" asked the rooster.

"I see a table set with lovely food and drink," answered the donkey, "and a band of robbers sitting around it enjoying themselves."

"We ought to trade them places," said the rooster.

So the animals held a council meeting to figure out how to get rid of the robbers, and they finally came up with a plan. The donkey stood with his forefeet on the windowsill, the dog jumped up on the donkey's back, the cat climbed on top of the dog, and the rooster flew up and sat on the cat's head. Then, when they were ready, at a given signal they all began to make their music: the donkey brayed, the dog barked, the cat meowed, and the rooster crowed. It was the most horrible noise you've ever heard! Then they crashed through the window into the room, glass flying everywhere.

The robbers were scared out of their wits when they heard the ghastly hullabaloo. They thought some kind of dreadful ghost had burst in, and they ran out into the forest fearing for their lives. The four musicians sat down at the table, helped themselves to everything that was left, and ate as if they were going to starve for the next four weeks. When they were finished they put out the lamp and found places to sleep that suited their nature and their idea of comfort. The donkey lay down on the manure heap in the yard, the dog settled behind the door, the cat curled up on the hearth by the warm ashes, and the rooster flew up into the rafters. And because they were tired after their long journey, they were soon asleep.

Midnight came and went. The house was dark and still. The robbers, who were watching from a safe distance, grew bold again.

"We shouldn't have let ourselves be stampeded like that," said the leader, and sent one of his men back to the house to scout around. Everything was quiet, so the robber went into the kitchen to light a candle. In the dark he saw the glowing, fiery eyes of the cat on the hearth, and thinking they were live coals, he held a match to them. But the cat didn't much like being poked in the eye and sprang straight at his face, spitting and scratching. The man was terrified and ran to the back door to escape, but the dog, who was lying behind the door, jumped up and bit his leg; and as the robber ran through the yard past the dung heap the donkey gave him a good kick with his hind foot. Then the rooster, up in the rafters, woke up because of all the noise and crowed, "Kikeriki!"

The robber ran back as fast as he could to his captain and reported, "In the kitchen there's a horrible witch who hissed at me and scratched my face with her long fingers, and at the door there's a man with a knife who stabbed my leg, and in the courtyard there's a black monster that beat me with a club, and on the roof there's a judge who cried out, 'Bring the rascal to me!' So I got away as fast as I could."

The robbers never dared to go back. But the four Bremen town musicians were so comfortable in the house that they never left. And the mouth of the last person to tell this story is still warm.

Source: Grimm KHM #27, 1857

A Cat and a Mouse Keep House
❧ Katz und Maus in Gesellschaft

A cat made the acquaintance of a mouse and spoke so eloquently of the affection and friendship she felt for her that the mouse was persuaded to make a common household with the cat.

"Before winter comes, we must lay in some supplies," said the cat. "Otherwise we'll go hungry, especially you, my dear mouse. There'll be little for you outside, and I worry that you'll get caught by one of the traps set for you and your kin indoors." The mouse agreed that they should follow the cat's advice, and they bought a small pot of goose fat. But where were they to store it?

After a great deal of consideration, the cat suggested the church. "No one would dare to steal something from a church," she said. "We'll put it under the altar and not touch it until we really need it." So the pot of goose fat was safely tucked away.

But the cat couldn't stop thinking about how delicious that goose fat would taste, and one day she said to the mouse, "By the way, mousie, I've been meaning to tell you that my cousin has had a baby, a little white tomcat with brown spots, and she's asked me to be the godmother. The baptism's today, and if you don't mind staying home alone, I'll be off to the church now."

The mouse answered a little wistfully, "Yes, of course you must go. Think of me if you get something good to eat. I'd like a sip of the christening wine myself." Now none of this was true—the cat had no cousin and no godchild. She went straight to the church, snuck under the altar to the pot of goose fat, and licked and licked until the skin on the top was all gone. Then she took a stroll over the rooftops and settled down in the sun to clean her whiskers.

When evening came she went home, and the mouse said, "You must have had a good time! Did everything go well?"

"It was a good start," answered the cat. "Tell me, what did they name the baby?" asked the mouse.

"Skinoff," answered the cat, and brushed her paw over her whiskers.

"Skinoff!" exclaimed the mouse. "How peculiar. Is it a common name in your family?"

"I don't know what's so odd about it," said the cat. "It's no worse than Crumbthief, the name your godchild has!"

It wasn't long before thoughts of the goose fat overcame the cat again.

"You'll have to do me the favor of looking after the house by yourself today," she said to the mouse. "I've been asked to be godmother at another christening, and since the child has a white ring around its neck I really can't say no."

The good-natured mouse agreed, and the cat went to the church, slinking along behind walls and through alleys. When she got to the church she snuck under the altar, and licked up the goose fat until the pot was half-empty.

"Nothing tastes as good as the food you eat yourself," she said as she cleaned her whiskers.

When she came home the mouse asked, "What name did they give this child, then?"

"Halfgone," answered the cat.

"Halfgone? I've never heard that before! I'll bet there's no saint's day for that name in the calendar!" said the mouse.

Soon after, the cat's mouth was watering again at the thought of the delicious goose fat hidden under the altar.

"Good things come in threes," she said to the mouse. "I've been asked to be godmother again, and this time the child is completely black except for its white paws. That coloring is very rare, so you won't mind if I go out again, will you?"

"Skinoff!" said the mouse. "Halfgone! Those names do make me wonder."

"Nonsense!" said the cat. "You've been sitting at home too long in your little grey house coat. People get strange notions if they never go out in the daytime." The mouse cleaned and tidied the house while the cat was away, but the greedy cat licked the goose fat until it was all gone and the pot was empty, right down to the bottom.

"Oh well," said the cat to herself, "Now that it's gone I won't be tempted to sneak out any more." When she came home that night, sleek and satisfied, the mouse asked right away what the third child had been named.

"You probably won't like this name either," said the cat. "They called it Allgone."

"Allgone!" cried the mouse. "That's the most curious name yet. I'm sure I've never heard it before. Allgone! What could that possibly mean?" She shook her head, curled up into a ball, and went to sleep.

After that, no one asked the cat to a christening again. Winter came and food was hard to find outdoors. The mouse remembered the goose fat and said to the cat, "Let's go get that pot of fat we put by for the winter. Now's the time to enjoy it."

"Oh you'll enjoy it all right," said the cat. "It will be just as good as sticking your pretty little tongue out the window." They set off together, and when they got to the church, they found that the pot was still there, but it was empty.

"Now I understand," said the mouse bitterly. "Now I see what's been going on. A fine friend you are! You ate it all up while you were at the christenings! First the skin off, next it was half-gone, and then—"

"Be quiet!" cried the cat. "One more word and I'll eat you up!" But the poor mouse already had "all gone" on the tip of her tongue, and as soon as the words were out of her mouth the cat grabbed her and gobbled her up. That's the way of the world, you see.

Source: Grimm KHM #2, 1857

The Kinglet and the Bear ❧
Der Zaunkönig und der Bär

Background: Zaunkönig, *"fence king,"* is the German name for the winter wren (Troglodytes troglodytes*), which is a very small, plain bird with a beautiful song. The name certainly suggests a much grander appearance than the bird actually has. The plot of this story is motivated by the Zaunkönig's misleading name. There is an even smaller songbird, of the family* Regulidae, *whose common English name, kinglet, can work the same way. For all their small size, wrens are very aggressive, quarrelsome birds.*

On a summer's day the bear and the wolf were taking a walk in the forest. The bear heard a bird singing a beautiful song and asked the wolf, "Brother wolf, what kind of bird is that singing so beautifully?"

"That's the king of the birds," said the wolf, "we must bow to him." (It was actually the kinglet.)

"If that is so," said the bear, "I would like to see his royal palace. Please take me there."

"The exact place is hard to find," said the wolf. "We'll have to wait until the queen comes home and see where she goes."

Soon the queen arrived, and the king, too, with food in their beaks to feed their children. The bear wanted to follow them right away, but the wolf held him by the sleeve and said, "No, you have to wait until the king and queen have left again. They're very fierce and won't like to be disturbed."

They took note of the place where the nest must be and went on with their walk. But the bear was so anxious to see the royal palace that he went back that afternoon. The king and queen had flown away, and the bear soon found the palace, a low little nest with five or six scrawny little baby birds in it.

Bitterly disappointed, the bear cried out, "This is a sad excuse for a king's palace! And you aren't king's children, either. You're fakes!" When the young kinglets heard this, they were very angry and screeched, "We're not, we're not fakes! Our parents are honest people. Those are fighting words, bear."

This threat frightened the bear. He went home and hid in his den. But the young kinglets kept screaming and screeching, and when their parents came home, they declared, "We won't eat, not as much as a fly's leg, even if we starve to death, until you call the bear to account. He was here and he called us names. He said we weren't real kinglets, we were fakes."

The old king said, "Now calm down. We'll settle this."

Then the king and queen flew to the bear's cave and the king called in to him, "Hey, old grumpy, why did you call my children names? You'll be sorry you did. It will take a bloody war to wipe out this insult."

Thus war was declared on the bear, who called up all the four-footed animals to fight on his side: the ox, the donkey, the cow, the deer, and whatever else walked on the ground. The kinglet, for his part, called together all flying creatures: not only the birds, great and small, but also the mosquitoes and the gnats, the hornets, the bees, and the flies.

When the time came to start the war, the kinglet sent scouts to find out who was the general in command of the enemy army. The mosquito was the wiliest scout. It buzzed around in the forest where the enemy was gathering and eventually settled under a leaf on the tree where the password was being given out. There stood the bear. He called the fox over and said, "Fox, you are the most cunning of all the animals, you shall be our general and lead us."

"Good," said the fox. "What will our signals be?"

No one had a suggestion, so the fox said, "I have a beautiful, long, bushy tail that looks almost like a red plume. If I hold it up high it means things are going well and the army must advance. But if I let it hang down low, run for your lives." The mosquito, who had heard it all, flew back to the kinglet and reported everything, down to the smallest detail.

When dawn broke on the day of battle, the army of four-footed animals took the field at a thundering run that shook the earth under their feet. The kinglet's army advanced through the air, humming and buzzing and shrieking in a truly terrifying way. As the two great forces met, the kinglet sent the hornet down with orders to get under the fox's tail and sting with all its might. At the first sting, the fox jerked one leg in the air, but he bore the pain and kept his tail high. The second sting made him drop his tail for a moment. The third sting was too much for him: he howled and tucked his tail between his legs. When the animals saw that, they thought all was lost and began run, each to its own home. And so the birds won the battle.

Then the king and queen flew home to their children and called, "Children, rejoice! Eat and drink to your heart's content. We've won the war."

But the young kinglets said, "We won't eat until the bear comes to our nest and apologizes and says that we're real kinglets."

The kinglet father flew to the bear's cave and called, "Hey, old grumpy, you have to come to my nest and apologize to my children and declare that they are indeed kinglets, or we'll break every rib in your body." The terrified bear crept to the nest and apologized. At last the young kinglets were satisfied, and they ate, drank, and made merry far into the night.

Source: Grimm KHM #102, 1857

The Fox and the Horse ❧ Der Fuchs und das Pferd

A farmer had a faithful horse that had grown old and couldn't do its work anymore. The farmer decided it wasn't worth its feed: "You're no use to me now," he told it, "but I'm not a hard-hearted man. Show me that you're still strong enough to bring me a lion, and I'll keep you. But for now, get out of my stable." And he chased the horse out into the open fields.

The horse sadly went to the forest to find a bit of shelter from the weather. There he met a fox, who said to him, "Why are you hanging your head like that and wandering around all by yourself?"

"Oh," said the horse, "stinginess and loyalty don't live together in the same house. My master has forgotten how well I have served him for so many years, and because I'm not much good for plowing anymore, he doesn't want to feed me and has chased me away."

"Without any consolation at all?" asked the fox.

"The consolation was bitter. He said if I was still strong enough to bring him a lion, he would keep me, but he knows I can't do that."

"There I can help you," said the fox. "Just lie down on your side, stretch yourself out, and stay absolutely still, as if you were dead."

The horse did what the fox had told him to do, and the fox went to the lion whose den was nearby. "There's a dead horse lying out there," the fox said to the lion. "Come with me and I'll show you. It will make a big meal for you."

The lion went with the fox, and when they got to the horse the fox said, "You can't really dine in comfort out here, can you? I'll tell you what: I'll tie its tail to you and you can drag it to your den and eat it at your leisure." The lion thought this was good advice. He stood next to the horse and stayed quite still so that the fox could fasten the horse to him. But the fox used the horse's tail to tie the lion's legs together, and twisted and knotted the hairs so tightly that the lion couldn't possibly get free. When he had finished, he slapped the horse on the shoulder and said, "Now pull!"

Then the horse jumped up all of a sudden and dragged the lion away. The lion started to roar, and roared so loudly that all the birds in the forest flew up in fright. But the horse just let him roar and dragged him over the fields to his master's door.

When the farmer saw what the horse had brought him, he had a change of heart and said to the horse, "You shall stay with me and live in comfort," and he fed the horse well until it died.

Source: Grimm KHM #132, 1857

The Fox and the Cat ❧ Der Fuchs und die Katze

It happened one day that the cat met Mr. Fox in a forest. She thought to herself, "He is clever and experienced and highly respected," so she greeted him in a very friendly way. "Good day, dear Mr. Fox. How are you? How's it going? Are you making out all right in these hard times?"

The fox arrogantly looked the cat up and down and took his time answering. Finally he said, "You shabby whisker-licker, you motley fool, you starvling, you mouse-hunter, what *are* you thinking? You have the impudence to ask *me* how I'm making out? What kind of education do *you* have? How many arts and subtle skills do *you* possess?"

"I have just one," answered the cat humbly.

"And what would that one be?" asked the fox.

"When the dogs are after me, I can climb a tree to save myself."

"Is that all?" said the fox. "I am master of a hundred arts and have a bag full of clever tricks besides. I pity you. Come with me, I'll teach you how to get away from dogs."

Just then a hunter came along with four hounds. The cat ran nimbly up a tree and climbed to the very top, where she was completely hidden by leaves and branches.

"Open your bag of tricks, Mr. Fox, open your bag," she called down. But the hounds had already grabbed the fox and held him fast.

"Well now, Mr. Fox," cried the cat, "Your hundred arts haven't done you much good. If you could have climbed up here like me you would have saved your life."

Source: Grimm KHM #75, 1857

The Wolf and the Fox ❧ Der Wolf und der Fuchs

The wolf had hired the fox as his servant, and the fox had to do whatever the wolf said because he was weaker than the wolf, although he would gladly have been rid of his master.

One day, when they were walking through the forest, the wolf said, "Red fox, get me something to eat or I'll eat you."

The fox answered, "I know a farm where there are a couple of young lambs. If you want, we could get us one." The wolf approved, so they went to the farm. The fox stole the lamb, gave it to the wolf, and ran off. The wolf ate the lamb but he wasn't satisfied with one, so he went to get the second lamb. Because he was clumsy about it, the lamb's mother spotted him and bleated and baaaaa-ed until the farmhands came running. They found the wolf and beat him until he limped and howled all the way back to the fox.

"You set me up there," said the wolf. "When I went to get the other lamb, the farmers caught me and beat me black and blue."

The fox answered, "It's your own fault for being such a greedyguts."

The next day they went out again, and again the greedy wolf said, "Red fox, get me something to eat or I'll eat you."

The fox answered, "I know a farm where the farmer's wife is making pancakes today. Let's get some of those." They went to the farm and the fox crept around the house looking and sniffing until he found the dish of pancakes on the windowsill. Then he took six pancakes and brought them to the wolf.

"Here's your dinner," said the fox and went on his way.

The wolf gulped down the pancakes in the blink of an eye and said to himself, "Those tasted like more." He went and pulled the whole dish down. It shattered into a dozen pieces, making such a noise that the farmer's wife came running. When she saw the wolf, she called the farmhands, who came running and beat the wolf so hard that he made his way back to the fox limping and howling.

"That was a nasty setup you led me into," he cried. "The farmers caught me and tanned my hide."

The fox answered, "It's your own fault for being such a such a greedyguts."

When they went out together on the third day, the wolf was so lame that he could hardly limp along, but again he said, "Red fox, get me something to eat or

I'll eat you." The fox answered, "I know a man who has just butchered and the salted meat is in a barrel in the cellar. We'll get some of that."

The wolf said, "This time I'll go in with you so you can help me get away if there's trouble."

"That's fine with me," said the fox and showed him the secret way to sneak into the cellar. There was plenty of meat and the wolf began to gobble it up, thinking to himself, "It will be a while before I'm finished here." The fox ate, too, but he kept looking around and often ran back to the hole where they had come in make sure he could still get through it.

Finally the wolf asked him, "Fox, why are you running back and forth and jumping in and out?"

"I have to make sure no one is coming," said the sly fox and added, "Just be careful not to eat too much."

The wolf said, "I'm not leaving until the barrel is empty." Just then the farmer, who had heard the noise the fox made jumping in and out, came into the cellar. The fox saw him and was out through the hole in no time. The wolf tried to follow, but he had eaten so much that he was to big for the hole and got stuck halfway. The farmer grabbed a big stick and killed the wolf. And the fox ran off into the forest, happy to be rid of old greedyguts.

Source: Grimm KHM #73, 1857

The Wolf and the Man ❧ Der Wolf und der Mensch

One day the fox was telling the wolf about how strong human beings are. "No animal can stand up to a man," he said. "Our only chance against them is to be wily and cunning."

"Not me," said the wolf. "If *I* ever get to see a man *I'll* go straight for his throat."

"I can give you that opportunity," said the fox. "Meet me tomorrow morning and I'll show you a human." The wolf turned up early the next morning, and the fox took him to the path where the hunter passed by every day.

First a discharged old soldier came along. "Is that a man?" asked the wolf.

"No," answered the fox, "that used to be a man."

After him came a little boy on his way to school. "Is that a man?" asked the wolf.

"No," answered the fox, "he'll grow up to be a man."

Finally the hunter came along, his double-barreled gun slung over his shoulder and his hunting knife at his side. The fox said to the wolf, "Look, there comes a man, he's the one you should attack, but I'm going back to my den."

The wolf charged at the man. The hunter thought, "It's a shame that I loaded my gun with shot instead of bullets," took aim, and fired the birdshot into the wolf's face.

The wolf howled, but he wasn't scared off. He kept coming and the hunter fired the second barrel. The wolf ignored the pain and leapt at the man. The hunter pulled his knife and gave him a couple of blows, right and left, that sent the wolf running back to the fox, bleeding and howling.

"Now, brother wolf," said the fox, "how did you make out with the man?"

"Oh," answered the wolf, "the man's strength wasn't at all what I expected. First he took a stick from his shoulder and blew into it so that something flew into my face and tickled terribly. Then he blew into the stick again, and it felt like my nose was hit by lightning and a hail storm. Then he pulled a shiny rib out of his side and hit me so hard that he almost killed me."

"You see what a boaster you are," said the fox. "Your words are a lot braver than your deeds."

Source: Grimm KHM #72, 1857

The Wolf and the Seven Little Kids ❧ Der Wolf und die sieben jungen Geislein

A mother goat had seven little kids, whom she loved dearly. One day, when she had to go out to get food, she called them all to her and said, "Dear children, I have to go to the market. Watch out for the wolf and don't let him in. Be on your guard because he often disguises himself, but you can recognize him by his rough voice and his black paws. If he gets into the house he will eat you up, hide and hair and all."

Soon after she had left, the wolf came to the door and called in his rough voice, "Dear children, unlock the door, I'm your mother and I've brought you treats."

But the seven little kids answered, "You're not our mother. She has lovely soft voice. Your voice is rough. You are the wolf and we won't unlock the door."

The wolf thought of a cunning trick. He went to a store, bought a big piece of chalk, and ate it to make his voice smooth. Then he went back to house where the seven little kids lived and called at the door in a soft voice, "Dear children, let me in, I'm your mother and I've got something for each of you."

But he had put his paw on the windowsill, and when the seven little kids saw it they said, "You're not our mother. Our mother doesn't have black feet like yours. You are the wolf and we won't let you in."

The wolf went to a baker and said, "Baker, cover my paw with fresh dough."

And when the baker had done that the wolf went to the miller and said, "Miller, dust some fine white flour over my paw." The miller didn't want to, but the wolf said, "If you won't do it, I'll eat you up." So the miller dusted his paw with white flour.

Then the wolf went back to the house where the seven little kids lived and called at the door, "Dear children, let me in, I'm your mother and I've got a present for each of you." The seven little kids demanded to see his paw first, and when they saw that it was as white as snow, and because the wolf's voice was so smooth, they believed it really was their mother. They opened the door and the wolf came in.

When the seven little kids saw the wolf they were terrified and tried to hide—the first under the table, the second in the bed, the third in the stove, the fourth in the pantry, the fifth in the cupboard, the sixth under a big bowl, and the seventh in the grandfather clock. But the wolf found them all and swallowed them up, except for the youngest one in the grandfather clock. He didn't find that one. Then the wolf left with a full stomach.

A little later the mother goat came home. The door stood open, the table and chairs and benches were overturned, the dishes were broken, the blanket and pillows had been pulled off the bed. What a calamity! The wolf had been there and had eaten her beloved children!

"Oh, oh, my seven kidlets are dead!" she cried sorrowfully.

At that the youngest little kid jumped out of the grandfather clock and said, "One is still alive, dear mother," and explained how the dreadful thing had happened.

Meanwhile, the wolf, very full and very sleepy, lay down in a green meadow in the sun and was soon snoring. But the old mother goat was wise and cunning and she thought there might still be a way to rescue her children. She said to the youngest little kid, "Get thread and a needle and scissors and follow me."

The two of them went out and found the wolf fast asleep in the meadow. "There's that wicked wolf," said the mother, "peacefully sleeping after eating my six children for his afternoon snack! Give me the scissors—with luck they'll still be alive in his belly." She carefully cut open the wolf's belly and the six little kids jumped out unharmed: the wolf had been so greedy that he hadn't stopped to chew them but had swallowed them whole. They hugged their mother and were overjoyed to be out of that dark prison. Then the mother goat sent them to get some big stones, and when they had filled the wolf's belly with them she sewed him up again. Then they all ran away and hid behind a hedge.

When the wolf finally woke up, he felt an unusual heaviness in his belly and said, "Something is rumbling and tumbling in my stomach. It's very strange. After all, I only ate six little goats." He thought a drink of fresh water might help, so he looked for a well. But when he bent over to drink, the stones inside him rolled forward and he lost his balance and fell into the water and drowned. When the seven little kids saw that, they came running and danced around the well for joy.

Source: Grimm KHM #5, 1819

Schwänke

(Comic Tales)

HCS '03

Hans in Luck ❧ Hans im Glück

When Hans had served his master faithfully for seven years, he decided it was time he went home to his mother, and as payment for his hard work, he got a lump of gold as big as his head. That much gold is heavy, but Hans tied it up in his handkerchief and went off happily enough with the bundle on his shoulder, for he certainly wasn't short of strength.

As he strolled along, thinking about what a fine gentleman he would be now that he was rich, he saw a man on a handsome horse riding toward him. Hans stood and gawked as the rider went by and said to himself quite loudly, "Riding must be a fine thing. You just sit there, don't stub your toes on stones, save wear and tear on your shoes, and get where you're going with no trouble at all." When the rider heard these words he pulled up and asked Hans where he was going. "I'm taking this lump of gold home to my mother, but it's a long walk!"

"Well," said the rider, "we could trade if you like. You give me your lump of gold and I'll give you my horse."

"That's a great idea," said Hans, "I'd love to trade." So he put down his lump of gold and the rider helped him up on the horse and put the reins in his hands.

"If you want to go faster, just click your tongue and say, 'hopp, hopp!' " the rider told him, and they went their separate ways.

For a while Hans rode happily, enjoying the view while the horse ambled along snatching the occasional mouthful of clover from the roadside. But then he decided they should be moving faster. He clicked his tongue and shouted, "Hopp, hopp!" At that the horse speeded up to a jolting trot, and before he knew what was happening Hans landed in the ditch.

A farmer driving a cow came along just then and caught hold of the horse before it could run away. "Riding isn't what it's cracked up to be!" said Hans to the farmer. "I could have broken my neck! I'm never going to get on that stupid nag again. Now your cow there, that's what I call a comfortable animal. You can stroll along behind her and you've got milk, cheese, and butter every day! I'd give anything to have a cow."

"We could trade if you like," said the farmer. "You give me your horse and I'll give you my cow."

"That's a great idea," said Hans, "I'd love to trade." So Hans took the cow and the farmer got up on the horse and galloped all the way home in case Hans changed his mind.

But Hans was completely content. He turned the cow in the direction of his mother's village and strolled along behind her, thinking happily that as long as he had a bit of bread he would always have butter and cheese to go with it and that whenever he was thirsty he would have milk to drink. Who could ask for more? To celebrate he stopped at the next inn for breakfast and ate all the food he had with him, lunch and supper both, and spent his last penny for half a glass of beer. Then he began walking again behind his cow, always heading home. The day got hotter and hotter. By midday Hans was in the middle of a moor, an hour or so from the next village, and so thirsty that his tongue stuck to the roof of his mouth. "Now's the time to milk my cow," he said to himself. "How lucky I am to have a refreshing drink walking right in front of me on four legs!" He tied the cow to a withered tree and put his leather cap on the ground underneath her to catch the milk. But he couldn't get a single drop of milk out of the cow, no matter how he tried. And because he was clumsy about it, the cow finally lost patience and kicked him so hard in the head with one of her hind feet that he was knocked senseless.

Luckily, a butcher came by just then pushing a young pig in a wheelbarrow. "What's your trouble, friend?" he asked Hans as he helped him up. Hans told him what had happened. The butcher passed a bottle to Hans and said, "A drink of this will make you feel better. But that cow is never going to give you milk. She's too old. The best you can do is butcher her."

"Oh my," said Hans, and rubbed his sore head. "I had no idea. There's probably a lot of meat on her, but I don't like beef, it's not juicy enough. A pig, now, that's good eating—hams and chops and ribs and the feet for pickling and all the sausages besides."

"Hans," said the butcher, "you're a good fellow and I'd like to help you out. I'll trade you my pig for your cow."

"That's a great idea!" said Hans. "I'd love to trade." So the butcher lifted the pig out of the wheelbarrow and went off with the cow, and Hans continued on the road home, driving the pig in front of him and thinking what a lucky fellow he was.

After a mile or so he met a man carrying a fat white goose under his arm. Once they had greeted each other and figured out that they were going in the same direction, Hans told him about all the lucky trades he'd made that day.

"You certainly know a good deal when you see one," said the fellow. "I'm taking this goose to a christening feast. Just feel how heavy it is. It's been fattened for eight weeks, and when the guests eat the roasted meat, they'll have to wipe the grease off their chins."

"Yes, it's a fat one," said Hans, hefting it in one hand, "but my pig isn't exactly skinny, either."

"About that pig of yours," said the fellow, looking carefully all around and shaking his head. "You may be in a bit of trouble. In the village I came through before I met you, the mayor had just had a pig stolen out of his sty. If that's the pig you've got, and they catch you, well, you'll have made a very bad bargain."

"Oh my goodness!" cried Hans, already seeing himself locked up in a dark cell. "You know your way around here and I don't. Please, help me. Trade me your goose for this pig."

"I'll be taking a big risk, but I'd hate to see you get into trouble just because you've been unlucky. Here, take the goose." The fellow handed the goose over to Hans and quickly drove the pig away down a small lane that branched off from the road.

"All in all," thought Hans to himself as he went on his way homeward, "I've made a good bargain. First there'll be the roast, and then there'll be drippings enough to make goose fat sandwiches for three months at least, and finally there are the beautiful white feathers that will make me a fine pillow on which I can sleep like a prince. My mother will be so happy!"

On the far side of the last village that lay between him and home, he saw a knife grinder standing by his cart and singing as his grindstone whirred around:

> *"Knives and scissors I sharpen with ease*
> *And I come and go wherever I please."*

Hans stopped and watched him for a while, and then said to him, "You must be a happy man to be singing at your work."

"I am," answered the knife grinder. "In my trade, a man always finds money when he puts his hand in his pocket. My living is guaranteed. But where did you buy that fine goose you're carrying?"

"Oh, I didn't buy it," said Hans. "I traded my pig for it."

"And where did you get the pig?"

"I traded my cow for it."

"And where did you get the cow?"

"I traded my horse for it."

"And where did you get the horse?"

"I traded a lump of gold as big as my head for it."

"And where did you get the lump of gold?"

"Oh, that was my wage for seven years of work," said Hans.

"Well, well," said the knife grinder. "You certainly know how to look out for yourself. But if you were a knife grinder, you could hear the money clinking in your pocket every time you stood up, and you'd be a made man."

"How do I go about becoming a knife grinder?" asked Hans.

"The main thing is, you need a grindstone. The rest will follow. Look here, I've got a stone that's just a bit damaged, and I won't ask more than your goose for it. Would that suit you?"

"How can you even ask?" answered Hans. "I'd love to trade! I'll be the happiest man on earth with money jingling in my pockets and no worries at all." Hans gave the knife grinder his goose, and the knife grinder gave Hans the damaged grindstone. Then he heaved up a large fieldstone that happened to be lying there and gave it to Hans, too. "Here you go," he said. "This is a good stone for hammering on. You can use it for beating crooked nails straight. See that you take good care of it."

Hans hoisted the two heavy stones onto his shoulder and walked off with a light heart. "What a lucky fellow I am," he said to himself. "I keep getting whatever I wish for. I must have been born on a Sunday." But soon he began to feel tired, for he had been on his feet since daybreak, and his stomach rumbled with hunger, for he'd eaten both lunch and supper for breakfast long ago. He dragged himself along and stopped frequently to rest, even though he was no more than a mile now from his mother's village. The stones seemed heavier and heavier, and he couldn't help thinking how much happier he'd be if he didn't have to carry them.

As slow as a snail he crept along until he came to a well by the side of the road. A drink of cool water seemed like a wonderful idea. Carefully, so as not to damage them, he laid the stones down on the well coping. But when he bent down to drink he accidentally nudged them, just a little, and the stones slid down the sloping edge and plopped into the water. And what did Hans do then? When he saw the stones sink down he jumped up full of joy. Getting rid of the stones had been his greatest wish, and now this, too, had been granted.

"No man on earth is luckier than I am!" he cried. And free of all burdens he ran home to his mother.

A man who can't do arithmetic will never be poor.

Grimm KHM #83, 1819; Uther

The Seven Swabians ❧ Die sieben Schwaben

Background: Schwaben ("Swabia" in English) is a region in southwestern German, bordering on Switzerland. The Swabians were a strong and warlike Germanic tribe that fought their neighbors for centuries, and Swabia was one of the most powerful duchies in medieval Germany. Funny stories and jokes about timid, simpleminded Swabians have been told in Germany since at least the sixteenth century (Keller). Swabians tell these stories themselves with complete good nature. They know that the jokes and tales spring from envy. The adventure with the hare is the most famous of many comic escapades, and it creates an unforgettable image: a line of seven frightened-looking men of all shapes and sizes hanging onto a long, long spear that is aimed at a harmless jack-rabbit.

Once there were seven men of Swabia who decided to set out into the world to seek adventures and to do great deeds together. The first was Mister Schulz, the second was Jackli, the third was Marli, the fourth was Jergli, the fifth was Michal, the sixth was Hans, and the seventh was Veitli. They wanted a weapon to take along, so they had a spear made—only one, but it was strong enough and long enough for all seven of them. They carried it together, one behind the other in a row, each gripping the shaft. The bravest and most heroic had to be first, so that was Mister Schulz. And at the end of the line came Veitli.

One evening in July, when they had gone a long way and still had a ways to go before they got to the village where they meant to spend the night, a hornet, or maybe it was a big cockchafer, flew past behind them, buzzing angrily in the twilight. Mister Schulz was so scared that he broke out into a cold sweat and almost let go of the spear.

"Hark, hark," he cried out to his companions. "By God, I hear a drum!"

Jackli, who was hanging onto the spear just behind him, smelled something, goodness only knows what, and announced, "There's certainly something out there, because I can smell the gunpowder in the air."

When he heard these words, Mister Schulz let go of the spear and started to run, leaping wildly over a fence that was in his way. Unfortunately, he landed on the teeth of a hay rake that happened to be lying on the ground, and the handle came up and smacked him in the face, hard.

"I surrender, take me prisoner, I surrender!" Mister Schulz hollered.

The other six jumped over the fence, too, falling all over each other and yelling, "If you surrender, I surrender! If you surrender, I surrender!"

After a while, when they noticed that they weren't being tied up and led away by the enemy, they realized that they had been fooled. And because they didn't want folks mocking and making fun of them, which would surely happen if the story got out, they swore a solemn oath together not to say a word about what had happened until one of them spilled the beans by accident.

Then they continued their expedition. The second danger that they encountered was a good deal worse than the first. They had been marching for several days and were crossing a field of bracken when they saw a jackrabbit sitting in the sun. He was sleeping with his big, glassy eyes wide open and his long ears standing straight up, the way jackrabbits do. The sight of this terrifying beast gave them all a horrible fright. They quickly took counsel among themselves to decide what would be the least dangerous thing they could do.

They wanted to run away, but if they did, maybe the monster would pursue them and gobble them up, hide and hair and all. So they concluded that they would have to fight a great and perilous battle, and do it right away while their courage was up. After all, well begun is half won, as the saying goes. The seven of them took hold of the spear, Mister Schulz at the head and Veitli at the tail. Mister Schultz wanted to wait just a bit longer, but Veitli, who was feeling quite brave at the end of the line, wanted to attack right away. He called out:

> *"Forward, in dearest Swabia's name,*
> *To hold back now would be a shame."*

Hans knew how to cap him, though:

> *"Sure, it's all right for you to talk,*
> *You're the very last man in this dragon stalk."*

Michal had something to add:

> *"The beast is foul, it isn't fair,*
> *I'll bet you it's the devil there."*

Then it was Jergli's turn:

> *"If it ain't him, it'll be his mother*
> *Or maybe the devil's stepbrother."*

Marli had an inspiration and said to Veitli:

> *"Go forward, Veitli, to the front*
> *I'll stand back while you bear the brunt."*

Veitli paid him no attention, so Jackli chipped in:

"Old Schulz will have to lead the way
For honor's sake, that's what I say."

At that Mister Schulz gathered his courage and spoke up in a very dignified tone:

"Don't think of death or of the grave,
Fortune goes always to the brave."

And then they charged the dragon. Mister Schulz crossed himself and called on God to help, but when that didn't make any difference and they were getting closer and closer to the enemy, he let out a yell of pure terror: "Aaaaaaaaaaaah!"

The noise woke up the jackrabbit, and scared him so that he hopped away. When Mister Schulz saw the rabbit deserting the field of battle he called out joyfully:

"Look, Veitli, look, look over there,
That is no monster, it's a hare."

Having survived this encounter, the intrepid band of Swabians looked for more adventure. They came to the mossy banks of the Mosel, a river whose still waters run very deep. There aren't many bridges over the Mosel, so mostly people cross by boat. The seven Swabians didn't know about the ferries, though, so they shouted to a fellow working on the far side of the river, asking him how to get across.

The man couldn't understand what they were saying because they were so far away and they had Swabian accents. So he called back, "Wait, wait," meaning that they should stay there while he came over to talk to them. But Mister Schulz thought the man was saying, "Wade, wade," and headed into the river. Before long he sank into the soft mud, and then under the rippling water, and only his hat reached the far shore, blown across by the wind. A frog sat down next to it and croaked loudly.

When the remaining six heard the frog, they said to each other, "That's our comrade, Mister Schulz, calling us. If he can wade over, so can we." They all rushed to jump into the water, and they all drowned. That's how a frog killed six men, and why none of the band of Swabians ever reached home again.

Grimm KHM #119, 1819

The Peasant's Wise Daughter
✺ Die kluge Bauerntochter

Once there was a poor peasant who owned no land. All he had was a very little house, no more than a hut, really, and one daughter. One day the daughter said to him, "Father, we should ask the king for a small piece of the grazing land so that we can make a garden and grow food for ourselves."

When the king heard how poor they were, he gave them a little corner of overgrown grassland. The girl and her father turned the sod, intending to plant barley and perhaps a few oats. When they had almost finished their hacking and hoeing they dug up a golden mortar out of the dark earth.

"Listen," said the father to his daughter, "Because the king was gracious and gave us this field we have to give the mortar back to him." His daughter disagreed with him.

"Father," she said, "If we give him the mortar without the pestle, we'll have to come up with the pestle, too. It would be better to say nothing." But her father refused to listen to her. He took the mortar to the king and explained how he had found it. The king took the mortar and asked whether he had found anything else.

"No," said the peasant. Then the king said he should have brought the pestle as well. The peasant explained that they hadn't found a pestle, but he might as well have saved his breath—he was put in prison, to sit there until the pestle showed up.

The servants who brought his bread and water every day heard the poor peasant wailing over and over again, "Oh, I should have listened to my daughter! Oh, if only I had listened to my daughter!" They reported this to the king and told him that the man would neither eat nor drink, but just kept crying, "I should have listened to my daughter!" The king ordered them to bring the prisoner, and he asked the peasant why he kept crying, "If only I had listened to my daughter!" What had his daughter said?

"Well, she said I shouldn't bring the mortar because I'd have to produce the pestle, too."

"If you've got such a wise daughter, let her come here," said the king. And so she had to appear before the king. He asked her if she really was wise and said he would give her a riddle. If she could solve the riddle, he would marry her. She said she was willing to try, and the king said, "Come to me not clothed, not naked, not riding, not driving, not on the road, not off the road. If you can do this, I will marry you."

The girl went home and undressed completely, and so she was not clothed. Then she took a large fishing net, sat down in the middle of it, and wrapped it around herself. So she was not naked. Then she hired a donkey and tied the end of the fishing net to its tail so that it had to drag her behind it, and so she was neither riding nor driving. And she made the donkey drag her along the center of the wagon track in such a way that no part of her touched the deep ruts made by the wagon wheels, and so she wasn't on the road and she wasn't off the road. When the king saw her coming like that, he said she had solved the riddle and met all his requirements. He released her father from prison, took her as his wife, and gave the royal treasury and estates into her care.

Several years went by, and then one day as the king was leaving the castle to review his troops, he met a group of farmers who had been selling wood in the town and had now pulled up their wagons near the castle gate. Some of them had oxen as draft animals and some had horses. There was a farmer who had three horses, and one of them was a mare with a young foal. The foal had run away from its mother and now lay under a wagon that had a pair of oxen hitched in front. The two farmers, the one with the mare and the one with the oxen, were making a lot of noise fighting about whom the foal belonged to. The one with the oxen claimed the oxen had produced the foal and it was his, while the other insisted that it was his mare's foal and it belonged to him. The argument was brought to the king, who ruled that where the foal lay, there it should stay, and so the farmer with the oxen got to keep the foal although it certainly wasn't his.

The farmer with the mare went away crying and lamenting. But he had heard that the queen was especially kind to farmers because she came from a poor peasant family herself, so he went to her and asked her to help him get his foal back.

She said, "If you'll promise that you won't give me away, I'll tell you what to do. Tomorrow morning, while the king is reviewing his troops, go and stand in the middle of the road where he will ride by. Take a big fishing net, and act as if you were fishing with it, and then empty it out as if it were full." And she told him what to say when the king asked him what he was doing.

So the next day the farmer stood fishing on dry land. When the king rode by and saw him he sent a messenger to ask what the foolish man was up to. The farmer answered, "I'm fishing." The messenger asked how he could fish where there was no water. "I can fish on dry land just as well as two oxen can produce a foal." The messenger brought this answer to the king, who had the farmer brought to him and said, "You didn't think this up yourself, did you? Tell me who gave you the idea."

The farmer didn't want to betray the queen, so he keep insisting that, God save him, he had thought it up himself. But the king's men thumped him and bullied him until he finally confessed that the queen had told him what to do.

When the king got home he said to his wife, "Why did you make me look like a fool? I don't want you as my wife anymore. Go back to the wretched little hut you came from." But as a parting gift, he said, she could take with her the one thing in the castle that was dearest to her.

"If that is your command, dear husband, I will obey," she said, and threw her arms around him and kissed him goodbye. Then she had wine brought with a strong sleeping potion mixed into it and said they should drink to their parting. The king took a large swallow, while she only sipped a little, and soon he fell into a deep sleep. As soon as she saw that he was fast asleep, she called a servant and told him to carry the king to the wagon that was waiting at the door. And then she drove the wagon home to her little hut. There she put the king into her bed, and he slept a day and a night straight through.

When he woke up, he looked around and said, "Where am I?" and called for his servants but no one came.

Finally his wife came to the bed and said, "My King, you allowed me to take with me from the castle the thing that is dearest to me. Nothing is dearer to me than you are, so I took you."

The king said, "Dear wife, I really was a fool," and took her back to the palace, where he married her a second time. And it's likely that they're still alive today.

Grimm KHM #94, 1837

Clever Else ❧ Die kluge Else

There was a man who had a daughter called Clever Else. When she grew up, her father said, "It's time we let her get married."

"Yes," said her mother, "If only some one would come along who wants her." Finally a man called Hans, who came from far away, asked for Else's hand, but only on the condition that she had a good head on her shoulders.

"Oh," said her father, "she's got plenty of brains."

"Yes," said her mother, "She can see the wind blowing down the street and hear flies coughing."

"All right," said Hans, "but if she's not a bright girl, I won't take her."

When they were sitting around the table after supper her mother said, "Else, go down to the cellar and get beer." So Clever Else took the pewter jug down from the wall and went to get beer, clapping the lid up and down to amuse herself on the way. Down in the cellar she got a little stool and put it in front of the barrel so that she wouldn't have to bend down and maybe hurt her back. Then she sat down, set the jug on the floor in front of the barrel, and opened the spigot. And while the beer ran into the jug, she rested her eyes by looking up at the wall. Looking around, she spotted a pickaxe that the stonemason had left behind, hanging right above her. Then Clever Else began to cry.

"If I marry Hans, and we have a baby, and it grows up, and we send it down to the cellar to get beer, then the pickaxe will fall on its head and knock it dead." She sat there and cried and howled as hard as she could about the coming misfortune. The folks upstairs were waiting for their beer, and after a while the mother said to the hired girl, "Go down to the cellar and see what's keeping Else."

The hired girl went and found her sitting in front of the barrel howling. "Why are you crying, Else?" asked the hired girl. "How could I not cry?" she answered. "If I marry Hans, and we have a baby, and it grows up, and comes down here to get beer, then that pickaxe might fall on its head and knock it dead."

The hired girl said, "What a clever girl our Else is!" and sat down beside her and started to cry about the future disaster herself. After a while, when the hired girl didn't come back and the folks upstairs were thirsty for their beer, the father said to the hired man, "Go down to the cellar and see what's keeping Else and the hired girl."

The hired man went down and found Else and the hired girl sobbing together. "Why are you crying?" he asked. "How could I not cry?" she answered. "If I marry Hans, and we have a baby, and it grows up, and comes down here to get beer, then that pickaxe will fall on its head and knock it dead."

The hired man said, "What a clever girl our Else is!" and sat down beside her and started to howl, too. Upstairs they were waiting for the hired man, and after a while the father said to the mother, "Go down to the cellar see what's keeping Else."

The mother went down and found all three of them wailing, and asked what the trouble was. So Else told her that her future child would probably be killed when it was old enough to be sent down to the cellar to get beer and the pickaxe fell on it.

Then her mother said, "What a clever girl our Else is!" and sat down and cried with them.

Upstairs the father waited for a while, but when his wife didn't come back, he said to Hans, "I'd better go down to the cellar myself and see what's keeping Else." And when he got down there and saw them all sitting and sobbing and found out they were crying about the child Else might have, that might be killed if it happened to be sitting in front of the beer barrel just when the pickaxe happened to fall down, he said, "What a clever girl our Else is!" and sat down and cried, too.

Hans waited upstairs alone for a long time, but when no one came he thought, "Maybe they're waiting downstairs for me. I should go down and see what's happening." When he got down there, he found all five of them in tears, each one howling and sobbing louder than the next one. He thought, "Something dreadful must have happened," and asked them what the calamity was.

"Oh, dear Hans," said Else, "if we get married and have a baby, and it grows up, and we send it down to the cellar for beer, and the pickaxe that got left up there happens to fall and break its skull, it would be dead, so how could we not cry?"

"Well now," said Hans, "that's enough good sense for me. You're such a clever girl, Else, that I'll take you." He grabbed her hand, took her back upstairs, and married her.

After they had been married for a while, Hans said, "Wife, I'm going to go out to work to earn us some money. And while I'm doing that, you can go out to the field and cut the rye so that we'll have bread."

"Yes, dear Hans, I'll do that," said Else. When Hans was gone, she cooked herself a nice pot of porridge and took it with her to the field. But when she got there, she asked herself, "What should I do? Should I cut first, or should I eat first?" She decided to eat first, and when she had emptied the pot and was very full of porridge she asked herself, "What should I do now? Should I cut first or should I have a nap first?" She decided to nap first, lay down in the rye field, and went to sleep.

Hans came home at the end of the day, but Else wasn't there. He thought, "What a clever Else I've got, she works so hard that she doesn't even come home to eat." After a while, though, when she still hadn't come home, he went out to see how much rye she had cut. And there she was, fast asleep in the rye, all of which was still standing. Hans hurried home and got a long piece of twine that was strung with small bells to scare birds away from the berry bushes. He wound it around her, and she never woke up. Then he ran home again, locked the door behind him, and sat down to do some work.

Night had fallen and it was dark before Else finally woke from her nap. When she stood up, the bells started tinkling, and they jingled with every step she took. The noise frightened and confused her, so that she wondered if she really was Clever Else, and asked herself, "Am I me, or aren't I?" But she didn't know the answer to her question and stood still for a while, overwhelmed by doubt.

Finally she thought, "I'll go home and ask whether I'm me or not. They'll know, for sure." She ran home and found the door locked, so she knocked on the window and called, "Hans, is Else in there?"

"Yes," answered Hans, "She's in here."

At that she became really frightened and said, "Oh, no! Then I'm not me!" She went to another house, but when the people there heard the bells they refused to open the door, not knowing what might be outside. She tried other houses, but nobody would let her in. So she ran out of the village, still jingling, and no one has seen her since.

Grimm KHM #34, 1857

Clever Gretel ❧ Das kluge Gretel

There was a cook whose name was Gretel. She wore shoes with red heels, and when she went out she would turn this way and that, admire her reflection in all the shop windows, and think to herself, "What a good looking girl you are!" And when she came home in high spirits, she would drink a glass of wine, and because the wine gave her an appetite, she would sample the best of her cooking until she was full, and then she'd say, "The cook has to know how the food tastes!"

It happened one day that her employer said to her, "Gretel, I've got a guest coming tonight. Cook two really tasty chickens for dinner."

"I'll do that, sir," answered Gretel. She killed two chickens and scalded them and plucked them and put them on the spit to roast over the fire. They began to get brown and crispy and were almost done, but the guest hadn't arrived yet.

Gretel called to her master, "If your guest doesn't come soon, I'll have to take the chickens off the fire, but it will be a dreadful shame if they aren't eaten while they're crisp and juicy."

The master said, "I'll run and get my guest right now." As soon as he was out the door, Gretel took the spit off the fire and thought to herself, "Standing beside the fire all that time makes a person sweaty and thirsty. Who knows when they'll be coming back. I'll just nip down to the cellar while I'm waiting and have a quick drink." She went to the cellar, drew a jug of wine from the barrel, and took a hearty swallow. "This wine seems to be just right to go with the chicken," she said, "but I'd better make sure," and took another. Then she went back upstairs and put the chickens back over the fire, brushed them with butter, and turned the spit briskly.

But they smelled so delicious that she thought, "Something might be missing—I'd better check the seasoning," swiped her finger over the sizzling skin and licked her finger. "My goodness, these chickens are tasty," she said. "It would be a shame and a scandal not to eat them right now!" She ran to the window to look for her master and his guest, but they weren't coming. She went back to the chickens and said to herself, "That one wing is burning. I'd better eat it—otherwise it will go to waste." So she cut it off and ate it and it was delicious. "I should eat the other one, too," she said, "Otherwise the master will notice that something is missing." After she had eaten the second wing, she went to the window again to look for her master, but he still wasn't in sight. "Maybe they're not coming at all," she thought. "They've probably stopped somewhere on the way." And then she said to herself, "Cheer up, Gretel. One of the chickens is partly eaten already, so you just have another drink and finish it up. Once it's gone you can stop worrying about it. It's a shame to waste good food."

She ran back down into the cellar, took a healthy drink, and ate the chicken up with great enjoyment. When the first chicken was nothing but bones and her master still hadn't come home, Gretel looked at the second chicken and said to herself, "Those two chickens were a pair and shouldn't be separated. What's right for the one is fair for the other. And it wouldn't hurt to have another drink." So she took another hearty swallow of the wine and let the second chicken join the first.

When she was halfway through the second chicken, her master came home and called, "Hurry up, Gretel, my guest will be here in a minute!"

"Yes, sir," Gretel called backed. "I'll dish up right away." The master checked to see that the table had been set, picked up the big carving knife, and went out into the hall to sharpen it. Just then the guest arrived and knocked politely at the door.

Gretel ran to see who it was, and when she saw the guest, she put her finger to her lips and said, "Shh, shh! Get away as fast as you can without letting my master see you. He invited you to supper but what he really has in mind is to cut your ears off. Listen—you can hear him sharpening his knife!" The guest did hear the sound of a knife being whetted and tiptoed back down the stairs as quickly as he could. Then Gretel ran shrieking to her master and shouted, "That's a fine guest you invited!"

"What do you mean, Gretel? What happened?"

"He grabbed both chickens from the platter as I was bringing them from the kitchen and ran off with them!"

"What a thing to do!" said the master. "He could at least have left one for me so I'd have something to eat." He called after the guest to wait, but the guest pretended not to hear him. So the master ran after him, waving the knife that he was still holding and crying, "Just one, just one!" meaning that the guest should leave him one of the chickens and not take both. But the guest thought his host was talking about his ears and ran as if a fire had been lit under him to get both of his ears safely home.

Grimm KHM #77, 1857

Clever Folk ✥ Die klugen Leute

Story note: I have long argued that gender is not an essential element of any folktale. I've reversed the gender roles in this tale, and since there are as many foolish men in the world as there are women, the story is just as funny this way.

There once was a foolish farmer who had a very capable wife. Marrying her was the smartest thing he had ever done, and their farm prospered because she made all the decisions. One day the wife said to her husband, "Hans, I'm going to visit my mother for three days. If the cattle dealer shows up and wants to buy our three cows, go ahead and sell them, but only if you can get two hundred talers* for them, not a penny less. If he won't pay two hundred talers, tell him to come back when I'm home again."

"Oh, go on, have a safe trip," said her husband, "I can manage that."

The next morning the cattle dealer came. When he'd looked at the cows and heard the price he said, "Fine, it's a deal. I'll take them with me right now." He unfastened the chain and drove the cows out of the barn. But just before he got to the yard gate the farmer grabbed his sleeve and said, "You have to give me the two hundred talers, or I can't let you take them."

"Right," said the cattle dealer, "only I forgot to bring my money bag. But don't you worry. I'll just take two of the cows with me now, and the third I'll leave with you as a pledge. That way you can be sure I'll come back with the money."

This made sense to the farmer, so he let the dealer go with two of the cows and thought to himself, "Won't Trina be pleased when she sees how clever I've been."

The farmer's wife came home on the third day and asked right away whether the cows had been sold. "Of course, Trina dear," the farmer answered, "and for two hundred talers, just like you said. They're not really worth that much, but the man took them without arguing."

"Where's the money?" asked his wife.

"Oh, I don't have the money yet," answered the farmer. "He forgot to bring his wallet, but we'll get the money soon. He left me good security."

"What did he leave?" asked the wife.

"One of the three cows. He won't get her until he's paid for them all, and I was clever about it. I kept the smallest one because she eats the least."

The farmer's wife was furious. "You are the silliest fool that ever walked on God's green earth! I've a good mind to leave you and let you manage the farm by

---

*A taler is a coin that was the official currency in German territories into the eighteenth century. The English word "dollar" is derived from "taler."

yourself—you'd soon starve! But I'm your wife, and I feel sorry for you. I'm going to go to my sister's inn at the crossroads and I'll stay there for three days, and if someone comes along who is sillier than you are, then I'll come home. But if not, I'm going back to my mother for good."

So the farmer's wife went to the inn, sat down on a bench where she could watch the road, and waited for whatever would come along. The first thing she saw was a hay wagon with a woman standing up in the middle of it instead of sitting comfortably on the bundled hay or walking and leading the oxen. "This may be just what I'm looking for," thought the farmer's wife, and she jumped up and ran back and forth in front of the wagon as if she'd lost her wits.

"What do you want, friend?" asked the woman. "I don't know you. Where are you from?"

"I fell down from heaven, and I don't know how to get back up. Could you drive me there?"

"No," said the woman, "I don't know the way. But if you come from heaven maybe you can tell me how my husband is. He's been up there for three years already so you've probably seen him."

"Oh yes, I've seen him, but he's not happy. They've made him the shepherd, and the sheep give him a lot of trouble. They wander away into the mountains and get lost in the thickets and he has to run after them through the bushes and try to gather them in again. His clothes are so torn and ragged that soon they'll fall right off him. There aren't any tailors up there to mend them—St. Peter won't let them in, as you know from the fairy tale."

"Who would have thought it!" cried the woman. "You know what? I'll go get his Sunday coat, it's still hanging at home in the wardrobe. He can wear it up there and look respectable. If you'll be good enough to take it to him?"

"That won't work," said the farmer's wife. "You can't bring presents into heaven, they get taken away outside the gate."

"Well, listen," said the woman, "I sold my wheat yesterday for a pretty price, and I'll send him the money. If you put the bag in your pocket no one will notice."

"Well, I'll give it a try, to oblige you," said the farmer's wife.

"Just sit down and wait for me here," said the woman. "I'll drive home to get the money and I'll be back soon. I'm standing up instead of sitting on the hay, you know, because that makes the load lighter for the oxen." And she got the oxen moving again and drove away.

"Well, she's a natural fool," thought the farmer's wife. "If she brings the money, it will be good luck for my husband." Before long the woman came running back with the money and watched while the farmer's wife stuffed the bag deep down into her pocket. Then she thanked her a thousand times for being so obliging and left.

When the silly woman got home, she found her son, who'd just come in from the fields. She told him about the surprising things she had learned and added, "I'm so happy that I found a chance to send my poor husband something. Who would have thought he could lack for anything in heaven?"

Her son was totally astonished. "Mother," he said, "It's not every day that someone comes down from heaven. I'm going to try to find that kind woman before she goes back. She can tell me what it looks like up there, and what kind of work there might be." So he saddled his horse and rode away as fast as he could go.

He found the farmer's wife sitting under a willow tree counting the money in the bag. "Have you seen the woman who came down from heaven?" the young man called.

"Yes," answered the farmer's wife, "but she's on her way back and she's climbing up that mountain there because heaven is closer from the top. You can still catch her if you ride fast."

"Oh," said the young man, "I've been working hard all day and the ride here has worn me out. You know what she looks like, so do me a favor. Take my horse and persuade her to come back here. I'd like to talk to her."

"Aha!" thought the farmer's wife, "here's another one with no wick in his lamp."

"I might as well oblige you," she said, got up on the horse, and rode off at a fast trot.

The young man sat there until it was dark, but the farmer's wife didn't come back. "Oh, well," he thought, "the woman from heaven must have been in a hurry and didn't want to turn back, and the other woman must have given her the horse to take to my father." He went home and told his mother what had happened: that he'd sent the horse to his father so he wouldn't have to walk everywhere.

"You did the right thing," his mother told him. "You've got young legs and can easily go on foot."

When the farmer's wife got home she put the horse in the stable next to the third cow. Then she went to her husband and said, "Hans, you're in luck. I found two people who are even sillier fools than you. So I've come back. Go feed the animals and supper will be ready in an hour." Then she got a glass of buttermilk, sat down in the grandfather chair by the fire, and said to herself, "That was good business, getting a fine horse for two skinny cows, and a pocketful of money to boot. If foolishness always paid this well, I'd be a rich woman."

Grimm KHM #104, 1857

The Master Thief ❧ Der Meisterdieb

One day an old woman and her husband were sitting in front of their small cottage, resting from their work. Suddenly a magnificent coach drawn by four coal-black horses arrived at their door and a richly dressed man stepped out. The old farmer stood up and went to ask how he might serve him. The fine gentleman took the old man's hand and said, "I would like to eat some plain country food. If you'll make me a dish of potatoes the way you cook them for yourselves, I'll sit down at table with you and eat them with pleasure."

The old man smiled and said, "You must be a nobleman, a count or duke or perhaps a prince. Distinguished gentlemen sometimes have such desires."

The old woman went into the kitchen and began to grate potatoes for potato dumplings, while the farmer invited the visitor into the garden, where he had some work to finish up. He had dug holes there and now began to plant trees in them.

"Have you no children who could help with such work?" asked the stranger.

"No," said the farmer. "I did have a son, but he went off a long time ago and I have no idea where in the wide world he might be. He was a spoiled child, clever and cunning, but unwilling to learn anything useful and full of bad tricks. In the end he ran away, and I've heard nothing from him since."

The old man took a sapling, set it into a hole, and drove a pole in next to it. And when he had filled the hole with dirt and stamped it down, he tied the little tree to the pole, bottom, middle, and top, with a rope of twisted straw.

"Tell me," said the gentleman, and pointed to a crooked, twisted tree bent so far over that it nearly touched the ground, "Why don't you tie that tree to a pole to make it grow straight?"

The old man smiled and answered, "You don't know much about gardening, do you, sir? That tree is old and gnarled and full of knots. No one could straighten it out. Trees have to be trained up while they're young."

"It's the same thing with your son," said the gentleman. "If you had trained him when he was young, he wouldn't have run away. By now he must be stiff and gnarled, too."

"Very likely," replied the old man. "It's been so long since he left."

"Would you still recognize him if he came back?" asked the stranger.

"Probably not his face," the farmer answered. "But there is a sign I'd know him by: he has a birthmark shaped like a bean on his shoulder."

At that the stranger took off his coat, bared his shoulder, and showed the farmer the birthmark.

"Good heavens," cried the farmer, "You are in truth my son," and a great rush of love for his child filled his heart. But then he doubted. "How can you be my son? You're a fine gentleman with wealth in abundance! How did you come by it?"

"Oh, father," said the son, "the sapling wasn't tied to a pole and so it grew crooked, and now it's too late to make it straight. I became a thief. But I don't steal like a common thief. I'm a master thief. No lock nor bolt can keep me out. Anything I want is mine. I don't steal from the poor, only from the overabundance of the rich, and I don't take anything that comes easily. If the theft doesn't require cleverness and cunning, I don't touch it."

"My son," said the father, "I don't like it. A thief is a thief. You'll come to a bad end." Then he led the visitor into the house and when the old woman heard he was her son she cried tears of happiness. But when she found out he was a thief, she cried for grief. Finally she said, "Even if he is a thief, he is still my son, and I am glad to have seen him once more."

They sat down at the table together and ate the simple fare the son hadn't tasted for many years. His father said, "If our lord the count in his castle over there finds out who you are and what you do, he won't rock you in his arms as he did at your baptism. You'll be swinging at the end of a rope instead."

"Don't worry, Father, I know my business. The count won't harm me. In fact, I'll go and see him today myself."

Toward evening the master thief got into his carriage and drove to the castle. The count received him with civility because he thought his visitor was a gentleman. But when the thief introduced himself, he grew pale and sat in silence for a while.

Finally he said, "You are my godson, and for that reason I'll give you mercy instead of justice. You boast that you're a master thief, so I'll test your skill. If you fail the test, you'll have to marry the rope-maker's daughter and the crows will croak your wedding music."

"My lord count," answered the thief, "give me three tasks, as difficult as you can make them, and if I don't succeed you may do with me as you like."

The count thought for a few moments. Then he said, "First, you must steal my favorite horse from its stall. Second, after my wife and I have gone to bed you must steal the bed sheet out from under us and the wedding ring from her finger without our noticing. Third, you must steal my parson and sexton from the church. Mark carefully what I say, for your neck is at stake."

The master thief went to the nearest city, where he bought the clothes of an old peasant woman. When he had put them on, he dyed his face brown and painted wrinkles on it. No one would have recognized him. Finally he filled a small keg with old Hungarian wine and mixed in a very strong sleeping potion. The keg he put in a pack-frame that he hoisted onto his back, and then he walked with slow, unsteady steps to the count's castle.

It was dark when he arrived. He sat down on a stone in the courtyard, coughing like a consumptive old woman and rubbing his hands together as if he were freezing. In front of the stable door, a dozen soldiers sat around a fire. One of them noticed the woman and called, "Come closer, little mother, and warm yourself at our fire. You can spend the night here if you've nowhere else to sleep." The old woman tottered over to them, asked one of the soldiers to lift the pack-frame off her back, and sat down by the fire.

"What do you have in that keg?" one of the soldiers asked.

"As good a wine as you've ever tasted," she answered. "I sell it to make my living. For money and a few kind words I'll give you some."

"Hand it over, then," said the soldier, and as soon as he'd emptied the glass he called for more. The others gladly followed his example.

"Hey, you fellows in the stable," shouted one of them. "There's a little old woman out here with wine that's even older than she is. You should have some, too. It'll warm your bellies better than our fire will."

So the old woman carried her keg into the stable and found the count's favorite horse standing saddled and bridled and chained to a post. One guard sat in the saddle, a second held fast to the bridle, and a third was clutching the horse's tail. She poured wine for them until her keg was empty. And it wasn't long before the man holding the bridle let go, sank to the ground, and began to snore. The one holding the tail lost his grip too and lay down in the straw snoring even louder. The one in the saddle stayed sitting, but his head sagged forward until his nose almost touched the horse's neck, and he breathed so heavily in his sleep that he sounded like a pair of bellows. The soldiers outside had fallen asleep long since, and lay motionless on the ground like stones.

When the master thief saw that they were all asleep, he put a rope into the hand of the man who had been holding the bridle, and a fistful of straw into the hand of the man who had been holding the horse's tail. But what was he to do with the man on the horse's back? If he tried to lift him down, he might wake up and give the alarm. The master thief looked around and saw ropes hanging from two metal rings fastened to the walls. Quickly he unbuckled the saddle girth, tied two of the ropes to the saddle and pulled the sleeping rider on the saddle up off the horse. Then he wound the ropes around the post and fastened them. So far so good. The chain was no trouble at all, but iron horseshoes on the cobblestones would make enough noise to wake the castle. So the master thief wrapped rags around the horse's hooves before he led it carefully out of the stable and across the castle yard. Then he swung himself up on the horse and galloped off into the night.

Early next morning the master thief rode up to the castle just as the count got out of bed and went to his bedroom window. "Good morning, my lord!" called the thief. "Here is the horse I stole from its stall. You can see how well your soldiers are sleeping, and if you go into the stable you'll see that your guards have made themselves comfortable."

The count had to laugh, but then he said, "You've succeeded once. The second time you won't be as lucky, and I warn you that if you meet me as a thief, I shall treat you as a thief."

That night when the countess went to bed, she closed the hand with her wedding ring tightly and the Count said, "All the doors are locked and bolted. I'll stay awake and wait for the thief. If he tries to get in through the window I'll shoot him dead."

But under the cover of darkness, the master thief went out to the gallows, cut down a poor sinner who hung there, and carried him back to the castle. There he leaned a ladder against the wall under the bedroom window, set the corpse up on his shoulders, and began to climb. When the face of the corpse appeared in the bedroom window the count, who was lying in wait in his bed, fired his pistol at him. Right away the thief let the corpse fall, ran down the ladder himself, and hid in a dark corner. The moonlight was so bright that the thief could easily see the count climb down the ladder and carry the dead man into the garden, where he began to dig a hole to bury him in.

"Now's my chance," thought the thief. He stole out of his corner, nimbly climbed the ladder again, and stepped into the countess's bedroom. "My dear," he began, speaking in the count's voice, "the thief is dead. But he was my godson, and more a trickster than an evildoer, and besides I feel sorry for his poor parents. Rather than have him publicly dishonored when this story gets out, I'll dig his grave in the garden tonight myself. Give me the bed sheet to wrap his body in, and I'll bury him like a dog." The countess gave him the bed sheet.

"You know," continued the thief, "I feel moved to generosity. Give me your wedding ring as well. Since the poor soul risked his life for it, let him have it in his grave." She didn't want to refuse the count, so she reluctantly pulled the ring from her finger and handed it over. The thief left her room with both the sheet and the ring and was safely home before the count finished his grave digging in the garden.

The count made a very unhappy face when the thief brought him the bed sheet and the ring next morning.

"Can you work magic?" he asked him. "I buried you myself. Who brought you out of the grave and back to life?"

"You didn't bury me," said the master thief and explained in detail how it had all come about. The count had to admit that he was a clever and cunning thief.

"But you're not finished yet," he added. "You still have a third task, and if you can't accomplish it then nothing will save you." The master thief simply smiled.

That night, with a long sack on his back, a bundle under his arm, and a lantern in his hand, he went to the village church. The sack was full of crabs and the bundle was full of short candles. He sat down in the graveyard, pulled a crab from the sack, and stuck a candle on its back. Then he lit the candle, put the crab down, and let it crawl away. He took a second crab out of the sack, did the same with it, and continued until the sack was empty.

Next he put on a long dark robe that looked like a monk's cowl and glued a grey beard to his chin. When he was completely unrecognizable he took the empty sack, went into the church, and climbed up into the pulpit. The clock in the church tower struck midnight.

As the twelfth stroke died away, he cried out in a very loud voice, "Harken, ye sinners, the end of the world has come, the day of judgment is at hand, hear ye, hear ye. If you want to come to heaven with me, crawl into my sack. I am Peter, the keeper of the gates of heaven. Look ye, out there in the graveyard the dead are wandering, gathering up their bones. Come, come and crawl into my sack, the world is ending."

His shouting rang through the whole village. The pastor and the sexton, who lived closest to the church, heard it first, and when they saw the wandering lights in the graveyard, they were certain that something unusual was happening and went into the church. They listened to the sermon for a while, and then the sexton nudged the pastor and said, "It wouldn't be a bad idea to take this opportunity to go to heaven together the easy way before the day of judgment comes."

"I was just thinking the same thing," said the pastor. "If you like, we could go now."

"Certainly," answered the sexton, "but as parson you have precedence. Lead the way and I'll follow you."

So the pastor climbed the stairs to the pulpit where the thief was holding the mouth of the sack open, and he crawled in first and the sexton crawled in after him. Quickly the thief tied the sack shut, grabbed it by the knot, and dragged it down the pulpit steps. And every time the heads of the two fools bumped on a step, he called, "We're up on top of the mountains already." Then he dragged them through the village and whenever he pulled them through a puddle he'd shout, "We're going through the wet clouds." And when he finally dragged them up the castle stairs, he shouted, "We're on the stairway to heaven and we'll soon be at the gates." When he got to the top, he pushed the sack into the dovecot and as the doves fluttered around he said, "Can you hear? The angels are flapping their wings because they're so happy." Then he closed the bolt on the door and left them there.

The next morning he went to the count and told him that he had accomplished the third task too and had stolen the pastor and the sexton from the church. "Where did you leave them?" asked the count.

"Oh, I left them in a sack in the dovecot and they think they're in heaven."

The count climbed into the dovecot himself to make sure the master thief had told the truth.

After he had let the pastor and the sexton out, he said, "You are an arch-thief and you have won your case. This time you'll escape with a whole skin, but leave my country as fast as you can, and never come back. For if you set foot here again, you can count on being hanged."

The master thief said goodbye to his parents and went back out into the wide world. No one ever heard from him again.

Grimm KHM #192, 1857

The Three Lazybones ✿ Die drei Faulen

A king had three sons. He loved all three equally and didn't know which of them he should name as his heir. When the time came for the king to die, he called all three of his sons into his presence and said, "Dear children, I have thought long and hard about which of you should succeed me, and now I have decided: the laziest one of you will be king after my death."

Then the eldest son said, "Father, the kingdom is mine. For I am so lazy that when I lie down at night I can't even be bothered to close my eyes so that I may fall asleep."

The second son said, "Father, the kingdom is mine. For I am so lazy that when I sit by the fire to keep warm, I will let my heels burn rather than make the effort to pull my legs back."

The third son said, "Father, the kingdom is mine. For I am so lazy that if I were about to be hanged, with the noose already around my neck, and someone put a sharp knife into my hand so that I might cut the rope, I would let myself be hanged rather lift a hand."

When the father heard that, he said, "You will be the king."

Grimm KHM #151, 1819

The Post-horn ❧ Das Posthorn

One very cold winter day a postillion was driving his mail coach through the Black Forest along a hollow way.* From his high perch he saw a wagon in the distance, so he picked up his post-horn to blow the signal that would warn the wagoner that the mail coach was coming. Mail coaches had the right of way on any road, and the wagoner was supposed to stop and let it pass. But however hard he blew, the postillion could not get a single note out of the horn. The wagon came deeper and deeper into the hollow way, and because neither of them could move aside for the other, the postillion drove right over it. To make sure that such an inconvenience wouldn't occur again, he took his horn in his hand and played all the songs he knew, thinking that the horn must be frozen shut and that his warm breath might thaw it out. It didn't help, though. None of the notes he blew into the horn came out.

Toward evening the postillion finally came to the inn where the horses would be changed for the next stage and another driver would take over from him. He ordered a half pint of wine to warm himself, and because a wedding was being held at the inn and the main room was full of guests, he took his wine into the kitchen, sat down by the warm hearth, hung his horn on a nail in the wall, and chatted with the cook.

Suddenly the horn began to blow on its own. First it played the signal that postillions use when someone is supposed to give way, several times. Then it played all the songs he had blown into it along the way. They had frozen inside the horn and now they were thawing out one by one. It was quite a concert, and it ended with the chorale, "Now all the woods are sleeping," which was the last song the postillion had played.

From Meier 1852

*A hollow way is a narrow, unpaved road that has been used for so many centuries that its surface has worn down well below the level of the surrounding countryside.

All Lies ❧ Ein Lügen-Märchen

There once was a man who heard young birds cheeping in a hollow tree and climbed up to get the nest. But the hole was too small for his hand to reach through. So what did he do? He quickly crawled in and took the nest. But there he sat, stuck inside the tree, because the hole was only big enough for a little bird. What was he to do? He went home and got an axe, and then he crawled back into the tree and chopped at the hole until it was big enough for him to crawl out comfortably with the bird's nest in his hand. That was a piece of work, I'll tell you!

And if you don't want to believe me, you can suit yourself.

From Meier 1854

Till Eulenspiegel

Background: Till Eulenspiegel was probably born in a book in Germany in 1510. Although he began as a literary invention, he quickly became part of folklore as Germany's most famous folk hero and trickster. He has moved comfortably back and forth between oral and literary traditions for the past five centuries. His surname, Eulenspiegel, or Ulenspiegel, means "owl mirror." In English, he is known as Till Howleglass, or Owlyglass, "glass" meaning mirror in this case.

My source for these stories is J. M. Lappenberg's edition of the text printed in 1519, which was attributed to Thomas Murner. There are many variations on the spelling of Till Eulenspiegel's name. Till Eulenspiegel is the most common contemporary form, so I have used that throughout instead of the Thyl Ulenspiegel in the 1519 text of Lappenberg's edition. In the last story, "The End of Till Eulenspiegel," I have, of course, left the name in the inscriptions on the gravestone as they occur.

First Story

Till Eulenspiegel was born near the forest called Melme, in the land of Saxony, in the village called Knetlingen. His father was Claus Eulenspiegel and his mother was Ann Wibcken. After his mother had recovered from childbirth, they sent the baby to Ampleuen to be baptized, and the master of the castle, Till von Utzen, stood godfather. (Ampleuen is the castle that was broken up fifty years before by the people of Magdeburg with help from the other towns around because it had become the stronghold of a band of robbers. The churches and the village became the property of the worthy Arnold Pfaffenmeyer, abbot of St. Egidien.)

When Till had been baptized and they were carrying him back to Knetlingen, his godmother, who was holding the baby, fell off a narrow footbridge across a little pond that wasn't much more than a mud puddle. It's the custom to bring a newly baptized baby from the church to the public house for a celebration and to toast the baby with beer that the father will have to pay for. Till's godmother had drunk a few too many beers. So she fell into the water with Till and got so covered with muck that the baby almost suffocated. The other women helped them out and went back home to Knetlingen where they washed the baby clean in a kettle.

So Till Eulenspiegel was baptized three times in one day: once in the font, once in the puddle, and once in a kettle with warm water.

The castle in Celle (see page 69).

Second Story

As soon as Till Eulenspiegel was old enough to walk, he spent most of his time playing with the other children, tumbling around on the grass like a monkey. And when he reached the age of three he started to play tricks on people, making so much mischief that all the neighbors got together and complained about him to his father.

His father went to find Till and asked him, "Why do all the neighbors accuse you of being a rascal? What have you been up to?"

Till answered, "Dear father, I haven't done anything to anybody. I can prove it to you. Get your horse, and I'll sit behind you and won't say a word. We'll ride through the streets together and you'll see, people will tell lies about me and accuse me of all sorts of things."

So his father did as Till suggested. But as they rode through the town, Till raised his backside in the air, pulled up his smock, and stuck his bare bum out for everybody to see before he sat down again. Of course all the folk in the street and at their windows pointed at Till and called, "Shame on you! Dirty rascal!" Till said to his father, "See? You know I've just been sitting quietly behind you, but listen to them."

Till's father gave it another try, this time putting Till in front of him on his horse. And this time Till made dreadful faces, opening his mouth as wide as it would go, baring his teeth like a monkey, and sticking his tongue out at the passers by. The people who saw him called out, "Just look at him! What a rascal!"

So Till's father said to him, "You must have been born at an unlucky hour. You sit still, don't say a word, don't do anyone any harm, and still people accuse you of mischief."

Third Story

Claus Eulenspiegel moved his family into the district of Magdeburg on the River Saale, and not long afterward, he died. Till and his mother stayed on in the village where they had settled because this was where Ann Wibcken, Till's mother, had been born. They were poor, but Till wouldn't learn a trade. Even at the age of sixteen he spent his time fooling around and learning silly tricks instead. One of them was tightrope walking. He practiced in the attic of the house where his mother couldn't see him, because she had no patience for this foolishness and threatened to beat him whenever she caught him at it.

One time when she knew he was on the tightrope she took a big stick and tried to knock him off the rope with it. But Till quickly ran along the rope to a window, climbed through, and sat on the roof where she couldn't reach him. After that he gave up the tightrope for a while, but it wasn't long before he was at it again.

Till's mother lived in a house with a courtyard that ran down to the river Saale, and Till ran a rope from the roof beam of his mother's house to the house just across the river. A lot of people, young and old, noticed the rope and came to see what curious or astonishing trick Till might be up to this time. Well, Till walked out on the rope until he was right over the river and started to show off, confident that his mother couldn't see him from inside the house and couldn't do much to him even if she did. But just when his performance was at its best, his mother snuck up to the attic where the rope was tied and cut the rope loose. Her son Till fell into the river with a huge splash. The people watching laughed and made fun of him and the boys yelled things like, "Hey! Enjoy your bath! Take a good long soak! You sure worked hard to get it!"

Till was so annoyed by their laughter and ridicule that he didn't even mind his unexpected ducking. All he could think about as he got himself out of the water was how to pay them back.

Fourth Story

The next day Till Eulenspiegel took his revenge. He stretched his rope across the river from a different house and told everybody that he was going to perform again. A lot of people, young and old, soon gathered. Till addressed the crowd, asking that each one of the boys there give him his left shoe because he needed the shoes for an especially fine trick. They all believed him, and the boys took off their left shoes and gave them to Till. There were almost twice five dozen—that is, 120—boys, so there was a big pile of shoes. Till strung all the shoes together on a cord and climbed onto his rope with them. Everybody watched to see what he would do with the shoes, and the boys began to be a little anxious about getting them back. Till sat on his rope and fiddled about a bit until he was ready, and then called down, "All of you watch out, and each of you find your own shoe!" And with that he cut the cord and the shoes tumbled to the ground, all jumbled together.

Everybody rushed over to the shoes and scrabbled for his own. Over here one said, "This one's mine!" and over there one answered, "You're lying, it's mine!" and everywhere they got in each other's way and began to punch each other and knocked each other down and screamed and cried and laughed until even the old men started slapping faces and pulling each other's hair.

Eulenspiegel sat above the scuffle on his rope and laughed and called down, "Hey, there! Yesterday I got to go swimming, today you get to play hunt the slipper!" Then he ran to the end of the rope and climbed off, leaving the crowd to skirmish over the shoes.

He was afraid to show his face in the village for a month afterward and stayed at home with his mother, mending shoes for a cobbler in a nearby town. His mother was happy that he seemed to be settling down and began to hope that perhaps he might still amount to something. She didn't know about the trick in the air that had grounded him.

Eighth Story

One of Till Eulenspiegel's neighbors was a penny-pinching farmer who had played a nasty trick on Till and the other children out of pure stinginess. A few days afterward, this farmer ran into Eulenspiegel on the street and said, "When are you going to come for a visit again?"

"When your hens play tug-of-war, four at a time, for a piece of bread," answered Eulenspiegel.

"That will be a while, then," said the farmer.

"Maybe not," said Eulenspiegel, and went on his way.

He watched, and he waited, and one day when the farmer's hens were out feeding in the lane he grabbed his chance. He had twenty-some pieces of string and tied them together in twos, knotting each pair together in the middle so that there were four ends. Then he tied a bit of bread to each end of string and laid the strings out crosswise in the lane with only the bread showing. The flock of hens came pecking and clucking along, and when they saw the bits of bread they gobbled them up. But they gobbled up the string, too, and couldn't swallow the bread all the way down because there was another chicken pulling at the other end of the string trying to swallow the piece of bread it had picked up. The bread stuck in their throats because the pieces were big ones, so there they were in sets of four, the entire flock of chickens, choking and pulling. They looked exactly as though they were play tug-of-war.

Ninth Story

One day, Eulenspiegel and his mother went to a fair in another village. Eulenspiegel drank enough to get drunk, and then wandered away to find a quiet corner where he could safely have a little nap. In the yard of one of the houses he came across a bunch of beehives, some of which were empty. He crawled into one of the empty hives and settled down to sleep for a bit. In fact, he slept from noon until midnight. His mother had looked for him, but when she couldn't find him anywhere she thought he'd gone home.

That same night two thieves came to steal honey. One said to the other, "I've always heard that the heaviest beehive has the most honey in it." So they lifted the hives, one after another, until they got to the one Eulenspiegel was sleeping in. It was by far the heaviest, so they said, "That's the best one," and heaved it up and carried it away

Meanwhile Eulenspiegel had woken up and figured out what they were up to. It was really dark, dark enough that the two thieves could barely see each other. Eulenspiegel reached out of the beehive and gave the hair of the man at the front a sharp tug. He, of course, thought that the man behind him had done it, and began to swear at him. The man behind him said, "Are you dreaming, or sleepwalking? How could I have pulled your hair? I can barely carry this beehive with both hands, let alone one."

Eulenspiegel laughed to himself and thought, "This game should be fun to play." He waited until they'd gone the length of a field, and then he yanked the hair of the thief behind him. That man, of course, thought that the thief at the front had done it, and got angry himself: "Here I am, practically breaking my back, and you're pulling my hair out!"

"You're lying!" answered the first thief. "How could I have pulled your hair? I can hardly see the road in front of me. And besides, *you* just pulled *my* hair."

So they squabbled back and forth as they stumbled through the dark with the beehive, each accusing the other. After a little while, when their tempers were really hot, Eulenspiegel reached forward again and pulled the first thief's hair so hard that his head banged against the beehive. That was enough! The first thief dropped his end of the beehive and punched the other thief on the nose. The second thief let go of the beehive, too, and threw himself at the first thief, knocking him to the ground. They rolled around in the dark until they got separated and neither could find the other. Then each went his own way, muttering and grumbling, leaving the beehive where it lay. Eulenspiegel peered out, but when he saw that it was still dark, he went back to sleep and slept until broad daylight. Then he crawled out of the beehive and had no idea where he was. So he followed a road until he came to a castle, where he found work as a page.

Twenty-Sixth Story

Eulenspiegel played such wild tricks in Celle, a city in the Duchy of Lünenburg, that the duke banished him and gave orders that if Eulenspiegel set foot in that land again he was to be arrested and hanged. But Eulenspiegel didn't let that stand in his way—if his road led through Lünenburg, then through Lünenburg he went.

On one occasion, Eulenspiegel went with a horse and a two-wheeled cart that he'd acquired to a small village near Celle and waited for the duke to pass that way. There he saw a farmer plowing a field. Eulenspiegel went up to the farmer and asked him who owned the field that he was plowing.

The farmer answered, "I do. I inherited it."

Then Eulenspiegel asked the farmer how much he'd charge for a cartful of dirt from that field.

"A schilling," said the farmer.

So Eulenspiegel gave him a schilling and shoveled dirt into his cart until it was full. Then he climbed into the cart, wriggled himself down into the dirt, and drove to the castle in Celle on the River Aller. When the duke came riding by, there was Eulenspiegel in his cart, up to his shoulders in dirt. The duke said, "Eulenspiegel, I banished you from my land and gave orders that you should be hanged if you were found in it."

Eulenspiegel answered, "Your grace, I'm not in your land. I'm sitting in my land, that I bought for a schilling from a farmer who said he had inherited it."

The duke said, "Drive your cartful of earth off my soil and never come back, or I'll hang you, horse and cart and all."

Instead of driving away, Eulenspiegel climbed out of the cart, jumped on his horse, and rode out of Lünenburg. He left the cart standing in front of the castle. So some of the land in front of the bridge still belongs to Till Eulenspiegel.

Twenty-Seventh Story

Eulenspiegel did some astonishing things in the country of Hessen. He had traveled all over Saxony and became so well known that he didn't have much chance of pulling off any of his tricks there. So he went to Hessen and wound up in Marburg at the court of the landgrave. When the landgrave asked him what he did for a living, Eulenspiegel answered, "Your lordship, I'm a practitioner of the arts."

The landgrave was delighted because he thought Eulenspiegel meant the arts of alchemy, in which the landgrave himself had a strong interest. So he asked Eulenspiegel directly, was he an alchemist? Eulenspiegel answered, "No, your lordship, I'm a painter, a painter without equal, for my work is better than the work of any other."

The landgrave said, "Let us see some of your work."

"Yes, your lordship," answered Eulenspiegel and pulled from his sack a number of canvases and some other pieces of art that he had bought in Flanders.

The landgrave liked the things Eulenspiegel showed him and said to him, "Dear master, what would you charge to paint this hall with murals showing the lineage of the landgravine of Hessen, my wife, and how it brings me the friend-ship of the king of Hungary and other princes and lords, and how far back the con-nection goes? The whole thing should look as magnificent as you can possibly make it."

"If your lordship were to give me the work," answered Eulenspiegel, "it would probably cost four hundred guilders."

The landgrave said, "Fine. Do a good job and we'll pay you for it, and give you a bonus as well."

So Eulenspiegel took the commission and a first payment of one hundred guilders to buy pigments and hire assistants. Before he actually started the work, he set the condition that no one except his assistants was to enter the hall while he was working, so that his art would not suffer from interruption. Then Eulenspiegel made a deal with his three assistants: they were to say nothing, no matter what he did, and do no work themselves, but be paid all the same. Their only task would be to amuse themselves by playing draughts. The assistants, of course, were happy to agree.

After three or four weeks, the landgrave wanted to see what the master and his helpers were painting, and whether it would be as good as the samples he'd been shown. So he said to Eulenspiegel, "Dear master, we long to see your work. Won't you take us into the hall and show us your painting?"

Eulenspiegel answered, "Yes, your lordship, I will. But first I must warn your grace of one thing. If anyone who looks at my paintings is not of legitimate birth, he will see nothing at all."

"How astonishing!" said the landgrave, and they walked into the hall.

Eulenspiegel had covered the wall he was supposed to be painting with a long piece of linen cloth. Now he pulled it back a little and pointed at the wall with a small white stick. "Your lordship will see that this figure here is the first landgrave of Hessen, a member of that ancient and noble Roman family, the Colonnas, who was married to a duchess of Bavaria, herself the daughter of Justinian the Generous who later became emperor. And here your lordship will see his heir, Adolphus. Adolphus sired Wilhelm the Black, and Wilhelm sired Ludwig the Pious, and so on until we come to your princely grace's own self. I am confident that no one could find fault with my painting. In its artistry, colors, and composition it is in every way worthy of its illustrious subject."

The landgrave, who could see none of what Eulenspiegel had described, thought to himself, "Even if it means I'm a bastard, I can't see anything there except the plain white wall." But he said, "Dear master, we are very pleased with your work, although we ourselves don't know enough to judge its artistic qualities," and left the hall. When he next saw his wife, she asked him, "My dear lord, now that you've seen your freelance painter's work, tell me, what is he painting, and how do you like it? I have my doubts about the whole thing—he looks like a charlatan to me."

The landgrave answered, "My dear wife, I think his work is very nice, very suitable. You must do him justice."

"Then, dear sir, should we not see it for ourselves?" asked his wife.

"Certainly, with the master's permission," answered the landgrave.

The landgravine summoned Eulenspiegel and desired to see his paintings. Eulenspiegel first warned her, as he had warned her husband, that anyone whose birth was in any way illegitimate would be able to see nothing of his work. Then the landgravine, accompanied by eight ladies-in-waiting and the woman who was her court fool, entered the hall. Eulenspiegel drew back the cloth that covered the wall and pointed out all the ancestors of the landgravine, just as he had for her husband. But the landgravine and her ladies-in-waiting were silent. None of them said a word of praise or blame. Each one was afraid she might be of illegitimate birth on either her father's or her mother's side. At last, the fool spoke up and said, "Master painter, it may mean I'm a bastard, but I don't see any painting."

Eulenspiegel laughed, but he thought to himself, "This isn't going to work out. When fools tell the truth, then I must in truth be on my way."

The landgravine went back to her husband, who asked her how she had liked the painting. She answered, "Gracious sir, it pleases me as much as it pleases your grace. But our fool doesn't like it. She says she sees no painting, and our ladies-in-waiting say the same. I'm afraid there's knavery in this business." The landgrave was very much struck by what his wife had said, and he began to suspect that he had been swindled. But he sent word to Eulenspiegel that the work should be finished quickly, for he wanted his whole court to look at the painting so that he could see which of his knights were base-born and which were truly noble. The base-born would forfeit their rank and estates.

When Eulenspiegel heard this, he gave his assistants a holiday, got another hundred guilders from the paymaster on account, and left town. The next day when the landgrave asked for his painter, he was gone. Then the landgrave and all his court went into the hall to find out if anyone could see the painting, but no one could honestly say he did.

The landgrave said to his speechless courtiers, "Now we see clearly that we have been deceived. I had hoped Eulenspiegel would not trouble us, but he came here and we've gotten off lightly at the cost of two hundred guilders, for he's a scoundrel through and through. But he had better not cross our borders again."

So Eulenspiegel got away from Marburg, and wanted nothing more to do with painting.

Story note: The landgravine of Hessen whose ancestry the landgraf wants painted is logically Saint Elisabeth, the daughter of the king of Hungary, who married Ludwig VI in 1221. Her story is told as one of the Wartburg legends in this book.

Twenty-Eighth Story

From Marburg Eulenspiegel traveled through Bohemia to Prague. This happened when there were still good Christians in that land, before Wyclif's heresy came from England to Bohemia and was spread by John Huss. In Prague Eulenspiegel gave out that he was a great scholar, one who could answer questions nobody else could even explain. He had notices written to advertise himself and posted them on the doors of the churches and colleges. The rector of the university, the professors, and all the learned doctors and masters were seriously annoyed by Eulenspiegel's announcements, and they met together to figure out questions that Eulenspiegel couldn't possibly answer. They thought the best way to attack him would be to humiliate him publicly. In proper academic fashion, they determined and decided and agreed and assented and concluded and ordered that the rector should pose the questions. Then they sent their beadle to tell Eulenspiegel that he should come the next day and in the presence of all the members of the university answer the questions that the rector gave him in writing. If he refused this test or if he wasn't clever enough to answer the questions, he would be declared an imposter.

Eulenspiegel said to the beadle, "Go tell your masters that I will do as they ask, and that I expect I'll prove as competent as I always have."

The next day all the learned men assembled, and Eulenspiegel showed up with his innkeeper and an escort of useful fellows, just in case the students threatened him with violence. He was told to stand at the raised lectern and to answer the questions that the rector would put to him.

First the rector asked him to state how much water there is in the sea and to prove his answer. If he could not answer the question, he would be condemned and punished as an ignoramus and an enemy of knowledge.

But Eulenspiegel was quick-witted as always: "Honorable rector, if you will stop all the rivers from running that flow into the sea, I can easily measure, prove, and tell you exactly how much water there is in the sea. It's a very straightforward piece of reasoning."

The rector couldn't stop the rivers from running, so he withdrew the question. He was embarrassed, but he went ahead with the second question: "Tell me, how many days have passed from Adam's time until today?"

Eulenspiegel again had a ready answer: "Just seven days. And when those seven days have passed, another seven days begin, and so it will be until the end of time."

Then the rector asked his third question: "Tell me, where is the center of the earth?"

Eulenspiegel answered, "Right here, where I stand. You can measure the distance with a string, and if I'm off by the length of a straw I'll admit I'm wrong."

Rather than do the measuring, the rector conceded the question. But he was clearly angry when he asked the fourth question: "Tell us then, how far is it from earth to heaven?"

Eulenspiegel answered, "Not very far. If someone were to speak or call down from heaven, you could hear him from here. If you'll climb up there, I'll call softly from down here, and you'll be able to hear me. If you can't hear me, then we'll know I'm wrong."

The rector had to let this answer stand, and he went on to his fifth question: "How big is the sky?"

Eulenspiegel didn't take long to answer: "I'm absolutely certain it's a thousand fathoms wide, and a thousand ells high. If you don't believe me, take down the sun, the moon, and the stars and measure the space that's left. You'll find I'm right, even though you don't want to agree with me."

What were they to say to that? Eulenspiegel was too clever for them all, and they had to admit that they were beaten. But he didn't stay around to gloat for long. He was worried that they would get him drunk and he would give away the game. So he took off his long scholar's gown and left Prague to go to Erfurt.

Forty-Eighth Story

When Eulenspiegel came to Berlin, he took a job as a tailor's assistant. The tailor told him, "If you want to sew, do it well, and make sure that the stitches can't be seen."

Eulenspiegel said he would, and took his needle and the garment he was to finish and crawled under a large tub. There he folded a seam over his knee and began to sew.

The tailor stood watching this, and said to him, "What are you doing? That's a strange place to sew."

Eulenspiegel said, "Master, you said I should sew stitches that no one could see, and if I work under this tub no one can see them."

The tailor said, "No, my dear assistant, stop sewing like that and start sewing where I can see you."

Two or three days later, when evening came, the tailor was tired and wanted to go to bed. On the worktable lay a farmer's coat of rough gray cloth, the kind that's called a "wolf." It was only half-finished, and the tailor tossed it to Eulenspiegel and said, "Finish up the wolf and then go to bed yourself."

Eulenspiegel answered, "Yes, you go ahead, I'll do a good job."

The tailor went to bed without giving it another thought. But Eulenspiegel took the coat and cut it up into pieces that looked like a wolf's head and body and legs. He stretched the pieces over some sticks so they really did look like a wolf, and then he went to bed.

The next morning the tailor got up, woke Eulenspiegel, and went down to his workshop where he saw the wolf. He was surprised, but he knew at once that it wasn't a real wolf. Then Eulenspiegel came in and the tailor said to him, "What the devil have you made out of the jacket?"

"A wolf, just as you told me to," answered Eulenspiegel.

"I didn't mean this kind of wolf," said the tailor. "I was talking about the coat—we call that kind of coat a wolf."

"Dear master," said Eulenspiegel, "I didn't know that. If I'd known what you meant, I would much rather have made the coat than the wolf."

The tailor let it go at that, since the coat was past mending. Four days went by before he decided to have another early night. Although he himself was tired, he thought it was too early for his hired man to go to bed. So he threw him a coat that was all finished except for the sleeves and said, "Baste the sleeves in," and went to bed. Eulenspiegel stuck the sleeves into the armholes of the coat, wrapped the coat around the roasting spit on the hearth, and turned the spit in front of the fire all night, basting the coat regularly with bacon fat. Every now and then he would check the sleeves, but they were still loose. When the tailor came down the next morning, Eulenspiegel paid no attention to him, but kept turning and basting.

"What the devil are you playing at?" asked the tailor?

"I'm not playing," answered Eulenspiegel. "I've been working all night trying to get the sleeves basted into this coat as you told me to, but they're still loose. You must have known this wouldn't work. Why did you waste my time when I could have been sleeping?"

The tailor said, "Don't blame me! How could I know you would misunderstand what I said? I meant that you should sew the sleeves onto the coat."

Then Eulenspiegel said, "If you keep on saying one thing and meaning another, how do you expect me to understand you? If you'd said what you meant, I could have sewn the sleeves into the coat easily enough and got a few hours sleep besides. Now you'll have to do the sewing yourself—I'm going to bed."

"Oh, no!" said the tailor. "I'm not paying you to sleep." And the quarrel went on, but while the tailor was insisting that Eulenspiegel owed him money for the bacon fat and firewood he had used, Eulenspiegel gathered his things together and walked off down the road.

The End of Till Eulenspiegel: How Eulenspiegel Was Buried

Till Eulenspiegel fell ill in Mölln, and there he died in the year 1350. He played tricks even on his deathbed, and his burial was as unusual as his life. When everybody was gathered in the churchyard they put his coffin on the two ropes lying ready and started to lower it into the grave. But the rope under the foot end broke and the coffin fell so that Eulenspiegel landed on his feet at the bottom of the grave. All the bystanders said, "Let's leave him standing like that. He was peculiar in life, so let him be peculiar in death." So they left him upright and filled in the grave, and set a gravestone on it with a picture of an owl with a mirror in its claws, and over the picture of the owl they carved an inscription:

> *Move not this stone with profane hands.*
> *Here Ulenspiegel buried stands.*
> *Anno Domini MCCCL.*

[*Eule*, or *Ule*, means "owl," and *spiegel* means "mirror." Eulenspiegel, or Ulenspiegel, means "owl's mirror."]

Eulenspiegel's grave was much visited by journeying craftsmen and other travelers in the centuries after his death. So many people came to see it that the gravestone was moved to the wall of the church to protect it from souvenir hunters and vandalism. In 1592, one visitor described the stone as standing right next to the church. According to his report, the inscription on the stone read:

> *In this place this stone was raised,*
> *Beneath lies Eylenspiegel in his grave.*
> *Think of me,*
> *You who pass by,*
> *For on this earth*
> *You may become as I.*

An owl and a mirror were carved in the two corners of the stone above the inscription.

A chronicle written in 1631 describes the stone as standing just to the left of the church door. It was protected by a wooden enclosure that had recently been rebuilt because visitors kept cutting off splinters of the wood to take with them as a cure for toothache. Travelers visiting Eulenspiegel's grave also reported that after the stone had been moved and enclosed for protection, craftsmen on their journeyman travels would stop in Mölln and hammer a nail into the old linden tree that stood by the place where Eulenspiegel had been buried, to show that they had been there. Eventually the bark of the tree was entirely covered by the iron nail heads.

Today, early in the twenty-first century, Eulenspiegel's gravestone stands in a niche in the west wall of St. Nikolai Church, to the left of the door that was bricked in when the main entrance was moved to the south wall, behind protective iron bars. Carved into the stone is the figure of a man with an owl in one hand and a mirror in the other.

The inscription reads:

> In the year 1350 this stone was raised,
> Beneath leans Tylle Ulenspegel in his grave.
> Consider this well,
> You who pass by,
> For whatever I was on this earth,
> You must become as I.

The carving on the stone dates it to the early seventeenth century. Because Till Eulenspiegel's grave was a tourist attraction from the beginning, perhaps not as early as 1350 but certainly before 1519, the town undoubtedly renewed the stone several times. The renovations would account for the different inscriptions that have been reported.

The church stands on the north side of the town square, next to the Rathaus (built in 1373). In the cobblestone square below the church are the fountain that would have been the main public source of water and the town's whipping post. One of the narrow alleys between the old half-timbered brick houses facing the square is called Till-Eulenspiegel-Gang. Next to the fountain a bronze Eulenspiegel made by the sculptor Karlheinz Goedtke and put there in 1951 lounges grinning on a stone plinth. Eulenspiegel's upturned thumb and his feet gleam like gold, the patina of the bronze worn away by the hands of the many travelers who come to see him and touch him for good luck.

Zauber-
märchen

(Fairy Tales)

HCS '03

Hansel and Gretel ❧ Hänsel und Grethel

On the edge of a huge forest lived a poor woodcutter. He was so poor that he could barely feed his wife and his two children, Hansel and Gretel, and finally a time came when he couldn't manage even that. As he tossed and turned in bed one night, unable to sleep for worry, his wife said to him, "Listen, husband. Tomorrow morning give the two children a bit of bread, take them deep into the heart of the forest, light a fire for them, and leave them there alone. We can't afford to feed them any longer."

"No, wife," said the man. "How can I leave my own dear children to be eaten by the wild beasts of the forest?"

"If you don't, we will all die of hunger together," said the woman, and she nagged at him until he gave in.

The two children were also still awake—they couldn't sleep for hunger—and heard what their mother said to their father. Gretel thought, "That's the end of us," and started to cry , but Hansel said, "Don't fret, Gretel. I'll find a way to help us." He got up and put on his jacket, opened the lower half of the door, and slipped outside. The moon was shining brightly, and the white pebbles on the ground gleamed like silver pennies. Hansel picked up as many as would fit in his pockets. Then he went back into the house. "Cheer up, Gretel, and go to sleep," he said and got back into bed and fell asleep.

Early the next morning, before the sun was even up, the mother came and woke the two children. "Get up, we're going to go into the forest. Here's a piece of bread for each of you, but save it for your noon meal." Gretel tucked the bread under her apron because Hansel had his pockets full of stones and they set out into the forest. After they had gone a little way, Hansel stopped and turned back to look at their house, and soon he did it again, and then again, until his father said, "Hansel, what are you looking at? You'll get left behind. Pick up you feet and pay attention."

"Oh, Father, I'm looking at my white cat. It's sitting on the roof and wants to say goodbye to me."

"You fool," said his mother, "that isn't your cat, it's just the morning sun shining on the chimney."

But Hansel hadn't been looking back at his cat at all. Each time he'd stopped, he'd dropped one of the shiny pebbles on the path.

When they deep in the forest the father said, "Now gather some wood, children. I'll make a fire to keep us warm." Hansel and Gretel gathered a small mountain of dry branches and twigs. They lit the fire, and when the flames burned high the mother said, "Now lie down by the fire and sleep. We're going to cut wood. Wait here until we come back and get you."

Hansel and Gretel sat by the fire until noon, when they ate their bits of bread. They thought their father was still in the forest because they heard the sound of his axe, but it was really a branch that he had tied to a tree and that was knocking in the wind. They waited until evening, but their mother and father failed to come. No one came to get them and take them home.

When the night grew dark, Gretel began to cry, but Hansel said, "Just wait a bit until the moon comes up." And when the moon came up, he took Gretel's hand, and there were the pebbles shining like newly minted silver pennies to show them the way. They walked all night, and when morning came they were back at their father's house. Their father was happy to see his children again because leaving them alone like that had made him sick at heart. The mother pretended to be happy, too, but secretly she was angry.

Not long after, the cupboard was bare again and Hansel and Gretel heard their mother say to their father at night, "The children found their way back once, and I let it be. But now we're down to our last half-loaf of bread again. You must take them deeper into the forest tomorrow so that they can't find their way back. There's no other help for us." The man felt heartsick and thought to himself, "Surely it would be better to share your last bit of food with your children." But because he had agreed once already, he really had no choice.

The children overheard this conversation and Hansel got up to collect pebbles again, but this time when he got to the door he found their mother had locked it. But he comforted Gretel and said, "Go to sleep, Gretel, I'm sure the good Lord will help us." Early the next morning they got their little piece of bread, even smaller than last time. On the way into the forest Hansel crumbled his piece in his pocket and stopped quite often to drop some crumbs. "Why do you keep stopping and looking back, Hansel?" asked his father.

"I'm looking at my pigeon. It's sitting on the roof and wants to say goodbye to me."

"You fool," said his mother, "that's not your pigeon, that's the rising sun shining on the chimney."

But Hansel crumbled up all of his bread and dropped the crumbs along the way.

Their mother led them deeper into the forest to a place they had never been before. There they were supposed to sleep by a big fire until evening when their parents would come to get them. At noon Gretel shared her piece of bread with Hansel because he had used his to mark their way. The afternoon passed, and the evening passed and no one came to get the poor children. Hansel comforted Gretel and said, "Wait until the moon comes up, then I'll see the crumbs of bread and they'll show us the way home."

The moon came up but Hansel couldn't find his breadcrumbs. The thousands of birds in the forest had found them and pecked them all up. Hansel thought he could find the way home without them and Gretel followed him, but they soon lost themselves in the deep forest. They walked the whole night through and all of the next day until they were so tired that they had to sleep. Then they walked for another day, but they still hadn't come to the edge of the forest, and they were terribly hungry because they had eaten nothing except a few small berries that they found on the bushes.

On the third day they came to a little house made entirely out of bread, and the roof was made of cake and the windows were made of clear sugar. "We'll stop here, Gretel, and eat until we're full," said Hansel. "I'll have a piece of the roof and you can have a piece of window—it will be nice and sweet." But as Gretel started to nibble the sugar pane a soft voice inside the house called:

> *"Nibble, nibble mousekin,*
> *Who is nibbling at my housekin?"*

The children answered:

> *"The wind, the wind wild,*
> *Heaven's own child,"*

And they kept eating. Gretel broke out a whole round windowpane and Hansel ripped a big piece of cake from the roof. Suddenly the door opened and an old, old woman came creeping out. Hansel and Gretel were so startled that they dropped the food they held. But the old woman shook her head and said, "Oh my, what dear children, where did you come from? Come inside with me, I'll make you comfortable," and she took their hands and led them into the little house. There she served them delicious food, milk and pancakes with sugar, and apples and nuts. And then she showed them two soft little beds. Hansel and Gretel lay down in them and thought they were in heaven.

But the old woman was really a wicked witch who lay in wait for children and had built the bread house as bait, and when she got hold of children, she killed them and cooked them and ate them, and that was a real feast day for her. So she was very glad that Hansel and Gretel had come her way.

Early in the morning she got up and went to look at the two children sleeping peacefully in their beds. "What a fine catch," she mumbled happily. "They'll make a very tender dish." Then she grabbed Hansel and put him into a small pen, so when he woke up he found himself fenced in as if he were a chicken, with only enough room to take a couple of steps. But Gretel she shook awake and said to her, "Get up, you lazy girl, fetch water and go to the kitchen and cook something tasty. Your brother is over there in a pen. I'm going to fatten him up and eat him when he's ready, so you'll have to feed him." Gretel was very frightened, but she had to do what the wicked witch told her. Every day Hansel got the most delicious food so that he would get fat, but Gretel got nothing but crab shells. Every day the old woman came and said, "Hansel, stick your finger out so I can tell whether you're fat enough yet." But Hansel always poked a little bone through the fence instead of his finger, and the witch wondered why he was still so thin and didn't seem to be fattening up at all.

After four weeks she said to Gretel one evening, "Hurry up and fetch some water. Your brother may be fat enough or not, tomorrow I'll butcher him and boil him. In the meantime I'll set some bread dough so that we can bake as well." Poor Gretel went off, sad at heart, to get the water in which Hansel would be boiled.

Early the next morning Gretel had to get up, light the fire, and put on the big kettle full of water. "Now pay attention," said the witch. "I'm going to make a fire in the bake oven and then push the bread in." Gretel wept bitter tears, thinking, "It would have been better if the wild animals had eaten us in the forest."

When the bread was done the old woman said to Gretel, "Look inside the oven to see if the bread is nicely brown. My eyes are weak and I can't see far. If you can't see either, sit on the baker's peel and I'll push you in. Then you can move around in there and get a good look."

Once she got Gretel into the oven, the witch meant to shut the door behind her. Then Gretel would be baked and the witch would eat her, too. But Gretel cleverly said, "I don't understand what you want me to do. Show me—you sit on the baker's peel and I'll push you in." The witch sat on the peel, and because she was such an old, old woman she didn't weigh much and Gretel could push her in easily, as far the handle of the peel reached. Then Gretel quickly shut the oven door and put the iron bar across it. The witch in the oven started to scream and wail, but Gretel ran away and the witch died a miserable death.

Gretel ran straight to Hansel, unlocked the pen, and cried, "Jump out Hansel, we're saved!" Hansel sprang out like a captive bird released from its cage. They cried for joy and kissed each other happily. Gretel had discovered that the little house was full of precious jewels and pearls so they filled their pockets and then they left to find the way home.

After they had walked for some hours they came to an enormous lake that they couldn't cross, but the Gretel saw a white duck swimming to and fro and called to it, "Dear little duck, carry us on your back."

When the duck heard Gretel, she swam over to them and carried Gretel across, and then she went back for Hansel. After that it didn't take long for them to find their house. Their father was very glad to see them. He hadn't had a single happy day since his children had been left in the forest. But their mother had died.

The jewels the children brought made them all rich for the rest of their lives, and they never had to worry about getting enough to eat ever again.

Source: Grimm KHM #15, 1837

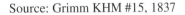

Aschenputtel

Background: Aschenputtel is the German Cinderella. The name, which varies a little in different German dialects, means a person who gets dirty from spending time close to the ashes (Aschen) of the hearth—a kitchen boy or kitchen maid, for example. The word is not gender specific, and in the earliest known references to the German story, which go back to the sixteenth century, Aschenputtel is a boy. The German variation of this famous fairy tale is very different from the version most widely known in North America, the Disney story based on Charles Perrault's "Cendrillon." There is no pumpkin, the slipper isn't made of glass, and instead of a fairy godmother there is a magic tree. Aschenputtel is a much stronger, more active character than Cinderella: she commands magic and tricks her family and the prince to rescue herself.

Once there was a rich man who lived happily with his wife and their only child, a daughter. But the wife fell ill, and when she was close to death, she called her daughter to her bedside and said, "My child, I have to leave you. Plant a tree on my grave, and when you wish for something, shake the tree and you'll have it. And if ever you are in trouble I'll send you help. Be good, and always do your best."

After she had said these things she closed her eyes and died. The girl planted a tree on her mother's grave and watered it daily with her tears, and in a very short time it grew strong and beautiful.

Soon the snow covered the grave with a soft, white cloth, and when the spring sun had pulled it off again, the man married for a second time. His new wife had two daughters of her own who were lovely and fair of face but nasty and foul of heart. Life became very hard for the girl.

"That stupid goose has no right to be in the sitting room!" her stepmother said. "People who want to eat must earn their bread. Off with her to the kitchen." The stepsisters took away the girl's fine clothes and gave her an old grey smock and a pair of wooden shoes to wear instead. "That's good enough for you," they said, and laughed at her.

The poor girl had to get up before dawn, carry water, light the fire, cook the meals, and wash the clothes, and all the while her stepsisters tormented and mocked her. They even made extra work for her by throwing dried peas and lentils into the ashes of the kitchen fire, which she had to pick out one by one before she could go to sleep. And when each long day finally came to an end, the girl had no bed to go to, but had to sleep in the ashes next to the kitchen hearth to keep warm. As a result she was always sooty and dirty, and so they called her Aschenputtel.

A time came when the king announced that a grand ball would be held, with feasting and dancing for three days, and that his son, the prince, would choose a wife from among the guests. All the eligible young ladies in the kingdom were invited, including the two stepsisters. They were very pleased and excited at the prospect. They called to Aschenputtel, "Come up here, brush our hair, polish our shoes, and buckle our buckles, for we're going to dance with the prince!"

Aschenputtel did her best for them, but when she was finished they asked her mockingly whether she wouldn't like to go to the ball, too. "Of course I would," answered Aschenputtel, "but I've got no clothes to wear."

"No, you don't, and a good thing, too," said the older sister. "It would be a shame and a disgrace to have people look at you and know you are our sister. You belong in the kitchen, not in a ballroom. Here's a bowlful of lentils to pick over before we come home. If there's even one bad one left among them you'll be in trouble."

The stepsisters left for the ball with their mother, but Aschenputtel poured the lentils into a big heap on the hearth. Then she went out the back door that led to the garden and called, "You tame doves, you turtledoves, all you birds of the air, come and help me sort these lentils,

> the good ones in the pot
> the bad ones in your crop."

First two white doves came to the kitchen window, then the turtledoves, and finally all the birds under heaven flew in, and they settled around the heap of lentils. Pick, pick, pick, pick, they put the good ones in the bowl and ate the bad ones until the whole heap was gone—it took less than an hour—and they flew out the window again.

The doves stayed a moment and said, "Aschenputtel, if you want to see your sisters dance with the prince, climb up into the dovecote." Aschenputtel followed them and climbed to the very last rung of the ladder. From there she could see her sisters dancing with the prince, and thousands of glittering, twinkling lights. When she had looked her fill she climbed down again with a heavy heart and lay down to sleep in the ashes.

The next morning the sisters came down to the kitchen and were angry when they saw that Aschenputtel had finished sorting the lentils, for they'd expected to scold her. So instead, out of malice, they began to tell her about the glories of the ball and how much they had enjoyed themselves: "The prince, who is the most handsome man on earth, danced with us and one of us is sure to be his bride."

"I saw all the lights glittering," said Aschenputtel. "It must have been splendid."

"What? How did you manage that?" asked the older sister.

"I went up to the dovecote."

The stepsister grudged her even that much pleasure and immediately ordered that the dovecote should be torn down.

Then Aschenputtel had to dress and adorn her stepsisters for the second day of the ball. While she was brushing their hair and polishing their shoes and buckling their buckles, the younger sister, taking pity on her, said, "Once it's dark you can come to the palace and look in through the windows if you like."

"Oh, no, she can't!" the older sister said. "That will just make her lazy. Here, you, here's a sack of split peas to keep you busy. Sort out the bad ones, and be quick about it, for if they're not done by tomorrow morning, I'll throw them into the ashes and you'll go hungry until you've picked them all out."

The sisters went to the ball, and Aschenputtel went to the kitchen, where she emptied the sack of split peas onto the hearthstone. Then she went out the back door that led to the garden and called: "You tame doves, you turtledoves, all you birds of the air, come and help me sort these peas,

> the good ones in the pot
> the bad ones in your crop."

First the two white doves came to the kitchen window, then the turtledoves, and finally all the birds under heaven flew in, and they settled around the heap of peas. Pick, pick, pick, pick, they put the good ones in the pot and ate the bad ones until the whole heap was gone—it took even less time than before—and they flew out the window again.

Then Aschenputtel went to her mother's grave in the garden. She shook the tree she had planted and said:

> "Shake and shiver little tree,
> Throw gold and silver over me."

All at once a splendid silver dress lay on the grave, and pearls, and silken stockings with silver clocks, and silver slippers. Aschenputtel carried the lovely things into the house, quickly washed and dressed herself, and went to the ball. She was so beautiful in her silver gown that her stepsisters and stepmother thought she must be a princess from another country. They certainly didn't think of Aschenputtel sitting at home in the ashes of the kitchen fire, sorting split peas.

The king's son came to greet her, took her hand with royal courtesy, and danced with her. After that, he danced only with her, and she danced only with him, until evening came and she wanted to go home. The king's son asked to go with her because he wanted to see where she came from, but Aschenputtel slipped away from him into the shadows. Back at home she laid the silver dress and everything that went with it on her mother's grave and said to the tree:

"Shake and shiver little tree,
Take these fine things back from me."

The tree took them at once, and Aschenputtel in her old grey smock and wooden shoes went into the house to rub ashes on her face and hands and lie down next to the hearth as if she had never been anywhere else.

The next morning the stepsisters came into the kitchen looking sullen. "Did you have a wonderful time at the ball?" asked Aschenputtel.

"No," answered the sisters. "There was a foreign princess there, and once the prince met her, he paid no attention to anyone else."

That day Aschenputtel dressed her sisters for the third time, brushing their hair and polishing their shoes and buckling their buckles, and when they had left for the ball, she washed herself clean and went to her mother's grave again and spoke to the tree:

"Shake and shiver little tree,
Throw gold and silver over me."

The dress that fell from the tree this time was made of cloth-of-gold and embroidered with precious stones. The silken stockings had golden clocks and the slippers were gold, and when Aschenputtel was dressed, she shone like the midday sun.

When she got to the palace, the king's son was already standing on the steps waiting for her. If the guests had been astonished at her beauty yesterday, they were even more astonished today, and the stepsisters stood in a corner pale with envy. If they had known that this was Aschenputtel, they would have died of envy.

Aschenputtel danced with the prince until she was weary and wanted to go home. As he had the night before, the prince asked to go with her, and as she had the night before, Aschenputtel slipped away from him. But the prince had coated the stairs with pitch so that she could not run away as quickly, and one of her golden slippers stuck to it. She left the slipper behind and ran home, where she give the dress back to the tree, dirtied her face and hands with ashes, and lay down by the hearth.

Only a little while later her stepsisters came home and called for her to light their way. Yawning as if she had just been sleeping, Aschenputtel carried a lamp for them and heard one of them say to the other, "I wonder who that accursed princess was. I wish she were dead and buried! The prince danced only with her, and after she left he didn't want to stay any longer and the party was over."

"It was as if someone had blown the lights out," agreed her sister.

But the prince took the golden slipper from the stairs thinking that he would use it as a clue to find his vanished partner. He announced that he would marry the young woman whom the shoe fit, and for the next day or two the slipper was tried on all over town, but it was too small for everyone. Indeed, some of the hopefuls wouldn't have been able to get a foot into it even if two slippers had been made into one.

Finally it was the turn of the two stepsisters, and they were confident that the shoe would fit one of them, for they both had dainty feet. The oldest went into her room to try on the slipper, but found that her big toe was too long. Her mother, who had gone with her, handed her a knife and said, "Cut off your toe. When you're the queen you'll never have to walk again." So the oldest sister cut off her toe and squeezed her foot into the shoe and went back to show it to the prince. He lifted her onto his horse and rode away with her. But as they passed the grave in the garden, the two white doves sitting in the tree called out

> *"Cooroo, cooroo*
> *There's blood in the shoe,*
> *The shoe is too small.*
> *She's not the right bride at all."*

So the prince looked down and saw the red stain on the toe of the shoe. He turned his horse and took the false bride back.

Now it was the younger sister's turn. When she tried the shoe on, her toes fit in, but her heel was too big. Her mother handed her the knife and said, "Cut a piece off your heel. When you're the queen you'll never have to walk again." So she cut off a piece of her heel, squeezed her foot into the shoe, and went back out to the prince. He put her on his horse and rode away with her. But as they passed the grave the two white doves called out again,

> *"Cooroo, cooroo*
> *There's blood in the shoe,*
> *She's the wrong bride, you'll find.*
> *You've left the right bride behind."*

And when the prince looked down he saw the red stain on the heel of the shoe, so he turned his horse a second time and brought the false bride back.

"Is there another daughter in the house who could try on the shoe?" he asked.

"No," said the father, "There's just a dirty little kitchen maid who belonged to my dead wife, and she couldn't possibly be the one you're looking for."

The prince said she should be brought in any case, but the stepmother objected that the girl was far too dirty and not fit to be seen. Still, the prince insisted, so they called for Aschenputtel.

Aschenputtel washed her face and hands and came and curtsied to the prince, who handed her the golden shoe and said, "Try it on, and if it fits, you will be my wife." Aschenputtel stepped out of her heavy wooden shoes and pushed her left foot lightly into the golden slipper. It fit as though it had been made for her. And as she straightened up, the prince looked at her face and recognized her as his beautiful dancing partner. "She is the right bride," he said.

The stepmother and her two daughters went white with shock and fear, but the prince lifted Aschenputtel onto his horse and rode away with her. And as they passed by the grave the two white doves in the tree called out:

> *"Cooroo, cooroo,*
> *There's no blood in the shoe,*
> *The shoe fits just fine.*
> *You've got the right bride this time."*

Source: Grimm KHM #21, 1812, 1819, and 1857

The Golden Goose ❧ Die goldene Gans

There was a man who had three sons. The youngest of them was called Simpleton and was despised and mocked and slighted at every opportunity. One day the eldest son went into the forest to cut wood, and before he left his mother gave him a fine big honey cake and a bottle of wine to take with him in case he got hungry or thirsty. When he got into the forest he met a little grey old man who wished him good day and said, "Give me a piece of the cake you have in your pocket and a drink of your wine, for I am very hungry and thirsty."

But the clever son answered, "If I give you my cake and my wine, I'll have nothing left for myself. Take yourself off!" And he left the little man standing there and went on his way to the part of the forest where he meant to cut wood. There he started chopping down a tree, but it wasn't long before one of his strokes went wrong and the axe cut his arm badly enough that he had go home to get it bandaged.

Then the second son went to cut wood in his brother's stead, and his mother gave him a fine big honey cake and a bottle of wine, too. When he got into the forest, he met the little grey old man, who asked him for a piece of cake and a drink of wine. But the second son said, "Whatever I give you I won't have for myself. Take yourself off!" And he left the little man standing there and went on his way. But almost as soon as he began to chop down a tree, he missed his stroke and the axe cut his leg so badly that he had to be carried home.

Then Simpleton said, "Father, let me go out and cut wood for a change."

His father answered, "Your brothers know what they're doing, and they've hurt themselves. Leave it alone."

But Simpleton kept asking until finally his father said, "All right, go ahead. If you hurt yourself you might actually learn something." His mother gave him a dry oatcake that had been baked in the ashes and a bottle of sour beer, and off he went. When he got into the forest he met the little grey old man, who greeted him and asked, "Give me a piece of your cake and a drink from your bottle, for I'm very hungry and thirsty."

Simpleton answered, "I only have an ashcake and sour beer, but if that suits you we can sit down and eat." So they sat down, and when Simpleton took out his ashcake, it had become a honey cake, and the sour beer in his bottle had become good wine. They ate and drank, and then the little man said, "Because you have a good heart and willingly share what is yours, I will give you good luck. Do you see that old tree? Cut it down, and you'll find something in the roots." And then he left.

Simpleton cut down the old tree, and when it fell, there was a goose with feathers of pure gold sitting among the roots. He lifted the goose up and took it with him to an inn, where he meant to spend the night. When the innkeeper's three daughters saw the goose, they were very curious about this marvelous bird and each of them wished she had one of its golden feathers.

The eldest daughter thought, "When there's a chance, I'll pull out a feather for myself," and when Simpleton left the room she took hold of the goose's wing. But her fingers stuck to it and she couldn't let go. Then the second daughter came to pull a golden feather for herself, but the moment she touched her sister her hand stuck fast and she couldn't pull it loose. Finally the third daughter came to get herself a feather. The other two cried, "Keep away, for heaven's sake, keep away!" but she thought, "If they can do it, so can I," and reached out to push past her sister. And as soon as she touched her she was stuck, too. So they all had to spend a very uncomfortable night next to the goose.

The next morning Simpleton took his goose and left, not at all concerned about the three girls who had to follow him willy-nilly. A little way down the road they met the pastor, and when he saw the procession he said, "Shame on you, you dreadful girls! You shouldn't be chasing after that young fellow for all the world to see!" He took the youngest by the hand to pull her back, but as soon as he touched her he was stuck, too, and had to follow along himself.

A short while later the sexton came along and saw the pastor close on the heels of the three girls. He called to him, "Pastor, where are you off to? Don't forget we have a baptism today," and ran over and took hold of his sleeve. And, of course, he stuck fast.

Then two farmers carrying their hoes came down the road and the pastor called to them to pull him and the sexton loose. But they had hardly touched the sexton before they were stuck, too, and now there were seven running after Simpleton and his golden goose.

Eventually they came to a city ruled by a king whose daughter was so serious that no one could make her laugh. For that reason the king had decreed that the man who could make her laugh could marry her. When Simpleton heard about the decree, he went with his goose and its human tail to the king's daughter. And when she saw that peculiar parade, she laughed so hard her stomach hurt. Simpleton expected to marry her on the spot, but the king didn't want him as a son-in-law, so he made all kinds of objections.

Finally he said that before he could have his daughter Simpleton would have to bring him a man who could drink a whole cellar of wine dry. Simpleton thought the little grey old man could probably help him, so he went back to the forest where he had cut down the tree. There on the stump sat a man with a very sad face. Simpleton asked him what his trouble was, and the man answered, "I have a dreadful thirst and I can't quench it. I can't stand cold water, and although I've drunk a barrel of wine it was just a drop in the bucket."

"I can help you out," said Simpleton. "If you come with me you'll be able to drink your fill." He led him to the king's wine cellar, where the thirsty man took one happy look at the huge barrels and began to drink. He drank and drank until his belly was as tight as a drum, and by the end of the day he had drunk the cellar dry. Then Simpleton demanded his bride, but the king still didn't want a common fellow whom everyone called a simpleton marrying his daughter, so he made another condition: Simpleton was to bring him a man who could eat an entire mountain of bread.

Simpleton didn't need to think about it. He went back to the tree stump in the forest, and there he found a man with a gloomy face who was pulling his belt in as tight as it would go. "I've just eaten a whole bake oven full of rye bread, but I'm so hungry that it made no difference—my stomach is still empty, and if I can't tighten my belt enough to close it I'll die of hunger," he said.

Simpleton was delighted. "If you come with me," he said, "you'll be able to eat till you're full." He led the man back to the courtyard of the palace where an enormous mountain of bread was piled up. The king had commandeered all the flour in the whole kingdom to bake it. The hungry man took one happy look and began to eat, and at the end of the day the mountain was gone, down to the last crumb.

Simpleton demanded his wife for the third time, but the king set yet another condition. He told Simpleton to bring him a ship that could sail both on water and on land. "When you sail it into the courtyard," he said, "you shall have my daughter as your wife." Simpleton went straight back to the tree stump in the forest. There sat the little grey old man with whom he had shared his cake.

The little man said, "I've drunk for you, I've eaten for you, and I will give you the ship you need. I do all this because you were compassionate toward me." Then he gave Simpleton a ship that could sail both on water and on land, and when the king saw it, he could withhold his daughter no longer. The wedding was celebrated, and after the king's death Simpleton inherited the kingdom and lived long and happily with his wife.

Source: Grimm KHM #64, 1857

Brier Rose ❧ Dornröschen

Long ago there lived a king and queen who said every day, "Oh, if only we had a child!" but none ever came. Then one day when the queen was bathing a frog crawled out of the water onto the land and said to her, "Your wish will be fulfilled. Before a year goes by you will bring a daughter into the world."

And it came to pass as the frog had said. The queen gave birth to a child who was so beautiful that the king couldn't contain his joy. He planned a great feast and invited not only his relatives, friends, and acquaintances, but also the wisewomen in the kingdom so that they would be well disposed toward his daughter. There were thirteen wisewomen in his kingdom, but he had only twelve golden plates for them to eat from, so one of them wasn't asked. The feast was celebrated with great splendor and at the end the wisewomen gave the child their magic gifts. The first gave her virtue, the second beauty, the third wealth, and so they went on, giving her all the things in the world worth wishing for.

But after eleven had spoken, the thirteenth wisewoman suddenly stepped into the great hall. She wanted revenge for not having been invited, and without greeting or even looking at anyone she cried out in a loud voice: "In her fifteenth year the princess will prick herself on a spindle and fall down dead." Without saying another word, she turned and left the hall. Everyone was horrified.

But the twelfth wisewoman, who still had her wish to make, stepped forward. She couldn't lift the curse, but she could soften it. She said: "The princess will not die, but she will fall into a deep sleep a hundred years long."

The king ordered that all the spindles in the entire kingdom be burned because he wanted to protect his daughter from this fate. But on the day of her fifteenth birthday the king and queen happened to be away from home, and the princess was left alone in the castle. She went exploring, looking into rooms and chambers as she liked, and finally came to an old, old tower. She climbed the narrow winding stairs and found a small door. A rusty key was stuck in the lock, and when she turned it, the door sprang open. There was a little room, and in it sat an old woman with a spindle busily spinning flax.

"Good day, old woman," said the king's daughter. "What are you doing there?"

"I'm spinning," said the woman and nodded her head.

"What's this thing you're twirling around?" asked the girl and reached for the spindle. She had hardly touched it before the spell took hold and she pricked her finger.

The instant she felt the prick she fell down into a deep sleep. That sleep spread over the whole castle. The king and queen, who had just come home, fell asleep, surrounded by their whole court. The horses in the stables, the hounds in the courtyard, the pigeons on the roof, the flies on the wall fell asleep. Even the fire flickering on the hearth became still and slept. The roast stopped sizzling, and the cook, who was just about to slap the kitchen boy, fell asleep with his hand in the air. Outside, the wind died down and not a leaf stirred on the trees. But all around the castle a brier hedge began to grow, and it grew higher year by year until it covered the whole castle so that nothing could be seen of it, not even the flag on the roof.

In the country around the castle people told stories about the beautiful sleeping Brier Rose, as she was called, and so from time to time princes came and tried to force their way through the hedge into castle. They never succeeded, for the briers clung together as if they had hands, and the young men were caught by them and couldn't free themselves; so they died a pitiful death.

After many years another prince came to that country and heard an old man telling about the brier hedge that was said to surround a castle where a beautiful king's daughter called Brier Rose had been sleeping for a hundred years, together with the king and queen and all their court. The old man also knew from his grandfather that many princes had already come and tried to force a way through the hedge, but all had been caught by the briers and died there. The prince said, "I'm not afraid. I will go and see the lovely Brier Rose." The old man tried to talk him out it but the prince wouldn't listen.

Now it happened that exactly one hundred years had passed and the day had come when Brier Rose was to wake up. When the prince approached the hedge, the briers were covered with large, beautiful roses that parted of their own accord to let him through unharmed and then closed behind him again. In the stable yard he saw the horses and the spotted hunting dogs lying asleep. The pigeons sat on the roof with their heads tucked under their wings. Inside the castle, the flies were sleeping on the wall, the cook slept with his hand still raised to smack the kitchen boy, and the maid sat fast asleep, nodding over the black hen in her lap ready for plucking. He went farther and found the whole court lying asleep in the great hall and the king and queen sleeping on their thrones. He went still farther and it was so quiet everywhere that he could hear himself breathing. Finally he came to the old tower and to the room where Brier Rose slept. There she lay, so lovely that he couldn't take his eyes off her. He bent down and kissed her.

At that very moment, Brier Rose opened her eyes and smiled at him. The king and queen and the courtiers woke up and looked at each other with astonishment. The horses in the stable yard stood up and shook themselves. The hounds jumped and wagged their tails. The pigeons on the roof took their heads out from under their wings and flew out into the fields. The flies on the walls started crawling again, the fire in the kitchen flickered into flames, the roast began to sizzle, the cook clouted the kitchen boy's ear so hard that he yelled, and the maid finished plucking the chicken.

The wedding of the prince and Brier Rose was celebrated with great splendor. And if they haven't died by now, they're living still.

Source: Grimm KHM #50, 1857

The Devil with the Three Golden Hairs ❧ Der Teufel mit den drei goldenen Haaren

There was once a poor woman who gave birth to a little son, and because the baby was born with a caul,* everyone knew that he would be lucky all his life. It was even foretold that in his fourteenth year he would marry the king's daughter. Now it happened that the king came to the village soon after the baby boy was born, although no one knew he was the king. And when he asked the people what news there was, they told him, "A few days ago a baby was born here with a caul. Whatever a child like that undertakes will turn out well. There's a prophecy about him, too, that in his fourteenth year he'll have the king's daughter for his wife."

The king, who had a wicked heart and was angry about the prophecy, went to the parents and pretended to be friendly. He said to them, "You are poor people and I am a rich man. Let me have your child, and I will look after it." At first they refused, but the stranger offered them a lot of gold, and they thought, "This baby is a good-luck-child and everything is bound to turn out for his best," so in the end they agreed and gave him the child.

The king put the baby in a box and rode on with it until he came to a deep river. There he threw the box into the water and thought, "That takes care of my daughter's an unexpected suitor." But the box didn't sink. It floated like a boat and not a drop of water leaked in. It floated all the way to a mill that stood two miles from the king's city, and there it got stuck on the mill-dam.

By good luck the miller's boy was standing there. He noticed the box and pulled it out with a hook, expecting to find treasure in it. But when he opened it, there lay a beautiful little boy, quite healthy and happy. He took the baby to the miller and his wife, and as they had no children, they were glad to keep the baby as their own. They took good care of the boy and he grew in health, strength, and virtue.

It happened one day that the king went into the mill to shelter from a storm, and he asked the miller and his wife if the tall boy there was their son. "No," they answered, "he's a foundling. Fourteen years ago he floated onto the mill-dam in a box and the mill-boy pulled him out."

---

*Sometimes a child is born with a part of the inner membrane that encloses the baby before birth still on its head, that is, with a caul. In folk belief, a child born with a caul will be lucky all its life.

Then the king knew it was none other than the good-luck-child he had thrown into the water, and he said, "Good people, could the boy take a message for me to the queen? I will pay him two gold coins for the service."

"As the king commands," answered the miller, and they told the boy to get ready. Then the king wrote a letter to the queen, saying, "As soon as the boy bringing this letter arrives, he should be killed and buried; and it must all be done before I return."

The boy started out with this letter, but he lost his way. At twilight, he came to a big forest. In the darkness he saw a small light. He went toward it, and found it was a small cottage. Inside, an old woman was sitting by the fire all alone. "Where do you come from," she asked him, "and where are you going?"

"I come from the mill," he answered, "and I am going to the queen to bring her a letter. But I've lost my way in the forest and I would like to spend the night here."

"You poor boy," said the old woman, "you have come to a robbers' den and when the robbers come home, they will kill you."

"Let them come," said the boy. "I'm not afraid. And I'm so tired that I can't go any farther." And with that he stretched himself out on a bench and fell asleep.

Soon afterward the robbers came home and were angry to find a stranger there. "Oh, come now," said the old woman, "he's an innocent boy who lost his way in the forest and I said he could stay the night. He's taking a letter to the queen." The robbers stole the letter out of his pouch and broke the seal. When they read the king's order that the messenger was to be killed, the hard-hearted robbers took pity on the boy, and their leader tore up the letter and wrote another one saying that when the messenger arrived he should be married to the king's daughter at once. Then they let him sleep out the night, and in the morning they showed him the right way.

When the queen read the letter, she did just what it told her to. She arranged a splendid wedding, and the king's daughter was married to the good-luck-child. And as the young man was both handsome and agreeable, they made a happy couple.

After some time the king returned to his castle and saw that the prophecy was fulfilled and the good-luck-child was married to his daughter. "How did this happen?" he asked. "I gave a very different order in my letter."

So the queen gave him the letter and said he could read for himself what was written there. The king read the letter and realized that it had been exchanged for his. He asked the boy what he had done with the letter entrusted to him and why he had brought a different one instead. "I know nothing about it," he answered. "It must have been switched during the night when I slept in the forest."

The king was very angry. He said, "It's not going to be this easy for you! Any man who wants my daughter must get me three golden hairs from the head of the Devil in Hell. Bring me what I demand, and you can keep my daughter."

But the good-luck-child wasn't worried. "I'll get those golden hairs," he told the king. "The Devil doesn't scare me." Then he said goodbye to his wife and set out to find Hell.

The road led him to a large town, where the watchman at the gate asked him what his trade was and what he knew. "I know everything," the good-luck-child answered.

"Then you can do us a favor," said the watchman, "and tell us why our market well, which once flowed with wine, has gone dry and does not even give us water to drink."

"You'll have the answer," the good-luck-child said, "just wait until I come back."

Then he went on and came to another town, and the watchman there asked him what his trade was and what he knew. "I know everything," he answered.

"Then you can do us a favor and tell us why a tree in our town that once bore golden apples now doesn't even put forth leaves."

"You'll have the answer," he said, "just wait until I come back."

Then he went on and came to a wide river that he had to cross. The ferryman asked him what his trade was and what he knew. "I know everything," he answered.

"Then you can do me a favor," said the ferryman, "and tell me why I have to keep rowing back and forth across this river day after day, year after year, and never get relieved."

"You'll have the answer," said the good-luck-child, "just wait until I come back."

When the good-luck-child had crossed the water he found the entrance to Hell. It was black and sooty inside and the Devil wasn't home, but his grandmother was there, sitting in a big armchair. "What do you want?" she said, but she didn't look so very wicked.

"I would like to have three golden hairs from the Devil's head," he answered, "otherwise I can't keep my wife."

"That's asking a lot," said she. "If the Devil comes home and finds you here, you're done for. But I feel sorry for you, so I'll see if I can help you."

She changed him into an ant and said, "Crawl into the folds of my skirt, you'll be safe there."

"That's fine," he said, "but there are three things I'd like to know, too: why a well that once flowed with wine has dried up and will not even give water; why a tree that once bore golden apples now doesn't even put forth leaves; and why a ferryman has to row back and forth across the river day after day, year after year, and never gets relieved."

"Those are hard questions," she answered, "but keep still and be quiet and pay attention to what the Devil says when I pull out the three golden hairs."

When evening came, the Devil came home. The minute he stepped in the door, he started sniffing. "I smell—I smell human flesh," he said. "Something isn't right." And he looked in all the corners and searched everywhere, but he could find nothing wrong.

His grandmother scolded him: "I've just swept and tidied and now you're pulling everything apart again. You're always smelling human flesh! Sit down and eat your supper."

When the Devil had eaten and drunk his fill, he was tired. He laid his head in his grandmother's lap and told her to pick the lice out of his hair. Before long, he fell asleep and began to snore. Then the old woman took hold of a golden hair, pulled it out, and tucked it in her pocket.

"Ouch!" yelled the Devil, "What did you do that for?"

"I had a bad dream," said the grandmother, "and I grabbed your hair."

"What did you dream, then?" asked the Devil.

"I dreamed that a market well that used to flow with wine has dried up and doesn't even give water. What could the cause be?"

"Hah! If they only knew!" said the Devil. "There's a toad sitting under a stone in the well, and if they killed it, the wine would flow again."

The grandmother began lousing him again and soon he was asleep and snoring loud enough to rattle the windows. Then she pulled out the second hair.

"Hey!" yelled the Devil, "What are you doing?"

"Don't get angry," she said, "I must have pulled your hair while I was dreaming."

"Well, what did you dream this time?"

"I dreamed that in a kingdom stood an apple tree that used to bear golden apples, but now it doesn't even put forth leaves. I wonder, why would that be?"

"Hah! If they only knew!" said the Devil. "There's a mouse gnawing at the root, and if they killed it, the tree would bear golden apples again, but if it gnaws at the root much longer the tree will die. But leave me alone with your dreams. If you wake me up again, you'll get your ears boxed!"

The grandmother made soothing noises and loused him some more until he was asleep and snoring again. Then she pulled out the third golden hair. The Devil jumped up and yelled and shook his fist at her, but she calmed him down and said, "Who can help having bad dreams?"

"Well, what did you dream?" he asked, because he was curious.

"I dreamed about a ferryman who complained that he had to row back and forth across the river, day after day and year after year, and never got relieved. Why would that be?"

"Hah! He's a fool!" said the Devil. "If someone comes and wants to be ferried over, the ferryman has only to put the oar in his hand, and then the passenger will have to row the boat and the ferryman will be free." And because she had the three golden hairs and the answers to the three questions, the grandmother left the old dragon alone and he slept until dawn.

When the Devil had gone out the next morning, the old woman took the ant from the folds of her skirt and gave the good-luck-child his human form again. "Here are the three golden hairs for you," she said, "and I suppose you heard what the Devil said to your three questions?"

"Yes, I heard it all," he said, "and I'll remember it well."

"So you have what you wanted," she said, "and you can be on your way." The good-luck-child thanked the Devil's grandmother for helping him in his need, and left Hell very pleased with his luck.

When he came to the river the ferryman asked for the promised answer. "Ferry me across first," said the good-luck-child, "and then I'll tell you." And when he was safely on the other side he passed on the Devil's advice: "The next time someone comes and wants to be ferried across, just put the oar in his hand."

He went on and came to the town where the barren apple tree stood. There he told the watchman what he had heard the devil say: "Kill the mouse that gnaws at the root and the tree will bear golden apples again." The watchman thanked him and as a reward gave him two donkeys laden with gold.

Lastly he came to the town where the well had dried up. He told the watchman what the Devil had said: "There's a toad sitting in the well under a stone. You have to find it and kill it, and then the well will fill with wine again." The watchman thanked him and gave him another two donkeys laden with gold.

Finally the good-luck-child got home to his wife, who was very glad to see him and to hear how well he had done. To the king he brought what he had demanded, the Devil's three golden hairs, and when the king saw the four donkeys laden with gold, he was happy enough and said, "Now the conditions are fulfilled and you may keep my daughter. But tell me, dear son-in-law, where did you get all that gold? It's a huge treasure!"

"I crossed a river," the good-luck-child said, "and found it there, lying on the river bank like sand."

"Can I get some, too?" asked the king eagerly.

"As much as you want," the boy answered. "There's a ferryman on the river. Let him ferry you over and you can fill your sacks on the other side." The greedy king set out in all haste, and when he came to the river he called the ferryman to take him across. The ferryman came and rowed him across the river, but when they got to the other side he put the oar in the king's hand and jumped out of the boat. So the king had to do the ferrying from that moment on.

Is he still ferrying?

If he is, it's because no one has taken the oar from him.

Source: Grimm KHM #29, 1857

The Shoemaker and the Elves ❧
Die Wichtelmänner

There was a shoemaker who, through no fault of his own, had become so poor that the day came when he had only enough leather left for one pair of shoes. He cut out the shoes that evening so that he could start work on them next morning; and because he had a good conscience, he went peacefully to bed and fell asleep.

The next morning the shoemaker went to his workbench, and there stood the shoes, completely finished. He was amazed and didn't know what to think. He picked the shoes up to look at them more closely: they were so carefully made that not a single stitch was wrong, and they looked like the work of a master craftsman.

A little later a customer came in, and he liked the shoes so well that he paid more than the usual price. So the shoemaker had enough money to buy leather for two pairs of shoes. He cut them out that evening, meaning to start work fresh in the morning. But when he got up the shoes were already finished. And he didn't have wait long for buyers, who gave him so much money that he could buy leather for four pairs of shoes. Early next morning he found the four pairs finished, too, and so it went on: whatever he cut out in the evening was always finished by morning, so that he soon had a respectable income again and in time became wealthy.

One evening, not long before Christmas, after he had finished cutting out the leather for the next day, the shoemaker said to his wife, "Why don't we stay up tonight to see who it is that's been lending us such a helping hand?" His wife agreed and lit a candle, and then they hid themselves in the corner of the room behind some clothes that were hanging there. At midnight, two naked little men came, sat down at the workbench, took the cut leather, and began to punch and sew and hammer so quickly with their nimble little fingers that the astonished shoemaker couldn't take his eyes off them. They didn't stop until all the shoes were finished and stood ready on the workbench, and then they ran off.

The next morning the shoemaker's wife said, "Those little men have made us rich, and we should show our gratitude. They're running around with nothing on and must be cold. Do you know what? I'm going to sew little shirts and jackets and vests and pants for them, and knit a pair of stockings for each of them. You can make them each a pair of shoes." He husband agreed, and that evening, when everything was finished, they put the presents on the workbench and then hid themselves in the corner to watch.

At midnight the elves came skipping in ready to work, but instead of cutout leather, they found the neat little clothes on the workbench. At first they were astonished, but then they seemed to be enormously pleased. Quickly the elves put on the pretty clothes, twitched and smoothed them into place, and sang:

"Aren't we fine in these new clothes?
We'll work no more on others' shoes!"

Then they hopped and danced and jumped over the chairs and benches and out the door.

They never came back again, but the shoemaker prospered in everything he undertook, and he and his wife fared well for as long as they lived.

Source: Grimm KHM #39, 1857. The Grimms put three stories about elves together as number 39 of the KHM. The first one is widely known as "The Shoemaker and the Elves." The second and third are legends and are included in the "Sagen" section of this book.

The Fisherman and His Wife ❧ Von dem Fischer un syner Fru

There once was a fisherman and his wife who lived together in a pisspot close by the sea. The fisherman went fishing every day, and he fished and he fished.

One day he was sitting there fishing, looking into the shining water. He sat and he sat.

Then suddenly the hook went down, deep under the water, and when he hauled it up, he found a big flounder on his line. The flounder said to him, "Listen, fisherman, I beg you to let me live. I'm not a real flounder, I'm an enchanted prince. What good would it do you to kill me? I wouldn't taste any good: put me back in the water and let me swim."

"Well now," said the man, "you didn't need to use so many words. I'd let any talking flounder go." With that the fisherman put the fish back into the shining water and the flounder went straight down to the bottom of the sea, leaving a long streak of blood behind him.

The fisherman stood up and went to his wife in the pisspot. "Husband," said the woman, "didn't you catch anything today?"

"No," said the man, "I caught a flounder who said he was an enchanted prince, so I put him back in the water."

"Didn't you wish for something?" asked the woman.

"No," said the man, "What would I wish for?"

"Oh," said his wife, "it's disgusting to live in a pisspot all the time, it stinks and it's cramped. You could have wished for a little cottage for us. Go back again and call him: tell him we want to have a little cottage. He'll do it, I'm sure."

"There's no use in going back," said the fisherman.

"Eh!" said his wife, "you caught him, didn't you? And you let him swim away. I'm sure he'll give us a cottage."

The man didn't really want to go, but he didn't want to cross his wife, either, so he went back to the shore. When he got there, the sea was all green and yellow and not so shiny anymore. But he stood by the water and said:

> "Manntje, Manntje, Timpe Tee,
> Flounder, flounder in the sea,
> Now my wife, that Ilsebill
> Wants something against my will."

The flounder swam up to him and said, "Well, what does she want, then?"

"Oh," said the man, "My wife says I should have wished for something before I let you go. She doesn't want to live in a pisspot anymore, she wants a little cottage instead."

"Go on home," said the flounder, "she's got what she wants."

So the man went home, and found his wife sitting on a bench outside the door of a little cottage. His wife took his hand and said to him, "Come in and see. Now isn't this a lot better?"

The cottage had a little hallway, and a wonderful little living room, and a bedroom with a bed in it, and a kitchen and a pantry all fitted out with dishes and pots and everything else a pantry should have. And behind the cottage was a little yard with hens and ducks and a little garden with vegetables and fruit.

"See," said the woman, "isn't it nice?"

"Yes," said her husband, "let's be content with this. Now we'll live very pleasantly."

"I'll think about that," said the wife. Then they had something to eat and went to bed.

After a week or two, the woman said, "Listen husband, the cottage is really a tight fit for us, and the yard and the garden are so small. The flounder could just as well have given us a bigger house. I'd like to live in a big stone castle. Go back to the flounder and tell him to give us a castle."

"Oh, wife," said the fisherman, "the cottage is plenty good enough, why would we want to live in a castle?"

"Go on," said the wife, "just go and tell him. The flounder can do it, I'm sure."

"No, wife," said the man, "the flounder already gave us the cottage, and I don't want to ask for more. It might make him angry."

"Oh, go on!" said the woman, "It will be easy for him and he'll be glad to do it. Just go and ask."

The fisherman's heart was heavy. He didn't want to go. He said to himself, "This isn't right." But he went anyway.

When he came to the sea the water was violet and dark blue and grey and thick, not green and yellow anymore, but it was still calm. He stood there and said:

> *"Manntje, Manntje, Timpe Tee,*
> *Flounder, flounder in the sea,*
> *Now my wife, that Ilsebill*
> *Wants something else against my will."*

"Now what does she want?" said the flounder.

"Oh," said the man looking miserable, "she wants to live in a big castle."

"Go on home, she's standing at the door," said the flounder.

So the fisherman went back and found his wife standing on the stairs of a big stone castle. She took him by the hand and said, "Come inside and see."

He went in with her, and inside the castle there was a huge entrance hall with a marble floor, and a lot of servants who opened the great doors, and beautiful tapestries on the walls, and golden chairs and tables, and crystal chandeliers. All the sitting rooms and bedrooms had carpets, and the tables were loaded with so much food and so much good wine that it seemed they might break. Behind the house there was a big yard with stables for horses and cows, and a coach house full of elegant coaches. There was a big, splendid garden with the loveliest flowers and fine fruit trees, and beyond that a park that must have been half a mile long, with stags and deer and rabbits and everything one could wish for.

"Now," said the wife, "isn't that lovely?"

"Oh, yes," said the fisherman, "Let's be content with this. We'll live in this beautiful castle and be satisfied."

"I'll think about that," said his wife, "and we'll sleep on it." And with that they went to bed.

The next morning the woman woke up at dawn and looked from her window at the round hills and green valleys outside. Her husband hadn't stirred yet, so she jabbed him in the side with her elbow and said, "Husband, get up and look out the window. See? Couldn't we be king of all this land? Go to the flounder and tell him we want to be king."

"Oh, wife," said the fisherman, "why would we want to be king? I don't want to be king!"

"Well," said the woman, "if you don't want to be king, I'll be king. Go to the flounder. I want to be king."

"Oh, wife," said the fisherman, "why do you want to be king? I don't want to ask him."

"Why not?" said the woman. "Go right now. I must be king."

"This isn't right, this really isn't right," thought the fisherman. He didn't want to go, but he went anyway. When he came to the shore the sea was all dark gray, and the water bubbled up from the deep and stank of something rotten. But he stood there and said:

> "Manntje, Manntje, Timpe Tee,
> Flounder, flounder in the sea,
> Now my wife, that Ilsebill
> Wants something else against my will."

"What does she want now?" said the flounder.

"Oh," said the fisherman, "she wants to be king."

"Go on home, she's king already," said the flounder.

So the man went home and when he came to the castle, it had become much bigger, with a tall tower and splendid decorations. There was a sentry at the door and soldiers were playing drums and trumpets. When he went inside, he saw that everything was made of marble and gold, and the curtains were velvet with big golden tassels. Then the doors of the great hall opened and there was the whole court. His wife was sitting on a high throne made of gold and diamonds, and she had a big golden crown on her head and held a scepter made of gold and precious stones in her hand. And on both sides of her stood her ladies in waiting in a row, each one a head shorter than the next one.

He went and stood before her and said, "Well, wife, are you king now?"

"Yes," said the woman, "now I'm king."

He stood and looked at her and when he had looked for a while he said, "Well, wife, let it be enough that you're king. Now we won't wish for anything more."

"Oh yes we will," said the woman all upset. "Being king is not enough. I want more. Go back to the flounder. I want to be emperor."

"Oh, wife," said the fisherman, "why do you want to be emperor?"

"Husband," she said, "go to the flounder. I will be emperor."

"Oh, wife," said the man, "he can't make an emperor. I don't want to ask the flounder that. There's only one emperor in the empire: the flounder can't make you emperor, he just can't."

"What?" said the woman. "I'm the king and you're only my husband. Go on, go right now. If he can make a king, he can make an emperor. Go!"

So the fisherman had to go. But although he went, he was scared, and he thought to himself as he walked, "This won't end well. Emperor is too shameless, the flounder will get tired of this."

When he came to the shore the sea was black and thick and bubbling up from the depths. A sharp wind was blowing, and the man was filled with dread. He stood there and said:

> "Manntje, Manntje, Timpe Tee,
> Flounder, flounder in the sea,
> Now my wife, that Ilsebill
> Wants something else against my will."

"Well, what does she want?" said the flounder.

"Oh, flounder," said the fisherman, "my wife wants to be emperor."

"Go on home," said the flounder. "She's emperor already."

So the fisherman went home, and when he got there he found the whole castle was made of polished marble with alabaster statues and gold decorations. Soldiers marched up and down in front of the door playing trumpets and beating kettledrums and snare drums. Inside, barons and earls and dukes were walking around as servants. They opened doors for him made all of gold. And when he went through the doors he saw his wife on a throne that was made of solid gold and about two miles high. She wore a huge golden crown set with diamonds and rubies. In one hand she held a scepter and in the other hand she held an orb and on both sides of her stood the rulers of vassal states in two rows, each one shorter than the next, from the very largest giant, who was two miles tall, down to the very smallest dwarf, who was as big as my little finger.

The fisherman went and stood before her and said, "Wife, are you emperor now?"

"Yes," she said, "I'm emperor."

He stood there and took a good look at her, and when he had looked for a while he said, "Well, wife, let it be enough that you are emperor."

"Husband," she said, "why are you standing there? I'm emperor now, but I want to be pope, too. Go to the flounder."

"Oh, wife!" said the fisherman, "what don't you want? You can't be pope, there's only one pope in Christendom. The flounder can't make a pope."

"Husband," she said, "I will be pope. Go right now. I must be pope today."

"No, wife," said the fisherman, "I don't want to tell him that, it's no good. It's too much. The flounder can't make you pope."

"Nonsense, husband!" said the wife. "If he can make an emperor he can make a pope. Go on, I'm emperor and you're only my husband. Get going!"

Then the fisherman was really scared. He went, but he felt faint, and he shivered and shook, and his knees wobbled. A strong wind blew over the land, and the clouds flew across the sky. It was as dark as if it were evening already. The leaves fell from the trees and the water foamed as if it were boiling and dashed against the shore, and far off he saw ships shooting distress signals as they tossed and danced on the waves. The sky still had a bit of blue in the middle, but on the sides it was as red as if a bad thunderstorm were coming. Desperate and frightened, the fisherman stood on the shore and said:

> "Manntje, Manntje, Timpe Tee,
> Flounder, flounder in the sea,
> Now my wife, that Ilsebill
> Wants something else against my will."

"Well, what does she want?" said the flounder.

"Oh," said the fisherman, "she wants to be pope."

"Go on home," said the flounder, "she's pope already."

So the fisherman went home, and when he got there he found a great church surrounded by palaces. He pushed his way through the crowd into the church. Inside, everything was lit by thousands and thousands of candles. His wife was dressed all in gold and sat on a throne three miles high. She wore three great golden crowns, one on top of the other, and all around her were princes of the church, and on both sides of her stood two rows of candles, each one smaller than the next. The largest was as thick and tall as the biggest tower, and the smallest was no more than a kitchen candle. And emperors and kings knelt before her and kissed her slipper.

"Wife," said the fisherman, "are you pope now?"

"Yes," she said. "I'm pope."

He stood and looked at her and it was as if he were looking at the bright sun. And when he'd looked at her for a while he said, "Well, wife, let it be enough that you are pope!" But she didn't answer him. So he said, "Wife, now be content. Now that you are pope, you can't become anything more."

"I'll think about that," said his wife. And with that they both went to bed. The fisherman slept soundly because he had walked a lot that day. But the woman couldn't get to sleep. She tossed and turned all night trying to figure out what she could be that was more than pope, but she couldn't think of anything. At last the dawn came, and when she saw the first red glow of morning, she sat up in bed and looked out the window. As she saw the sun rising she thought "Ha! I should be able to make the sun and the moon come up!"

"Husband," she said, and jabbed her elbow into his ribs, "wake up, and go to the flounder. I want to be like God."

The man was still half asleep, but he was so shocked that he fell off the bed. He thought he'd heard wrong, and rubbed his eyes and said, "Wife, what did you say?"

"Husband," she said, "if I can't make the sun and the moon come up, and have to watch them rise, I won't be able to stand it. I'll never have a moment's peace if I can't make them come up myself!" She gave him such a terrible look that a shudder went through him. "Go right now. I want to be like God!"

"Oh no, wife," the fisherman said, and fell to his knees before her. "The flounder can't do that. Emperor and pope he can make, but not God. I beg you, just go on being pope."

Then the woman became angry. Her hair stood out wildly around her head. She tore up her nightgown and kicked the fisherman and shrieked, "I can't stand it! I can't stand it anymore! Go! Now!"

The fisherman pulled on his pants and ran off like a madman. Outside, such a storm was raging that he could hardly keep his feet. Houses and trees blew over, the mountains shook and rocks broke off the cliffs and rolled into the sea. The sky was pitch black and full of thunder and lightning, and the sea rose in black waves as high as church steeples crowned with white foam. The fisherman stood on the shore and screamed into the wind, although he couldn't hear his own words:

> *"Manntje, Manntje, Timpe Tee,*
> *Flounder, flounder in the sea,*
> *Now my wife, that Ilsebill*
> *Wants something else against my will."*

"Well, what does she want?" said the flounder.

"Oh flounder," said the fisherman, "she wants to be like God."

"Go on home," said the flounder. "She's back in the pisspot."

And there they still are, to this very day.

Source: Grimm KHM #19, 1857

Frau Holle

There once was a widow who had two daughters. One of them was good-tempered and diligent, while the other was quarrelsome and lazy. Because the lazy one was the widow's daughter by birth, the woman loved her best. Her stepdaughter had to do all the work around the house and garden, and on top of that, she had to go out to the well by the road every day and spin and spin until her fingers were sore.

One day the stepdaughter's distaff came loose and fell into the well, sinking deep down into the water. When she told her stepmother what had happened, the woman scolded her harshly and said, "Since you dropped it, you'll have to get it back. We don't have distaffs to waste."

Back to the well the girl went, and not knowing what else to do, she jumped into the water.

The next thing she knew she was standing in the sunshine in a beautiful meadow full of flowers. She walked through the meadow until she came to a bake oven full of bread. The bread cried to her, "Take me out, take me out before I burn, I was done long ago!" The girl used a corner of her apron to open the door and pulled the bread out with the long wooden baker's peel that leaned against the oven.

Then she went on until she came to an apple tree heavy with fruit. The tree called to her, "Shake me, shake me, we apples are all ripe and so heavy that my branches will break!" So the girl shook the tree until the apples fell around her like rain and not one was left in the branches. Then she went on through the meadow until at last she came to a small house, with an old woman looking out through the door. The old woman had such large teeth that the girl was frightened and began to run away. But the old woman called after her, "Don't be afraid, child!

Come and stay with me. If you do all the housework and do it properly, you'll have a good life here. You'll have to be especially careful about making my bed and be sure to shake out the pillows and featherbed until the feathers fly, for then it snows in the world above. I am Frau Holle."

The old lady seemed sensible and kind, despite her big teeth, so the girl agreed to stay. She did her work well and shook Frau Holle's bedding so vigorously that she never heard a harsh word and had meat for her dinner every day. Still, although life with Frau Holle was a thousand times better than her life at home, the girl became homesick after a while, and told Frau Holle that she could stay no longer.

Frau Holle said, "It's only right and proper that you want to go home. And because you have served me so faithfully, I'll take you back up myself." She took the girl by the hand and led her to a large gate that opened for her, and as the girl passed under its arch a heavy rain of gold fell down on her and stuck to her so that she was covered with gold.

"This is your reward for working so hard," said Frau Holle and gave her back the distaff that had fallen into the well. Then the gate closed behind the girl and she found herself back in the world above, not far from her stepmother's house. The rooster perched on the well crowed:

"Kikeriki,
Here comes our Goldmarie!"

And because she came covered with gold, she was welcome.

When the stepmother heard the story about Frau Holle, she was determined that her favorite daughter should have the same good fortune. She sent the lazy girl to sit by the well and spin, but the girl didn't spin until her fingers were sore. Instead she just threw her distaff into the well and jumped in after it. Like her sister, she found herself in the sunny meadow and began to walk. When she came to the bake oven the bread cried out again, "Oh, take me out, take me out before I burn, I was done long ago!" But the lazy girl answered, "As if I'd want to burn my hands to help you out!" and passed on.

Next she came to the apple tree heavy with fruit, and the tree called to her, "Shake me, shake me, we apples are all ripe and so heavy that my branches will break!" But the lazy girl answered, "Not likely! One of those apples could hit me on the head!" and passed on. When she came to Frau Holle's house and saw the old woman at the door she wasn't frightened at all, because her sister had already told her about the big teeth, and she agreed to take service with Frau Holle right away.

For the first day she actually worked hard and did whatever Frau Holle said: the thought of the gold kept her going. But on the second day she began to slack off, and on the third day she didn't even want to get up in the morning! She also did a poor job of making Frau Holle's bed and didn't shake the pillows and featherbed until it snowed on earth. Frau Holle soon had enough of the lazy thing and told her she was dismissed. This suited the girl just fine, because she thought she'd get the gold next.

And indeed, Frau Holle led her to the same gate, but as the lazy girl passed under its arch a large kettleful of black, sticky pitch poured down on her. "That's the wage for your services!" said Frau Holle and closed the gate behind her. So the girl came home covered with pitch and the rooster on the well crowed:

"Kikeriki,
Here comes our Pitchmarie."

And the pitch stuck to her for the rest of her life.

Source: Grimm KHM #24, 1857; Bechstein #11

The Frog King 🐸 Der Froschkönig

There once was a king's daughter who went out into the forest and sat down beside a cool spring. She had a golden ball, which was her favorite plaything, and she threw the golden ball high into the air and caught it again, over and over. But once, when the ball had flown high into the air, it missed the hand she held out to catch it and fell to the ground, where it rolled to the edge of the spring and straight into the water.

The king's daughter was startled and watched it sink for a moment, and then it was gone. The spring was so deep that it seemed bottomless. The princess began to cry. "Oh, I'd give anything to have my ball back—my dresses, my jewels, my pearls, anything in the world."

Suddenly a frog stuck its head up out of the water and asked, "King's daughter, why are you weeping?"

"Oh," she said, "You nasty frog, what could you do to help me? My golden ball fell into the spring and I can't get it out."

The frog said, "I don't want your dresses or your jewels or your pearls, but if you'll take me as your companion and let me sit next to you and eat from your plate and sleep in your bed, and if you will love me and hold me dear, then I will bring you back your ball."

The king's daughter thought to herself, "What's the silly frog babbling about? He'll have to stay in the water won't he? But maybe he can get my ball back, so I'll say yes." So she promised the frog whatever he asked, as long as he got her golden ball back for her. The frog ducked his head back into the water and dived down; and it wasn't long before he came back up with the ball in his mouth and threw it onto the grass. As soon as the king's daughter saw her golden ball she snatched it up and ran happily back to the castle, not giving the frog another thought.

The frog called after her, "Wait, king's daughter, take me with you, you promised!" But she paid no attention.

The next day when the princess was sitting at the dinner table, she heard something coming up the marble stairs—splish, splash! Splish, splash! A moment later someone knocked on the door and called, "King's daughter, youngest, open the door." She ran to open the door, and there was the frog. She had forgotten all about him! Quickly she slammed the door and sat down again. But the king noticed that her heart was pounding and asked, "What has frightened you?"

"There's a nasty frog out there," she answered. "He got my golden ball out of the spring for me and in return I promised him that he could be my companion, but I never thought he'd be able to leave the water, and now there he is outside the door and wants to come in." Right then the frog knocked on the door a second time and called:

> *"King's daughter, open the door,*
> *Remember what you bargained for*
> *By the waters of the spring.*
> *King's daughter, open the door."*

The king said, "You have to keep your promises. Go and open the door for the frog." She did, and the frog hopped in. He followed her back to the table and once she'd sat down he called, "Lift me up and put me on a chair next to you." She didn't want to, but the king ordered her to lift him up, and so she did. When the frog was up on the chair he said, "Now push your golden plate closer to me so I can eat with you." And she had to do that, too. When the frog had eaten his fill he said, "Now I'm tired and want to sleep. Take me up to your room, make your bed ready, and lie down with me."

The king's daughter could hardly bring herself to touch the cold frog, and now he was supposed to share her bed! She began to cry, sobbing that she would not pick him up—never, never! But the king said that she had to, so there was no help for it, but in her heart she was furious. She picked up the frog with two fingers and carried him up to her room. There she lay down on her bed, but instead of putting the frog next to her, she threw him—splat!—against the wall. "There! Now you'll leave me alone, you nasty frog!"

But the frog didn't fall back down dead as she expected. When he hit the bed he became a handsome young king whom she was happy to take as her dear companion, and they went to sleep very pleased with each other.

The next morning a splendid carriage arrived pulled by eight horses with plumes on their heads. With it came faithful Heinrich, the king's servant, who was so grieved when the king was turned into a frog that he had put three iron bands around his heart to keep it from breaking with sorrow. The king got into the coach with the king's daughter, and the faithful servant stood up behind them and they set out for the king's own country. After they had driven a little way the king heard a loud crack behind him, and he turned and called, "Heinrich, I hear the carriage break."

> *"No, Sir, you're making a mistake,*
> *It's the band around my heart,*
> *That sorrow almost broke apart*
> *When you were a frog in the cool spring water,*
> *Before you were saved by the king's fair daughter."*

Once more, and once again the king heard a crack and thought it was the carriage, but each time it was another iron band breaking from faithful Heinrich's heart because his master was free from the enchantment, and happy.

Source: Grimm KHM #1, 1812

The Queen and the Frog ❧ De Koenigin un de Pogg

Once there were a king and queen who loved each other very much. The king had to go off to war, and the queen was left all alone in the castle with only her faithful maid for company. Every day the queen climbed to the top of the castle tower to look for her husband coming home, but she never saw him. And every day when she came down she cried, and her maid comforted her.

Sometimes the queen went out into the garden and sat under a plum tree that grew on the bank of the river. And when the plums were ripe, she shook them down from the tree and ate them. The juicy plums stained her fingers, so she went down to the river to wash them, but as she rinsed her hands her wedding ring slid off her finger and disappeared under the water. The queen sat down on the river bank and wept, because she took this as a sign that her husband was dead

Suddenly a big frog jumped out of the water and looked at her. "Lady queen," he said, "why do you weep?" But the queen was crying so bitterly that she didn't hear him. The frog hopped onto her foot and said again, "Lady queen, why do you weep?" At that the queen looked up and said, "You nasty old frog, why should I tell you? You can't help me."

"Oh," said the frog, "is that what you think? I know why you're crying. You've lost your ring."

The queen looked at him with more interest and said, "Oh, dear frog, if you know that, you must have found the ring. Could you bring it back to me?"

"Yes," said the frog, "I can do that, but you have to promise me something."

"I'll promise anything if only you'll bring me back my ring," said the queen.

"What I want is not a small matter," said the frog. "You must promise to take me as your husband."

The queen laughed, and thought to herself, "Stupid frog! As if that could ever happen!" But she said, "Yes, I'll do it, just bring me the ring."

The frog jumped back into the water with a splash. He was gone so long that the queen began to think he had lied to her. But finally he crept back out of the water with the ring in his mouth. The queen snatched the ring from him and quickly ran back to the castle. The poor frog, left sitting on the riverbank, called after her that her would come to her soon.

Two days later the queen was sitting in her room sewing a silken shirt for her husband when she heard a little knock on the bottom of the door and a voice saying, "Open the door for me, fairest queen."

"Oh," said the queen to her maid, "that must be the frog I told you about. Go and open the door for him." But the voice outside the door sang,

> *"Not the maid, fairest queen.*
> *Remember your promise by the stream,*
> *That you would take me as your husband."*

So the queen got up and opened the door.

The frog hopped in, and as soon as he was across the threshold he spoke again, "Lift me up on your chair, fairest queen."

"Just listen to the frog!" said the queen to her maid. "Still, he did bring me the ring back, so we'll do what he asks. Pick him up and put him on the chair."

But the frog sang,

> *"Not the maid, fairest queen.*
> *Remember your promise by the stream,*
> *That you would take me as your husband."*

The queen wrapped her hand in her silken handkerchief, picked up the frog, and put him on the chair.

Then the frog said, "Give me something to eat, fairest queen."

"Go get the frog some bread and milk," the queen said to her maid.

But the frog sang,

> *"Not the maid, fairest queen.*
> *Remember your promise by the stream,*
> *That you would take me as your husband."*

The queen went to the kitchen and brought the frog sweet milk and bread and butter. And when the frog had eaten till he was full he said, "Wipe my mouth for me, fairest queen."

"No," said the queen, "I won't do that. Maid, take the napkin and wipe his mouth for him." But the frog sang,

> *"Not the maid, fairest queen.*
> *Remember your promise by the stream,*
> *That you would take me as your husband."*

So the queen had to do it herself. When she had wiped his mouth the frog said, "Give me a kiss, fairest queen."

The queen almost fainted, and said to her maid, "You'll have to kiss him. I couldn't possibly!"

The frog looked very unhappy. Two big tears rolled down his face and he sang in a very quiet little voice;

> *"Not the maid, fairest queen.*
> *Remember your promise by the stream,*
> *That you would take me as your husband."*

The queen thought about her promise and said to her maid, "I never expected it would come to this. Go fetch me a cloth and tie it over my eyes so that at least I don't have to look at the creature while I kiss him." The maid blindfolded the queen, and the queen felt about for the frog with both hands. She shuddered when she picked him up, but she puckered her lips for the kiss—and then there was a loud Bang! The queen was so startled that she almost fainted again. Suddenly, her beloved husband stood before her, alive and well. After the queen had kissed him, very willingly this time, the king told her what had happened. While he was far away fighting in the war, a wicked witch had turned him into a frog and said that he would have to stay a frog until a princess gave him a kiss. The poor king had made his way home to his wife by water, swimming through streams and ponds and lakes, splashing through marshes and puddles, until he finally reached his own river in his own garden. For, he said, he was pretty sure that only his own wife would be willing to kiss him.

Source: Jahn

The Rosemaiden *ﻬ* Das Rosenmädchen

It's getting dark outside. Supper is over. Mother sits in front of the bed and spins. Father has a basket of dried corn and is rubbing the kernels from the cobs into a pail; the corn will feed their hens all winter. The children have pulled the settle over to the stove. Now and then they put a stripped corncob on the fire and flames leap up brightly as it catches. The lamp isn't lit, so the only light in the room is the flickering firelight.

"Father," says the oldest boy, "Wouldn't you like to tell us a story? It's only five o'clock and we don't want to go to bed yet. Won't you, please, if we're good and pay attention?"

"Yes, if you're quiet, I'll tell you one you haven't heard before."

"Start telling, we'll listen as quietly as mice."

"All right then, this is the story of the Rosemaiden."

Once there was a poor orphan who got lost and wandered farther and farther away from his village. At last a woodwife, one of the forest spirits, found him and took him to her house, and she kept him and cared for him like a real mother.

When the boy was almost grown up, he said one day, "Mother, I'm leaving. I want to look for the Rosemaiden."

"That's a long way, my son, and even if you get there, you'll still have to face the dragon who guards her." But the boy wouldn't stay, so his mother gave him a bell and said, "If you need to wish for something, ring the bell."

The boy walked a long, long, way, until one day he came upon a swarm of bees. He asked the bee queen if she knew where the Rosemaiden lived. She didn't, she said, but she could find out, and she sent all her bees out to look. They came back without the answer, but when the bee queen counted them, there was one still missing. Finally she came back, too, and she had good news: she had seen the Rosemaiden.

So the bee was sent to show the young man the way. She led him across a big, big meadow, and then they came to a forest. On the other side of the forest they came to a big castle, and that's where the Rosemaiden lived. The boy found work there as a gooseherd, and he always pastured his flock close to the garden. Here he saw the Rosemaiden every day as she walked among the flowers. She was very beautiful.

One day he heard that the Rosemaiden drove to the town every evening to go to the ball. That evening he took out his bell and rang it. Before the sound had died away, a copper horse appeared, all saddled and bridled, and a copper cloak lay across the saddle. The boy put on the cloak, mounted the horse, and rode to town. At the ball he danced only with the Rosemaiden, and she liked him very much. But before the ball was over, he stole away, mounted his horse, and rode home. The Rosemaiden told her mother about the handsome boy in the copper cloak; but she had no idea he was just the poor gooseherd, herding his geese close to the garden where he could catch a glimpse of her.

The next evening the Rosemaiden drove to the ball again. The gooseherd rang his bell again and a silver horse appeared, with a silver cloak lying across the saddle. He put on the cloak and rode to the ball. There he spent the whole evening talking with the Rosemaiden, which she enjoyed very much; but he ran away again before the ball was over and rode home.

The following morning the Rosemaiden told her mother more about the handsome boy who had worn a silver cloak this time. The mother wanted to meet to meet this young man, and asked her daughter whether she had marked him somehow. "No," said the Rosemaiden.

"Then next time take a little pitch with you, and when he dances with you, stick it into his hair." That evening the Rosemaiden took some pitch to the ball. When the gooseherd took out his bell and rang it, a golden horse appeared, with a golden cloak lying across the saddle. He quickly put on the cloak, mounted the horse, and rode to the ball. There he danced with the Rosemaiden all evening, and she managed to stick a little pitch in his hair. At the end of the ball, he quickly ran outside, sprang onto his horse, and galloped home.

The next morning the Rosemaiden told her mother that the handsome boy had worn a golden cloak this time and how she had managed to get the pitch into his hair. Meanwhile the gooseherd was casting stolen glances into the garden again, but when he drove his geese back to the castle that evening, the girl noticed that his hair was tangled and knotted, and she took a long look at him.

"You are the young man I danced with!" she cried joyfully. "Can you rescue us?"

"That I will happily do!" he replied.

The mother said, "Quickly then, let us flee. The dragon is still sleeping, but he will wake up soon!"

The gooseherd went out and rang his bell three times, and the copper horse, the silver horse, and the golden horse appeared, all saddled and bridled. He helped the Rosemaiden onto the golden horse and put the golden cloak around her. He put the mother on the silver horse and gave her the silver cloak. And then he mounted the copper horse and wrapped himself in the copper cloak. And they galloped away.

In the castle the dragon slept in an enormous barrel with three massive iron rings around it. His year's sleep was just ending. Suddenly one of the rings broke, then the second, and then the third, and each one sounded like a thunderclap. The dragon rubbed his eyes and looked around.

"Where is my Rosemaiden?" he roared. No one answered him. He jumped up and looked in all the rooms and in the garden, but no one was there. Then he hurried to the stable, led out his stallion, jumped on its back, and said, "Take me to the thief."

The stallion galloped like the wind and soon caught up with the three riders. The dragon snarled at the boy, "I could smash you to pieces, you little earthworm, but you're not worth the trouble." He took the boy's bell, the three horses, the Rosemaiden and her mother and started back to the castle. But he turned once and called back to the boy, just to mock him, "You could rescue the Rosemaiden if my mother gave you a horse like the one she gave me, but that will never happen!"

The dragon took his captives back to the castle and curled up in his barrel to sleep for another year, and the iron rings bound themselves around it. The Rosemaiden and her mother were lonely again. During the day the girl tended the garden, but she no longer went dancing in the evening. Instead, she thought about the young man who had tried to rescue her.

Meanwhile, he set out to find the dragon's mother. On his way he saw a raven caught in a net. The raven called to him, "Help me out. I'll repay you some day." The boy freed the bird, and it flew away. Farther along, he saw a fox caught in a trap.

The fox cried, "Help me, I'll repay you some day." The boy freed the fox, and it ran into the forest.

After a time the boy came to the seashore, and there he saw a fish flapping on the sand, gasping for breath. "Put me in the water!" cried the fish. "I'll repay you some day." The boy put the fish back in the water and went on.

Finally, he came to the little house in the woods where the dragon's mother lived. He knocked at the door and asked whether she had any work for him. "Oh, yes!" she said. "You can take my mare out to pasture every day. What pay do you want for a year's work?"

"Just a foal," said the boy. "So be it," said the old woman. "But if you ever fail to bring my mare home at night, even just once, you life will be forfeited." The old witch had hired many a man before him and had killed them all.

In the morning the boy took the mare out to pasture, but she disappeared almost at once. He searched for her all day in vain. Just before it began to grow dark, he saw the raven, told it the story, and said, "Help me if you can!"

The raven said, "The mare is in the clouds and has given birth to a foal. Sit on my neck and I'll take you to her." So the boy brought the mare and her foal back to the house and the old woman was astonished.

The next morning when he took the mare out to pasture, the same thing happened: the mare and the foal vanished and he searched for them until evening, in vain. Then he met the fox, and told it what had happened.

The fox said, "She's in a cave in the mountains and has given birth to a foal. Sit on my tail and I'll take you there." So the boy brought the mare and her two foals back to the house and the old woman was even more astonished.

On the third day, when he took the mare and her two foals out to pasture they vanished again, right before his eyes, and he searched for them in vain. Just before it began to grow dark he came to the seashore and stood staring sadly into the water.

Suddenly the big fish swam up to the surface and asked him why he looked so miserable, and the boy explained what had happened. "She's on the ocean floor," said the fish, "and has given birth to a foal. I'll take you down there." The fish took the boy in his mouth and carried him down to the bottom of the sea. So the boy was able to drive the mare and her three foals back to the house that night.

The old woman wondered more than ever how he had managed it, but she had nowhere else to hide the mare and her foals, so the boy took them out to pasture every morning and brought them back in the evening without further trouble until a year was up.

Then the old woman said, "Now choose yourself a foal." He took the oldest of the three, which had grown into a beautiful mare, and rode her back to rescue the Rosemaiden. As soon as he came near the palace, the mare began to whinny. The dragon's stallion in the stable heard her and whinnied back, stamping his feet so hard that everything trembled. That woke up the dragon in the barrel, because his year of sleep was over, too. The three iron rings snapped with a noise like thunder. The dragon heard the whinnying and ran to the stable, where the stallion had already broken loose and wanted to run to the mare.

The dragon grabbed the stallion's mane and swung himself up on his back, but the stallion reared up, high up on his hind legs. The dragon fell off and the maddened stallion trampled him to death beneath his hooves. Then he jumped the palace wall and ran after the mare.

Meanwhile, the boy had reached the palace and dismounted right away. He was in such a hurry to see the Rosemaiden that he didn't go around to the door but climbed right over the garden hedge. His mare turned around and started to run back to the old woman, and the stallion ran after her, but he could not catch her until she got back to the old mare and the other foals.

The boy was now master of the castle and had his bell and his three horses back, too. So he and the Rosemaiden had a splendid wedding, and if they haven't died in the meantime they're still alive today.

Source: Zaunert

The Goosegirl *&* Die Gänsemagd

Once there was an old queen whose husband had died long before and who had a beautiful daughter. As a child, the princess had been betrothed to a king's son in a faraway land, and now the time had come for her to travel there to be married.

The queen packed up cutlery and cups and plates and platters, all of gold and silver, and gems and jewelry and fine bed linens, everything a royal dowry should have, for she loved her child dearly. She also sent with her a waiting woman to be her traveling companion and keep her safe until she reached her bridegroom, and each of them had a horse for the journey. The waiting woman had an ordinary brown gelding, but the princess's white horse was called Falada and could speak. When the time came for them to leave, the old queen went to her bedroom and cut her finger with a little knife and let three drops of blood fall onto a white handkerchief. This she folded up and gave to her daughter, saying, "Dear child, keep this carefully. It will help protect you on the journey."

Then mother and daughter sadly said good-bye to each other. The princess tucked the handkerchief into her bosom, mounted her horse, and set out on the journey to her bridegroom. When they had ridden for an hour, she became thirsty and called to her waiting woman, "Dismount, and get me some water from the brook in my cup that you carry. I would like something to drink."

"If you're thirsty," said the waiting woman, "get off your horse and lie down on the bank to drink. I'm not going to be your maid."

The princess was so thirsty that she climbed down from her horse, bent over the brook, and drank from her hands because she could not use her golden cup. As she straightened up, she said, "Heaven help me!" and the three drops of blood answered, "If your mother knew, her heart would break." But the princess mounted her horse again and said nothing.

They rode on for a few more miles. The day was warm, the sun burned down on them, and the princess became thirsty again. Since they were riding by a river, she called again to her waiting woman. "Dismount, and get me some water in my golden cup."

But the waiting woman answered even more arrogantly, "If you want a drink, get it yourself. I'm not going to be your maid."

The princess was so thirsty that she got down from her horse and lay down on the riverbank to drink. She was crying a little because she was unused to such harshness, and when she sighed, "Heaven help me!" the drops of blood answered again, "If your mother knew, her heart would break." But as she leaned over the water, the handkerchief fell out of her bodice and floated away, and in her unhappiness the princess didn't notice.

The waiting woman saw it, though, and was glad that she now had power over the princess, for without the three drops of blood, the princess would be helpless against her.

When the princess came to mount her horse, Falada, again, the waiting woman said, "I belong on Falada and you belong on my nag." And the princess had to accept this. Then the waiting woman roughly ordered the princess to trade clothes with her, and finally the princess had to swear on her life that she would say no word about any of this at the court of her bridegroom. But Falada watched it all, and bore it in mind.

Now the waiting woman rode white Falada and the true bride rode the brown horse and finally they came to the royal place of the bridegroom. Their arrival was greeted joyfully. The young king ran to meet them and lifted the waiting woman down from Falada's back, thinking she was his bride.

The waiting woman was led up the stairs and the true princess had to stay behind in the courtyard. But the old king was watching from the window and saw how fine she was—delicate and truly beautiful. He went to the royal guest chambers and asked the bride about the woman she'd brought with her, the one standing in the courtyard.

"I picked her up on the road to keep me company. Give the girl some work to do—don't let her stand around idly." The king really had no work for her. The only thing he could think of was to let her help the little boy who was the gooseherd. His name was Konrad. And from that day on, the true bride had to help Konrad look after the geese.

A few days later, the false bride said to the young king, "Dearest husband, I beg you to do me a favor."

"I will be happy to," he answered.

"I want you to send for the knacker and have him cut off the head of the horse I rode here. It made me angry on the road." Actually, she was afraid the horse might speak about the way she had treated the princess.

So everything was arranged and Falada was about to die when the princess heard what was going to happen. She went to the knacker and promised him money if he would do her a small service. In the town wall there was a large, dark gate, almost like a tunnel because the wall was so thick. She had to go through that gate morning and evening with the geese, and she asked the knacker to nail Falada's head over the arch of it so that she might see the horse every day. The knacker promised to do as she asked, chopped off Falada's head, and nailed it over the arch of the gate.

Early the next morning as the princess and Konrad drove the geese out through the gate she spoke to her horse,

> *"O Falada, there thou hangest,"*

and the head answered:

> *"O royal maiden, there thou gangest.*
> *If thy mother knew,*
> *Her heart would break in two."*

Then she drove the geese out of the town and into the countryside. Once they were in the meadow, she sat down and unbraided her hair, which shone like pure gold. Konrad saw it and because it shone so beautifully he tried to pull a few hairs out. At that she said,

> *"Blow, blow little wind,*
> *Take Konrad's little hat,*
> *Make him chase it till I've bound*
> *My braided hair with ribbon round*
> *And pinned it up into a crown."*

And a wind blew up that snatched Konrad's hat and made him chase it all around the meadow. By the time he had caught it, she was finished combing and braiding, so he had no chance to snatch a couple of hairs for himself. Konrad was angry and refused to speak to her. They looked after the geese in silence until evening when it was time to go home.

The next morning, as they were driving the geese under the arch of the gloomy gate, the maiden spoke:

> *"O Falada, there thou hangest.,"*

Falada answered,

> *"Oh royal maiden, there thou gangest.*
> *If thy mother knew*
> *Her heart would break in two."*

Once they were out in the country, she sat down in the meadow again and began to comb out her hair, and Konrad came running to snatch some. She quickly said,

> *"Blow, blow little wind,*
> *Take Konrad's little hat,*
> *Make him chase it till I've bound*
> *My braided hair with ribbon round*
> *And pinned it up into a crown."*

The wind came up and blew Konrad's hat far away, and by the time he'd caught it, she had finished combing out and putting up her hair so he had no chance to snatch any. They looked after the geese in silence until evening.

But that night after they had brought the geese home, Konrad went to the old king and said, "I won't look after the geese with that girl any more."

"Why ever not?" asked the king.

"Oh, she annoys me all day long."

The king ordered Konrad to tell him what she had done to him, and Konrad said, "In the morning when we drive the geese through the dark gate, there's a horse head nailed there that she talks to. She says,

> *"O Falada, there thou hangest,"*

and the head answers:

> *"O royal maiden, there thou gangest.*
> *If thy mother knew,*
> *Her heart would break in two."*

And then Konrad told the king what happened in the goose meadow and how he had to chase his hat.

The king ordered him to drive the geese out again the next day, and went himself early in the morning to the gloomy gate and hid himself. He heard what the goosegirl and the head of Falada said to each other. Then he followed them to the meadow and hid behind a bush. The goosegirl sat down and unbraided her gleaming gold hair and said,

> *"Blow, blow little wind,*
> *Take Konrad's little hat,*
> *Make him chase it till I've bound*
> *My braided hair with ribbon round*
> *And pinned it up into a crown."*

A gust of wind came and blew Konrad's hat away so that he had to run after it, and the goosegirl combed and braided and pinned up her hair, all of which the king observed. Then he returned, unnoticed to the palace.

When the goosegirl came home in the evening, the king took her aside and asked her why she did these things. "I'm not allowed to tell you or anyone else. I've sworn on my life never to do so."

The king pressed her to tell him, and at last he said, "If you can't tell me, maybe you can tell it to the stove in the corner."

"Yes, that I'll do," she answered. She crept into the big tile stove that heated the entire room in the winter and she poured her heart out, describing everything that had happened and how the waiting woman had betrayed her. But the stove had a hole at the top where it went through the ceiling into the room above, and there the king waited and heard every word she said.

Then everything was all right. The goosegirl was dressed in royal robes again and her beauty was a wonder. The old king called his son and revealed to him that his bride was only a waiting woman, and that the true bride was the one standing here, who had been the goosegirl.

The young king rejoiced with all his heart when he saw her. A great feast was arranged, and all their family and friends were invited. At the high table the young king sat with the princess on one side of him and the waiting woman on the other. The waiting woman was dazzled by all the lights and finery and didn't recognize the princess.

When everyone had enough to eat and drink and was merry, the old king gave the waiting woman a riddle: How would she judge a woman who had betrayed her lord in the following way?— and he went on to tell what had happened, ending with the question, "How would you judge her?"

The false bride answered, "She deserves to be put naked into a barrel that has sharp nails sticking through on the inside, and two white horses should pull it through all the streets of the town."

"You are speaking of yourself," said the old king. "You have decided your own punishment and so it shall be done."

And that is what happened. The young king married his true bride, and they ruled their kingdom together in peace and happiness.

Source: Grimm KHM #89, 1857

Statue of a goosegirl in Schwalm folk costume on a fountain in Alsfeld.

The Ratcatcher walks through the center of Hameln daily.
"The Ratcatcher of Hameln" (p. 200)

"Little Red Cap" (p. 147): This is the cap that the Grimms were supposed to have in mind. It is part of the folk costume of girls in Schwalm. Regionalmuseum Alsfeld.

Ludwig the Springer, builder of the Wartburg. The Wartburg: Five Legends (p. 222)

The stone dated 1556 commemorating the loss of the children of Hameln. The inscription reads:
Centum ter denos cum magus ab urbe puellos duxerat ante annos CCLXXII condita porta fuit.
["This gate was built 272 years after a magician led 130 children out of the city."]
Museum Hameln. "The Ratcatcher of Hamlen" (p. 200)

The official length of the ell in Alsfeld on the town hall by the market as mentioned in "Table Set Yourself, Donkey Stretch Yourself, Stick Jump Out of the Bag" (p. 172)

"The Hare and the Hedgehog" (p. 13)

"Hans in Luck"
(p. 37)

"The Goosegirl"
(p. 128)

"The Ratcatcher of Hameln"
(p. 200)

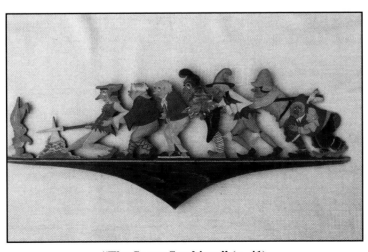

"The Seven Swabians" (p. 41)

The Marienkirche, Lübeck. "The Devil's Chapel" (p. 214)

Till Eulenspiegel's gravestone in Mölln. "The End of Till Eulenspiegel" (p. 76)

The Brothers Grimm in Hanau.

Saint Elisabeth with the basket of roses. "The Roses" (p. 226)

Ratcatcher House, Hameln

An inn sign, Alsfeld

A bake oven like the one in "Frau Holle" (p. 113) and "Hansel and Gretel." (p. 81) Hohenloher Freiland Museum.

A village well decorated for Easter. The green branches and flowers are a very old, pre-Christian tradition. The Easter eggs are a new custom. Hohenloher Freiland Museum.

Blown and decorated Easter eggs hung on a bouquet of branches. The eggs are the work of Elisabeth Schöning. Photograph by Klaus Schöning.

Two drop spindles and a high whorl spindle, with a skein of hand-spun singles (linen) boiled once. The cloth is hand-spun hand-woven linen. The work of Karen Braun. "Brier Rose" (p. 95); "Spindle, Shuttle, and Needle" (p. 169); and "The Three Little Men in the Woods" (p. 181)

Distaff dressed with a strick of flax ready to spin. "Frau Holle" (p. 113); "The Three Spinners" (p. 154)

A shoemaker's workbench. Regionalmuseum Alsfeld. "The Shoemaker and the Elves" (p. 104)

**The town square in Mölln with half-timbered houses and whipping post.
"Till Eulenspiegel" (p. 64)**

A thatched cottage in Gothmund.

The Wartburg. "The Wartburg: Five Legends" (p. 222)

Hunters in an ancient forest. "Little Red Cap" (p. 147)

The House in the Forest ❧ Das Waldhaus

A poor woodcutter lived with his wife and three daughters in a little hut at the edge of a great, wild forest. One morning as he was going to out to work, he said to his wife, "Have the oldest girl bring me my noonday meal in the woods, otherwise I won't get the work done. I'll take a bag of millet along and strew the grains on the path so she doesn't lose her way."

When the sun stood high above the trees, the girl set out with a pot of soup for her father. But the field sparrows and the wood sparrows, the larks and the finches, the blackbirds and the siskins had pecked up all the millet, and the girl couldn't find the path. She went on, though, deeper and deeper into the forest, trusting to luck, until the sun went down and it was night.

The trees rustled in the dark, the owls hooted, and she began to feel frightened. But then she saw a light shining far away among the trees. "There'll be good people living there, who will let me spend the night," she thought, and went toward it.

Before long she came to a house with lighted windows. She knocked and a gruff voice from inside called "Come in." So she stepped into the dark little entry and knocked on the inner door. "Come right in," called the voice, and she opened the door. An old man sat at the table. His head was propped on his hands, and his long white beard flowed over the table and almost down to the floor. Three animals were lying near the stove—a hen, a rooster, and a spotted cow. The girl told the old man what had happened to her and asked if she could stay the night. The man said,

> *"Pretty hen,*
> *Pretty rooster,*
> *And you, pretty spotted cow,*
> *What say you, now?"*

"Duks!" answered the animals, and that must have meant, "It's fine with us," because the old man said, "We have plenty of everything. Go into the kitchen and cook us some supper."

The girl did find plenty of everything in the kitchen and she cooked a good meal, but the animals never crossed her mind. She brought the full bowl to the table, sat down with the old man, and ate until she was satisfied. And when she was finished she said, "I'm tired now. Is there a bed I can sleep in?" The animals answered,

> *"You ate with him,*
> *You drank with him,*
> *You gave us neither sup nor bite,*
> *You look to where you'll sleep tonight."*

But the old man said, "Just go up the stairs and you'll find a room with two beds in it. Shake the featherbeds and put white linen sheets on them. Then I'll come up and go to bed, too."

The girl went upstairs and after she had shaken up the beds and put fresh linen on them, she lay down in one of them and went to sleep. After a while the old man came, held his candle so that the light shone on her, and shook his head. And when he saw that she was fast asleep, he opened a trap door and let her sink down to the cellar.

The woodcutter came home late in the evening and complained to his wife that he had gone hungry all day. "It's not my fault," she answered, "the girl went out before noon with your food. She must have lost the way. I'm sure she'll come home tomorrow." The next morning the woodcutter got up before dawn to go into the forest and told his wife to send their second daughter with his noon meal. "I'll take a bag of lentils with me," he said. "They're bigger than millet, so they'll be easier for her to see, and she won't lose her way."

At noon the girl took her father's food into the forest, but the lentils were gone—the birds of the forest had eaten every single one. She wandered around in the forest until night fell, and then she, too, came to the old man's house, where she asked for food and a bed. The man with the white beard asked the animals again,

> *"Pretty hen,*
> *Pretty rooster,*
> *And you, pretty spotted cow,*
> *What say you, now?"*

Again the animals said "Duks," and everything happened as it did the day before. The girl cooked a good meal, ate and drank with the old man, and didn't bother about the animals. And when she asked where she could spend the night they answered,

> *"You ate with him,*
> *You drank with him,*
> *You gave us neither sup nor bite,*
> *You look to where you'll sleep tonight."*

When she had gone upstairs, made the beds, and fallen asleep the old man came, looked at her, shook his head, and let her down into the cellar.

On the third morning, the woodcutter said to his wife, "Send our youngest child with my food today. She's always been a good, sensible girl. She'll stay on the path and not go buzzing off somewhere like her sisters. They're as hard to keep track of as wild bees."

Her mother didn't want to let her go and said, "Must I lose the last of my children, too?" "Don't worry," said her husband, "the girl won't get lost, she's got a good head on her shoulders. But just in case, I'll take peas along to mark the path. They're even bigger than lentils, she can't miss them."

But when the girl went out with a basket on her arm, the wood doves already had the peas in their crops, and she didn't know which way to go. She was worried, and kept thinking about how hungry her father would be if she didn't find him and how upset her mother would be if she didn't come home. Finally, when darkness had fallen, she saw the light and came to the house in the forest. She knocked on the door, was invited in, and asked if she could spend the night there. The man with the white beard asked his animals again,

> *"Pretty hen,*
> *Pretty rooster,*
> *And you, pretty spotted cow,*
> *What say you, now?"*

"Duks!" they said.

Then the girl went to the stove where the animals lay. She stroked the smooth feathers of the hen and the rooster, and scratched the spotted cow between her horns. And when she had made a good soup at the old man's bidding and put the bowl on the table, she said, "How could I eat my fill while these dear animals have nothing? There's plenty of everything outside. I'll look after them first." She brought barley and scattered it for the hen and the rooster, and she brought the cow a whole armful of sweet-smelling hay. "Enjoy you food, my dears," she said, "and when you get thirsty you can have a drink of fresh water."

With that she brought in a pail of water, and the hen and the rooster jumped up on the rim, stuck their beaks in, and then held their heads high, the way birds do when they drink. And the spotted cow took a hearty swallow, too. When the animals had been fed, the girl sat down with the old man at the table and ate what he had left her.

Before long, the hen and the rooster were tucking their heads under their wings, and the spotted cow was blinking her eyes. Then the girl asked, "Shouldn't we all go to bed?

> *Pretty hen,*
> *Pretty rooster,*
> *And you, pretty spotted cow,*
> *What say you, now?"*

The animals answered, "duks,

> *You ate with us,*
> *You drank with us,*
> *You gave us sup and bite,*
> *We wish you a good night."*

Then the girl went upstairs, shook the featherbeds and made them up with fresh linen. When she had finished, the old man came and lay down in one bed, and his white beard reached all the way to his feet. The girl got into the other bed, wished him a good night, and went to sleep.

She slept peacefully until midnight. Then there was so much commotion in the house that she woke up. There was cracking and rattling in the corners, the door sprang open and banged against the wall, the beams groaned as if they were being wrenched from their footings, the stairs seemed to be falling down, and finally there was a crash as though the whole roof had collapsed. But because it grew still again and she was unhurt, the girl stayed in bed and went back to sleep.

When she woke up in the morning to bright sunshine, what did she see? She was lying in a great hall, surrounded by royal splendor. The walls were covered with green silk embroidered with golden flowers, the bed was made of ivory and the coverlet of blue velvet, and on a chair next to the bed lay a pair of crimson slippers embroidered with pearls.

The girl thought she was dreaming, but three richly dressed servants came in and asked what her orders were.

"Go away," she answered, "I don't need you. I'll get up right now and make porridge for the old man and then I'll feed pretty hen, pretty rooster, and pretty spotted cow." She thought the old man must be up already and looked for his bed. There was someone lying in it, but it wasn't the old man. Instead she saw a stranger, and as she looked at him, noticing that he was young and handsome, he opened his eyes, sat up, and said, "I am a king's son. A wicked witch put a spell on me. I had to live in the forest as an old, grey man, all alone except for my three servants, who were changed into a hen, a rooster, and a spotted cow. The spell could only be broken when a girl came to us with such a loving heart that she was kind not only to humans but to animals as well. That was you. So last night at midnight the spell was broken and the old house in the forest was changed back into my palace. Will you do me another kindness and marry me?"

Then they both got up and the king's son told the three servants to go and bring the girl's mother and father to the palace for the wedding.

"But where are my two sisters?" asked the girl.

"I locked them in the cellar," he said. "Tomorrow they'll be taken into the forest, and there they'll have to work for a charcoal burner until they know better than to let poor animals starve."

Source: Grimm KHM #169, 1857

The Poor Miller Boy and the Little Cat ❧ Der arme Müllerbursch und das Kätzchen

There was an old miller who had neither wife nor children and ran his mill with the help of three journeymen. One day the miller said to them, "I'm old, and I want to start taking my ease and sit by the stove. All of you go off and find yourselves a horse each. I'll give the mill to the one who brings me back the best horse, on the condition that he'll look after me until I die."

The three of them set out together, but once they got outside the village, the two older ones said to the youngest, whose name was Hans, "You may as well stay here. There's not a chance in the world that you'll get hold of a horse."

For Hans was really just the lad-of-all-work and the general opinion was that he was more than a bit foolish. But Hans followed along anyway, and as the day darkened, they came to a cave where they decided to spend the night. The two clever ones waited until Hans was asleep and then snuck off, thinking they'd done something really smart.

Hans slept until the sun came up. When he opened his eyes, he panicked at first, because he had no idea where he was. And after he'd crawled out of the cave and wandered into the forest, he didn't feel much better. He thought, "Here I am, alone and abandoned. What chance do I have of getting a horse?"

He walked along thinking such gloomy thoughts until he met a small tabby cat that spoke to him in a friendly way: "Hans, where are you going?"

"Oh," he answered, "I'm looking for something, but I doubt you can help me."

"I know exactly what you want," answered the cat. "You want a fine horse. If you come with me and serve me faithfully for seven years, I'll give you the finest horse you could ever hope to see."

Hans thought to himself, "This is a very odd cat. But I'd like to know if she's telling the truth." So he went with the cat to her enchanted castle, where all her servants and attendants were cats too, and Hans was the only human being in the place. Cats cooked them supper, and served them at table, and a trio of cats played music while they ate—one played the bass, the second the violin, and the third the trumpet.

After they'd eaten, the cat said to Hans, "Come and dance with me." But Hans answered "I've never danced with a cat in my life, and I'm not going to start now!"

"All right," said the cat to her servants, "put him to bed." One cat showed him his bedroom, another took off his shoes, a third his stockings, and so on until the last one blew out the candle. The next morning the same thing happened in reverse: one cat put on his stockings, one his shoes, one washed his face for him, and one dried his face with its tail.

Hans was waited on hand and foot, but he, too, had to serve the cat. His job was to cut wood for the stoves and fireplaces, and for that work he had an axe of silver, and wedges and a saw of silver, and a copper mallet. He sawed and split wood and made kindling and ate and drank well and the years went by, years in which he never saw a human face.

One day the cat ordered him to cut the hay in her meadow. She gave him a silver scythe and a golden whetstone, but told him he had to bring them back along with the dried hay. When he came back with the silver scythe and the golden whetstone and the hay, he asked whether his time of service wasn't up yet, and couldn't he have the horse she had promised him?

"Not quite yet," answered the cat. "I want you to do one more thing for me. I want you to build me a little silver house." Outside he found a pile of silver wood and silver nails and a silver tape measure and plumb bob and square-edge and level and every other carpentry tool he might need.

So Hans built the little house for the cat and then he asked her again for his horse. Indeed, his time was up, although it had passed so quickly that he thought he had only been there half a year. The cat opened the door of the silver house and suddenly seven beautiful gleaming horses were standing there, so proud and spirited that his heart turned over with joy.

The cat said, "You will have one more meal with me, and then you must go home. But without your horse. I'll bring you the horse in three days' time." After they had eaten, the cat showed Hans the way to the mill. Hans went home in his old smock, which had acquired many more patches over seven years and grown far too short for him.

The other two journeymen were already there, each with a horse, although one of the horses was blind and the other was lame. "Where's your horse then?" they asked him, and laughed at him when he told them his horse would arrive in three days.

"Do you expect us to believe that? Look at you! Where would a ragbag like you come by a horse?" Even the miller said he looked too disgraceful to come into the house. Hans had to eat the few scraps they spared him for his supper outside, and slept in the goose pen on a bit of old straw. But when he woke up, he found that three days had passed and there was a great stir on the road.

Here came a coach pulled by six shining horses and followed by a servant who led a seventh wonderful horse for Hans. A splendid princess stepped out of the coach and went into the mill. You'll have guessed already that she was the little tabby cat Hans had served for seven years.

She asked for the lad-of-all-work, and when the miller said he was in the goose pen because he was too shabby to come into the mill, the princess had him brought in, all ragged and with straw in his hair. Her servant unbuckled a chest full of magnificent clothes, washed Hans, and dressed him, and when they were finished with him no king could have looked more handsome. Then the princess demanded to see the two horses that the other two hired men had brought back, the lame one and the blind one. She had her servant bring up the seventh horse and when the miller saw it, he declared he'd never had so fine a horse in the mill yard in his life.

"That horse is for Hans," said the princess. "Then the mill is his too," said miller. But the princess said the miller could keep his mill, and the horse too. She took her faithful Hans into the coach and drove away.

First they drove to the little silver house he had built. It had turned into a large palace all furnished with silver and gold. And then the princess married Hans. Now Hans was rich, so rich that he had plenty for the rest of his life. So nobody should say that a person who's foolish or simple won't amount to anything —that's the moral of this story.

Source: Grimm KHM #106, 1857

The Moon ❧ Der Mond

Long ago there was a country where the night was always pitch black. The night sky was like a dark cloth spread over the land because the moon never rose and the stars never shone there.

It happened that four young men from this country set out to travel and came to another country where at night, when the sun had gone down behind the mountains, there was a glowing ball high up in an oak tree. The ball shed a soft light far and wide, and although it wasn't as bright as the sun, people could see well enough to distinguish between one thing and another. The travelers stopped and asked a farmer who was driving by in his wagon what kind of light that was.

"That's the moon," answered the farmer. "Our mayor bought it for three silver talers,* and he hung it up in the oak tree. He has to put oil into it every day and clean it so that it always burns bright and clear. We pay him a taler a week to do that."

When the farmer had driven off, one of the travelers said, "We could use this lamp. There's an oak tree at home, just as tall as this one, that we could hang it in. What a pleasure it would be not to have to feel our way around in the dark!"

"You know what?" said the second one, "We should get a wagon and a horse and take the moon back with us. The people here can buy themselves another one."

"I'm a good climber," said the third one. "I can easily bring it down."

The fourth one brought a wagon pulled by two horses, and the third one climbed up the tree, drilled a hole in the moon, pulled a rope through the hole, and let the moon down into the wagon. Then they covered it with a blanket so that no one would know they had stolen it. They brought the moon back safely to their country and put it high up in a tall oak. Everybody, old and young, was glad to see the new lamp shedding its light over the fields and through the windows of their houses. The dwarfs came out of their caves in the mountains to admire it and the brownies in their little red jackets danced round dances in the meadows.

The four young men who had brought the moon filled it with oil every day, trimmed the wick, and got paid a taler a week. But eventually they grew old, and when one of them got sick and foresaw that he would die, he ordered that one quarter of the moon should be buried with him because it was his property. When he was dead, the mayor climbed up into the tree and cut off one quarter of the moon with his hedge clippers and put it in the coffin.

*A taler is a coin that was the official currency in German territories into the eighteenth century. The English word "dollar" is derived from "taler."

The moon gave less light, but not noticeably so. When the second man died, he was buried with the second quarter, and there was less light again. It was even weaker after the death of the third man, who also took his quarter with him. And when the fourth man was buried the old darkness returned. If people went out at night without lanterns, they bumped into each other.

But when the four quarters of the moon came together again in the underworld where darkness had always reigned, the dead became restless and awoke from their sleep. They were astonished to find that they could see again in the pale moonlight. They got up happily and took up their old ways again. Some played cards, some went dancing, others ran to the inns where they drank wine, got rowdy, and started to fight. The noise grew worse and worse until it could be heard up in heaven.

The noise was so loud that Saint Peter, who guarded the heavenly gate, thought the underworld was rising in rebellion, and he called together the heavenly hosts. But the enemy never came, so he got on his horse and rode out through the heavenly gate down to the underworld. There he calmed down the dead, commanded them to go back to sleep in their graves, took the moon away with him, and hung it up in the sky.

Source: Grimm KHM #175, 1857

Rapunzel

There once were a woman and her husband who were very happy together except for one thing: they had no children, although they had wanted them for years. But at last, the wife had reason to hope that their dearest wish would be fulfilled. In the attic of their house there was a small window that overlooked the garden of a fairy. The garden was full of wonderful flowers and herbs and vegetables of many different kinds, but no one dared go into it. The woman often stood at this window looking at the loveliness of the garden and dreaming about the child they would soon have.

One day when the woman was standing at the back window looking down into the garden she noticed a bed of the kind of wild lettuce called rapunzel.* She knew she couldn't get any, but she craved it so much that she began to waste away with longing. Her husband, seeing her grow thin and pale, became worried and asked her what was wrong.

"If I can't get some rapunzel to eat from the fairy's garden, I shall die," she told him.

The woman's husband loved her dearly, and he decided to get her the rapunzel, whatever the cost might be. One evening he climbed over the high wall and cut a handful of rapunzel. The woman quickly made it into a salad and ate it ravenously. It tasted so good that the next day she wanted it three times as much. Her husband could see that she would have no peace until he got her more rapunzel, so he climbed into the garden again. But this time he was horrified to find the fairy standing there. She was very angry that he had dared to enter her garden and even worse, to steal from it.

Leonhardsturm, built in 1380 in Alsfeld.

The man excused himself as best he could, explaining that his wife was pregnant and how dangerous it was to deny her what she longed for. Finally, the fairy said, "I will overlook what you have done, and will even permit you to take as much rapunzel as you want, if you will give me the child your wife is carrying."

*The English name for rapunzel (*Valetrianella locusta*) is lamb's lettuce.

In his fright the man agreed to this terrible pact. Three months later, his wife was delivered of a baby girl, and moment the child was born, the fairy appeared, named the child Rapunzel, and took her away with her.

Rapunzel grew to be the most beautiful child under the sun. When she was twelve years old, the fairy shut her up in a high tower that had no door and no stairs, only a small window way up at the top. When the fairy wanted to come in, she stood at the foot of the tower and called:

> *"Rapunzel, Rapunzel!*
> *Let down your long hair."*

Rapunzel had splendid hair, as fine as spun gold. When the fairy called, Rapunzel would unbind her hair, wind it around the window latch, and let it fall down to the ground far below. The fairy then used it to climb up the tower.

One day a king's son was riding through the forest where the tower stood. He saw Rapunzel standing by the high window and heard her singing. She was so lovely and sang so sweetly that he fell deeply in love with her. But he despaired of ever meeting her because the tower had no door, and no ladder would be long enough to reach her. Still, he went into the forest every day hoping to catch a glimpse of her until one day he saw the fairy come to the tower and heard her call,

> *"Rapunzel, Rapunzel!*
> *Let down your long hair."*

Then he saw what kind of ladder it took to get into the tower, and he carefully remembered the words the fairy had said. The next evening, he went to the tower as soon as it was dark and called up:

> *"Rapunzel, Rapunzel!"*
> *Let down your long hair."*

She let her hair fall, and when it reached the ground, he climbed up to her.

Rapunzel was frightened at first, but soon she grew to like him so well that she agreed he should come every day. She told him, "I would gladly go with you, but I don't know how I can get down. If you bring some thin rope with you every time you come, I will braid a ladder out of it, and when it is finished, I will climb down and ride away with you."

So the king's son came every evening and the two were merry and glad together.

The fairy knew nothing about it until one day Rapunzel said to her, "It's an odd thing, Godmother, my clothes are becoming much too tight and don't fit me anymore."

"You wicked child!" cried the fairy. "What have you done?" She realized at once how she had been betrayed, and she was furious. She grabbed Rapunzel's beautiful hair, wound it around her left hand a couple of times, snatched up a pair of scissors in her right hand, and—Snip, Snap!—Rapunzel's hair was gone. Then she banished Rapunzel to a wasteland where she lived wretchedly. After a time, Rapunzel gave birth to twins, a boy and a girl.

In the evening of the day when she had cast out Rapunzel, the fairy knotted Rapunzel's hair around the window latch, and when the king's son came and called,

> *"Rapunzel, Rapunzel!*
> *Let down your long hair,"*

The fairy let down the hair. The king's son climbed up as usual, but he was astonished to find the fairy waiting for him instead of his beloved Rapunzel.

"I have news for you, you villain!" said the angry fairy. "Rapunzel is lost to you forever!" In despair, the king's son threw himself off the tower. He survived the fall, but the briars at the foot of the tower blinded him. Sadly he wandered in the forest, eating nothing but berries and roots, and doing nothing but weep.

After several years, he came to the wasteland where Rapunzel lived meagerly with her two children. He heard her voice as she sang to them, and thought surely he knew it. At the same moment, Rapunzel recognized him and ran to embrace him, weeping for joy. Two of her tears fell on his eyes, and they became clear again, so that he could see as well as ever. The king's son took Rapunzel and the children home to his kingdom, where they all lived long and useful lives.

Source: Grimm KHM #12, 1812, 1857

Little Red Cap ❧ Rotkäppchen

Once there was a little girl who was so delightful that everyone loved her. The one who loved her best of all was her grandmother. She gave the child every pleasing thing she could think of, including a cap made of red velvet. Because this cap suited the child so well and because she refused to wear any other, people began to call her Rotkäppchen, "Little Red Cap."

One day the child's mother said to her, "Here, Little Red Cap, take this cake and this bottle of wine to Grandmother. She's been sick and needs something to build up her strength again. Behave yourself, give her a kiss from me, and keep your eyes on the path, or you'll fall and break the bottle, and then your poor, sick Grandmother will get nothing."

"I'll do exactly what you've said," Little Red Cap promised.

Little Red Cap's grandmother lived out in the forest about half an hour's walk from the village, and soon after the girl entered the forest, she met the wolf. Little Red Cap had no idea what a wicked animal he was, so she wasn't the least bit frightened of him.

"Good morning to you, Little Red Cap," said the wolf.

"Thank you, wolf, good morning to you."

"Where are you going so early in the day?"

"To my grandmother's house."

"And what have you got in your basket?"

"Cake and wine for my poor, sick grandmother. Yesterday was baking day at our house, and I'm taking her something to eat so that she can get her strength back."

"Little Red Cap, where does your grandmother live?"

"Farther on in the forest, about fifteen minutes from here, under the three tall oak trees. There's a hedge of hazelnut bushes around the house, but you probably know that," said Little Red Cap.

The wolf thought to himself, "Tender little girl, a very tasty morsel, but how do I go about getting it?" He walked along with Little Red Cap for a while, and then he said, "Little Red Cap, look at the beautiful flowers blooming here in the woods. You're walking as seriously as if you were going to school. I'll bet you haven't even noticed that the birds are singing. Take a look around you—the forest is a very pleasant place to be."

Little Red Cap looked up from the path and saw the sunlight dancing through the leaves of the trees and the wildflowers nodding their heads. She thought, "If I brought Grandmother a bunch of flowers, she'd be pleased. I can spend a few minutes here and still be at her house in plenty of time." She left the path and began picking flowers. Every time she picked one, it seemed to her that there were even lovelier blossoms further on, and so she moved deeper and deeper into the woods.

The wolf, however, went straight to the grandmother' house and knocked on the door. "Who is it?"

"Little Red Cap, with cake and wine, let me in."

"Just press down the latch," called the grandmother, "I'm too weak to get up." The wolf pressed down the latch, stepped inside, and without speaking another word went straight to the grandmother's bed and swallowed her up. Then he put on her clothes and her cap, got into her bed, and pulled the bed-curtains shut.

Meanwhile Little Red Cap picked flowers until she had as many as she could carry. At last, remembering what she was supposed to be doing, she went back to the path and hurried on to her grandmother's house. When she got there, she was surprised to find the door standing open. And when she stepped inside, things didn't look right.

"Goodness," she thought to herself, "I'm frightened. Usually I'm happy when I'm here." But she went up to the bed and pulled back the bed-curtains. There lay grandmother, her cap pulled right down on her forehead, looking very strange. "Oh, Grandmother, what big ears you have!"

"The better to hear you with."

"Oh, Grandmother, what big eyes you have!"

"The better to see you with."

"Oh, Grandmother, what big hands you have!"

"The better to grab you with."

"Oh, Grandmother, what an enormous mouth you have!"

"The better to eat you with." And with that, the wolf jumped out of bed, and gobbled up Little Red Cap.

Once he had swallowed his tasty treat, the wolf got back into bed and fell asleep. He snored so loudly that a hunter who happened to be passing by wondered, "Why is the old woman snoring like that? I'd better go in to make sure that she's all right." So he went in and when he came up to the bed, he saw the wolf, whom he'd been hunting for a long time. He was raising his gun when suddenly he thought, "Maybe he's eaten the grandmother and I can still save her." He put his gun down, picked up a pair of scissors instead, and carefully cut the wolf's stomach open. After a couple of snips he saw the red cap glowing, and after a few snips more the girl jumped out and cried, "Oh, how frightened I was! It was so dark in the wolf's belly." Then the grandmother, who was still alive, too, climbed out. Little Red Cap got some large, heavy stones that they put into the wolf's belly and then they sewed him up. When he woke up, he tried to run away, but the stones were so heavy that he fell down and died.

Then all three of them were very happy. The hunter skinned the wolf and took his pelt home, the grandmother ate the cake and drank the wine that Little Red Cap had brought, and Little Red Cap thought to herself, "Never again will I leave the path through the forest when my mother tells me not to."

There's another story, too, about the next time Little Red Cap met a wolf. She was taking fresh baking to her grandmother again when another wolf tried to talk her into leaving the path. But Little Red Cap was on guard and went straight to her grandmother's house. She told her grandmother that she had met a wolf, who had said "Good day" to her in a very friendly way. But from the wicked look in his eye, she thought he would have eaten her up if she hadn't been on the path where other people often traveled.

"Come," said her grandmother, "We'll lock the door so he can't get in."

A short while later, the wolf knocked at the door and called, "Let me in, Grandmother, I'm Little Red Cap, and I've got cake for you." But they didn't answer him, and they didn't unlock the door. So the wicked creature prowled around the house, looking for another way in, and finally he jumped up onto the roof. He planned to wait until Little Red Cap went home that evening, and then sneak after her and gobble her up under cover of darkness. But the grandmother figured out what he had in mind. There was a big stone trough in front of the house, and the grandmother said to Little Red Cap, "I cooked sausages yesterday, so get the pail, my dear, and carry the water I cooked them in out to the trough."

Little Red Cap carried water until the trough was full. Then the smell of sausages wafted up from the water and caught the wolf's attention. He sniffed and snuffled and looked down over the edge of the roof, and he stretched his neck out so far to see where the sausages might be that he lost his balance, slid off the roof, and landed in the big trough, where he drowned. And so Little Red Cap went home without a care, and no one did her any harm.

Source: Grimm KHM #26, 1837

Rumpelstiltskin ❧
Rumpelstilzchen

Background: This is perhaps the most famous spinning story of all. The two versions given here use three craft terms: strick, reel, and draw. A strick is a bundle of flax fibers that are ready to be arranged on a distaff and spun into linen yarn. A reel is used to remove the spun yarn from the bobbin, or spool, on the spinning wheel and wind it into a skein. Whether using a spindle or a wheel, the spinster's task is to draw out the fibers from the fiber supply and guide the twist.

The Grimms's manuscript notes made in 1810 give a short version of the story that begins and ends differently from the published version. The beginning and ending go like this:

There once was a little girl who was given a strick of flax to spin, but the thread she spun from it was gold, not linen, no matter what she did. She was very unhappy. She sat on the roof and spun for three days, getting nothing but gold. A little man came to her and said, "I will help you out of your trouble. A young prince will come by and will marry you and take you away, but you have to promise me your first child."

[. . . The prince marries the girl, they have a baby, and the little man comes to claim it. The girl can keep it only if she guesses the little man's name. . . .]

On the third night the girl sent her trusted servant into the woods, the little man seemed to have come from. She saw a little man riding around a big fire on a cooking spoon and calling out, "If the princess knew my name was Rumpenstünzchen!" and hurried home to tell her mistress. When the little man came at midnight, the princess tried all kinds of names. Finally she asked, "Would your name be Rumpenstüntzchen?" The little man was furious and said, "The devil must have told you that!" and then he flew out the window on his cooking spoon.

The Grimms suggest in their note on the story that the motif of spinning gold might be connected with the wretchedly hard work of making gold wire, which was generally done by poor, unmarried women.

There once was a miller who was poor, but he had a beautiful daughter. One day it happened that he was talking to the king, and to make himself seem important, he told the king, "I have a daughter who can spin straw into gold."

The king said to the miller, "That is an art that would please me. If your daughter is as skillful as you say, bring her to my palace tomorrow, and I'll see what she can do."

When the girl was brought to him, he led her to a room that was full of straw, gave her a spinning wheel and a reel, and said, "Now get to work, and if you fail to spin all this straw into gold by tomorrow morning, you will die." Then he locked the door, and she was left all alone.

There the poor miller's daughter sat, and for the life of her she couldn't figure out what to do. She didn't know how to spin straw into gold, and she became more and more frightened until finally she started to cry.

Suddenly the door opened, and a little man stepped into the room. "Good evening, Mistress Miller," he said, "Why are you crying so hard?"

"Oh," answered the girl, "I'm supposed to spin straw into gold and I don't know how."

"What will you give me if I spin it for you?" asked the little man.

"My necklace," said the girl.

The little man sat down at the spinning wheel and—whirr, whirr, whirr—three draws and the bobbin was full. He took the reel and wound the golden thread into a skein. Then he started the wheel and—whirr, whirr, whirr—three draws, and the bobbin was full again. And so it went on until dawn, when all the straw had been spun and the room was full of skeins of gold thread.

As soon as the sun came up the king unlocked the door. He was astonished and very pleased when he saw the gold, but greed grew in his heart. He had the miller's daughter taken to another room full of straw, bigger than the first, and ordered her to spin it all by the next morning if she valued her life.

The poor girl didn't know what to do and was crying again when the door opened and the little man reappeared. He said, "What will you give me if I spin the straw into gold for you?"

"The ring from my finger," answered the girl.

The little man took the ring, started the spinning wheel whirring, and spun all the straw into gleaming gold by morning.

The king was overjoyed at the sight, but he wanted still more gold. He had the miller's daughter taken to an even bigger room full of straw and said, "You must spin this roomful into gold tonight. If you succeed, you shall be my wife." To himself he thought, "She may be a miller's daughter, but I'll never find a richer wife in all the world."

When the girl was alone the little man appeared for the third time and said, "What will you give me if I spin the straw into gold for you?"

"I have nothing left to give," answered the girl.

"Then promise me your first child if you become queen."

"Who knows what will happen?" thought the miller's daughter, and because she could think of no other way to save herself, she promised the little man what he asked. The little man sat down and again he spun the straw into gold.

When the king came the next morning and found everything as he had wished, he married the girl, and the beautiful miller's daughter became a queen. A year later she brought a beautiful child into the world and never even thought about the little man until he suddenly stepped into her room and said, "Now give me what you promised."

The queen was horrified and offered the little man all the riches of the kingdom if he would let her keep the child. But the little man said, "No, something living is dearer to me than all the treasures in the world."

The queen began to weep so piteously that the little man felt sorry for her and said, "I'll give you three day's grace. If by then you know my name, you shall keep your child."

The queen spent the whole night thinking of all the names she had ever heard, and she sent out a messenger to inquire far and wide what other names there might be. When the little man came the next day she started with Kaspar, Melchior, and Balthazar and worked her way through the list of every name she knew, but to each one the little man said, "That's not my name."

On the second day she sent servants to ask the people living in the neighborhood of the palace what they were called and tried the most unusual and most peculiar names when the little man came again: "Are you called Ribbeast, or Muttoncalf, or Laceleg?" But each time he said, "That's not my name."

On the third day the messenger came back and reported, "I haven't found a single new name, but I came across a place between the edge of a forest and a high mountain, the kind of place where the fox and the hare bid each other good night, and there I saw a little house, and in front of the house was a big fire, and around the fire a ridiculous little man was hopping on one leg and singing:

> *Today I brew, tomorrow I'll bake,*
> *The next day the young queen's child I'll take.*
> *Nobody knows, none can proclaim,*
> *That Rumpelstiltskin is my name."*

You can imagine how happy the queen was when she heard the messenger's story.

When the little man came that evening and asked, "Well, my lady queen, what is my name?" she began with the most common names of all: "Is your name Kunz?"

"No."

"Is your name Heinz?"

"No."

"Could your name be Rumpelstiltskin?"

"The devil told you that, the devil told you that!" screamed the little man, and he stamped his right foot so hard that he drove it into the ground, all the way up to the top of his leg. Then in his rage he grabbed his left foot with both hands and tore himself in half, right up the middle.

Source: Grimm KHM #55, 1857

The Three Spinners ᴥ Die drei Spinnerinnen

There was a girl who was lazy and wouldn't spin. Her mother could say what she liked, but the girl simply refused to spin. One day her mother lost both her patience and her temper and slapped her daughter, at which the lazy girl started to cry loudly.

Now a rich lady happened to be driving by just at that moment, and when she heard the crying, she stopped her carriage, went into the house, and asked the mother why she was beating her daughter so hard that her howling could be heard all the way out on the street.

The mother was ashamed to reveal her daughter's laziness, so she said, "I can't get her to stop spinning, she wants to spin all the time, but I'm a poor woman and can't afford to buy the flax."

The rich lady said, "I love the sound of spinning and I'm never happier than when I hear the wheels purring. Give me your daughter to take home with me. I've got flax enough and she can spin to her heart's content." The mother was only too happy to agree, and the lady took the girl with her.

When they reached her house, the lady led the girl to three rooms that were filled from floor to ceiling with the finest flax. "Now spin this flax for me," said the lady, "and when you've finished, you shall marry my son. You are poor, but I won't let that stand in the way. Unflagging diligence is dowry enough."

The girl was dismayed. She couldn't spin all that flax, not if she worked from morning till night until she was three hundred years old. After her prospective mother-in-law left, she started to cry, and she sat and cried for three days without lifting a finger. When the lady came on the third day and saw no sign of spinning she was puzzled, but the girl had an excuse ready. She said she was so homesick for her mother's house that she just hadn't been able to work.

The lady accepted the story, but as she left she said, "Tomorrow you'll have to make a start."

Once the girl was alone again, she fell into despair because she had no idea what she should do to help herself. Miserably she wandered over to the window and looked out. There were three very odd-looking women coming down the street. The first had a ridiculously broad foot. Her other foot was normal, but this one was so splayed out that it looked like a giant goose foot. The second had a bottom lip so large that it hung down over her chin. And the third had an extremely broad thumb. The three of them stopped outside the window and asked the girl what the matter was. When she had told them her sad story, they offered to help her: "If you will invite us to your wedding, not be ashamed of us, call us your cousins, and seat us at your table, we'll spin up your flax for you in no time at all."

"I promise, with all my heart," the girl answered, "just come right in and start spinning." She let the three peculiar women in and made a small gap in the flax in the first room for them; and they sat down and began to spin. The first one drew the flax and worked the treadle of the spinning wheel, the second wet the thread, and the third twisted it and beat her finger on the table, and with every beat a skein of yarn fell to the floor, as finely spun as if it were silk. The girl hid the three spinners from the rich lady, but showed her such masses of spun yarn every time she came that the woman couldn't praise her enough.

When the first room was empty, they started on the second, and then they cleared out the third, and the work was done. As the three spinners took their leave of the girl, they reminded her, "Don't forget your promise—your happiness depends on it."

When the rich lady saw the empty rooms and the huge piles of yarn, she began to arrange the wedding at once. "I have three cousins," said the girl, "and because they've been very good to me, I'd like to share my happiness with them. Please let me invite them to the wedding and seat them at our table."

Her mother-in-law and the bridegroom said of course she could. And so when the feast began, the odd-looking three women arrived dressed in even odder-looking garments, and the bride said, "Welcome, dear cousins."

"My dear," said the bridegroom to his wife, "how did you come by such ugly relatives?" Then he went up to the one with the goose foot and asked her, "Why is your foot so broad?"

"From treadling the spinning wheel," she answered, "from treadling."

Then the bridegroom went to the second one and asked her, "Why does your lip hang down like that?" "From licking the thread," she answered, "from licking."

Then he asked the third one, "Why is your thumb so broad?" "From twisting the thread," she answered, "from twisting."

The bridegroom was horrified and declared, "Never again will my wife touch a spinning wheel." And so she was rid of the hated spinning once and for all.

Source: Grimm KHM #14, 1857; Uther

The Seven Ravens ❧ Die sieben Raben

There was a man who had seven sons and no daughter, although he had wished for a baby girl hard enough. At last his wife expected another child, and this time it turned out to be a girl. Their joy was great, but the baby was small and delicate, and because it was so weak they decided it should be baptized at once.

The father sent one of his sons running to the spring to get water for the christening. The other six went along, and because each of them wanted to be the one to draw the water, they scuffled and shoved and the pitcher fell into the well. They stood there and didn't know what to do, but none of them dared to go back home.

When they didn't come and didn't come, their father lost patience and said, "They've probably gotten distracted by some game and have forgotten all about the water, the young devils." He was afraid that the baby girl would die unbaptized, and in anger he cried, "I wish those boys would all turn into ravens!"

The moment he'd said the words, he heard a whirring of wings in the air above his head, looked up at the sky, and saw seven coal-black ravens flying away.

The parents couldn't undo the spell. They were sad about the loss of their seven sons, but they found consolation in their little daughter, who soon grew strong and became more beautiful every day. For a long time, she didn't know that she had brothers, because her parents were careful not to mention them. Then one day, by chance, she overheard people talking about her. "Oh, the girl is pretty enough," they said, "but she's to blame for the misfortune of her brothers."

The girl went to her father and mother and asked if she had ever had brothers and what had become of them. So the parents couldn't keep the secret any longer, but they also told her that what had happened to her brothers was fate, and not in any way her fault.

But the little girl thought about her brothers every day, and finally she secretly left her home and went out into the wide world to find her brothers, wherever they might be. She took nothing with her but a little ring to remember her parents by, a loaf of bread to eat when she was hungry, a jug of water to drink when she was thirsty, and a little chair to sit on when she was tired.

She walked and walked, a long, long way, until she came to the end of the world. There she found the sun, but it was burning hot, and terrible, and it ate small children. Quickly she ran away and came to the moon, but it was icy cold, and horrible, and ill natured, and when it noticed her, it said, "I smell, I smell human flesh!" Quickly she ran away and came to the stars, and they were kind and good, and each one sat on its own special chair. The morning star stood up and gave her a little chicken bone and said, "Your brothers are in the glass mountain. You can use this bone to unlock the door."

The girl took the bone, wrapped it up carefully in a handkerchief, and went on again until she came to the glass mountain. The door was locked, so she reached into her pocket for the bone. But when she unwrapped the handkerchief, it was empty, and the gift from the good stars was lost. What could she do now? She needed a key to open the glass mountain. So she took a knife, cut off her little finger, and put it in the keyhole, and unlocked the door.

As she stepped into the glass mountain, a dwarf came toward her and said, "My child, what are you looking for?"

"I'm looking for my brothers, the seven ravens," she answered.

"The ravens are not at home," the dwarf said, "but if you would like to wait until they return, please come in."

Then the dwarf set out the ravens' supper on seven little plates and in seven little cups, and the sister ate a crumb from each plate and took a sip from each cup, but into the last cup she dropped the ring she had brought with her.

Suddenly she heard a whirring and fluttering in the air, and the dwarf said, "Those are the ravens coming home." She barely had time to hide behind the door before seven glossy black birds flew in through the window. They went straight to the supper table, but as they began to eat and drink, they said one after the other, "Who has eaten from my plate? Who has been drinking out of my cup? A human mouth has touched it." And when the seventh raven drank to the bottom of his cup, the ring rolled toward him. He looked at it and recognized it as a ring belonging to his father and mother. "If only our sister were here," he said, "we would be freed from the spell."

When his sister heard his wish, she came out from behind the door, and suddenly all the ravens were human boys again. The eight of them hugged and kissed each other and happily went home.

Source: Grimm KHM #25, 1857

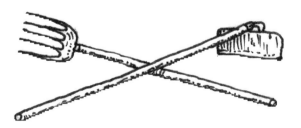

The Six Swans ❧ Die sechs Schwäne

Once a king was hunting in a great forest, and he chased a deer so eagerly that none of his people could keep up with him. When evening came, he stopped and looked around and saw that he was lost. He searched for a path but could find none. Then he saw an old woman, her head trembling with age, coming toward him. He didn't know it, but she was a witch.

"Good woman," he said to her, "could you show me the way through the forest?"

"Oh, yes, my lord king," she answered, "I can do that, but only on one condition, and if you do not meet it you will never get out of this forest and will starve to death here."

"What is the condition?" asked the king.

"I have a daughter," said the old woman, "who is as beautiful as any bride you might find. If you will make her your queen, I will show you the way out of the forest."

Fearing that he would be lost forever, the king agreed, and the old woman led him to her house where her daughter was sitting by the fire. She greeted the king as if she had expected him, and he saw that she was indeed very beautiful, but for all that, he didn't like her and could not look at her without an inward shudder. After he had lifted the girl up onto his horse, the old woman showed him the way, and the king returned to his palace and the wedding was held.

The king had been married once before and had seven children by his first wife—six boys and a girl whom he loved more than all the world. Because he feared that their new stepmother might not treat them well and might even harm them, he took them to a lonely castle deep in the middle of a forest. It was so hidden and the way to it so hard to find that the king himself couldn't have found it if a wisewoman had not given him a magic ball of yarn: when he threw the ball down in front of him, it unwound itself and showed him the way.

However, the king went to see his dear children so often that the queen eventually noticed his absence. She was curious and wanted to know what he did out in the forest all alone. She gave a great deal of money to his servants, and they gave away his secret and even told her about the ball of yarn that showed the way.

Now the queen had no rest until she discovered where the king kept the ball of yarn, and then she made small white shirts of the finest silk; and because she had learned witchcraft from her mother, she sewed a spell into each one. Then one day, when the king had ridden out to hunt, she took the little shirts and went into the forest with the ball of yarn showing her the way. The children saw her coming from far away and thought it was their father, so they happily ran to meet him.

But when the queen was close enough she threw a shirt over each of them, and the instant the shirts touched their bodies, they changed into swans and flew away over the forest. The queen went home well satisfied that she was rid of her stepchildren, but the girl had not come running with her brothers, and so the queen knew nothing of her.

When the king came the next day to visit his children, he found only his daughter. "Where are your brothers?" asked the king.

"Oh, father," she answered, "they have gone, and left me behind by myself." She told him that from her window she had watched her brothers fly away over the forest as swans, and she showed him the feathers they had dropped in the yard that she had gathered. The king mourned, but he never thought that the queen had done this wicked deed. And because he feared he would be robbed of his daughter as well, he wanted to take her home with him. But the girl was afraid of her stepmother and begged the king to let her stay in the castle in the forest for just one more night.

After the king left, the poor girl said to herself, "I can't stay here any longer —it isn't safe. I will go and look for my brothers." And when night came, she fled deep into the forest. She walked all night, and all the next day, until she was too tired to go any farther. Then she saw a little hut and climbed up to it. Inside she found a room with six little beds, but she didn't dare to lie down in any of them, so she crept underneath one instead and meant to sleep there on the hard floor. When the sun was about to set, she heard a rushing noise and saw six swans fly in through the window. They settled down on the floor and blew at each other until all their feathers were blown off, and then they took off their swan skins like shirts. The girl looked at them and was overjoyed to recognize her brothers. She crept out from under the bed and her brothers were equally happy to see her, but their joy didn't last long.

"You can't stay here," they told her, "this is a shelter for robbers. If they come home and find you, they will murder you."

"Can't you protect me?" asked their sister.

"No," they answered, "because we may take off our swan skins and take on human form every evening for only a quarter of an hour. Then we are changed back into swans."

Their sister cried and asked, "Couldn't I free you from the enchantment?"

"Ah, no," they answered, "the conditions are too hard. You may not speak for six years, nor laugh, and in those six years you must sew six shirts for us out of starflowers. If you say a single word during that time, all your work is wasted." And when they had said this, their quarter of an hour was up, and they flew out of the window as swans again.

The girl decided to set her brothers free, even if it cost her life. She left the hut, went deep into the forest, and spent the night in a tree. The next morning, she picked starflowers and began to sew. There was no one for her to talk to, and she didn't feel like laughing. She sat there and paid attention only to her work.

A long time had passed—months and years—when one day the king of that country went hunting in the forest and his huntsmen came to the tree in which the girl sat. They called up to her and asked, "Who are you?" She, of course, didn't answer.

"Come down to us," they said, "we mean you no harm." But she only shook her head. They kept pressing her with questions, so she took off her golden necklace and threw it down to them, thinking they might be satisfied and go away. But they didn't give up, so she threw them her belt, and when that didn't stop them, her garters, and then piece by piece everything she was wearing and could spare until she had nothing left but her shift. But the huntsmen would not be bought off. One of them climbed the tree and lifted the girl down, and they took her to the king.

The king asked, "Who are you? Why were you in that tree?" But she didn't answer. He asked again, in all the languages he knew, but she remained as mute as a fish. In spite of that, the king fell in love with her. He put his cloak around her, lifted her up in front of him on his horse, and took her to his castle. There she was dressed in rich clothing, and she shone in her beauty like the sun, but still she would speak no word.

The king had her sit beside him at dinner, and he liked her modesty and good manners so much that he said, "This is the woman I want to marry, and no other one in the world," and a few days later, they were wed.

Now, the king had a wicked mother who didn't like this marriage at all and who constantly spoke ill of his new wife.

"Who knows where this girl who can't speak comes from," she said. "I'm sure she's not a proper wife for a king. You should never have married her." A year later, when the young queen gave birth to her first child, the old woman took the baby away from her when she was sleeping and painted her lips with blood. Then she went to the king and accused his wife of being an ogre. The king refused to believe his mother and would allow no one to harm the queen.

As for the queen, she steadfastly kept sewing the starflower shirts and neither spoke nor laughed. The next time she gave birth, to a beautiful boy, her mother-in-law played the same trick, but still the king could not bring himself to believe that his wife was an ogre.

He said, "She is too gentle and good to do such a thing. If she were not mute and could defend herself, her innocence would be revealed." But when the old woman stole the third newborn child and accused the queen again, the king had no choice but to give his wife over to judgment, and the verdict was that she be burned to death.

The day came when the sentence was to be carried out, and it was the last day of the six years during which she could neither speak nor laugh. Five of the six shirts were finished, and the last lacked only the left sleeve. As she was led to the place of execution, she carried the six shirts over her arm, and when she stood on top of the pyre and the fire was about to be lit, she saw six swans flying toward her. With a rushing of their great wings, they settled at her feet so that she could throw the shirts over them, and as soon as the shirts touched them, the swan skins fell away and her brothers stood before her, strong and handsome. The youngest, though, was missing his left arm and had a swan's wing instead.

They embraced and kissed each other and then the young queen went to the king, who was much astonished, and spoke to him for the very first time. "Dear husband," she said, "Now I can tell you that I am innocent and have been falsely accused," and she told him about his mother's having taken their three children and hidden them. To his great joy the three children were brought to him, but the wicked mother-in-law was tied to the stake and burned to ashes. After that, the king and queen and her six brothers lived many long years in peace and happiness.

Source: Grimm KHM #49, 1857

Snow White ❧ Sneewittchen

Once upon a time in the middle of winter, as snowflakes fell from the sky like feathers, a queen sat sewing at her window. The window had a frame of ebony, and she was watching the soft snow mounding on the dark windowsill when she pricked her finger with her needle and three drops of blood fell onto the snow. The red looked so beautiful against the white that she thought to herself, "I wish I had a child as white as snow, as red as blood, and as black as ebony."

Not long after, she gave birth to a daughter. Because the child was as white as snow, as red as blood, and had hair as black as ebony, she was called Snow White. Sadly, as soon as the child was born, the queen died.

A year later, the king married again. His second wife was beautiful, but she was also proud, and arrogant, and so jealous of her beauty that she could not bear the thought that anyone else might be lovelier. She had a wonderful mirror, and when she looked at her reflection in its glass she would ask,

> *"Mirror, mirror on the wall,*
> *Who is the fairest one of all?"*

The mirror would answer,

> *"My Queen, you are the fairest one of all,"*

and the queen would be satisfied, because she knew that the mirror always spoke the truth.

As Snow White grew older, she became more beautiful with each passing year. When she was seven years old, she was as beautiful as the day is long, and lovelier than the queen herself. And the day came when the queen asked her mirror,

> *"Mirror, mirror on the wall,*
> *Who is the fairest one of all?"*

and the mirror answered,

> *"My Queen, you are the fairest here, it's true.*
> *But Snow White is a thousand times fairer than you."*

The queen went pale with shock, and then green and yellow with envy. And from that hour on, whenever she saw Snow White, her heart would twist in her breast with hatred. Her envy grew until she had no peace by day or by night. Then she called a huntsman to her and said, "Take the child out into the forest. I don't want to see her again. Kill her, and bring me her liver and lights* as proof that she is dead."

*Lights are the lungs of sheep, pigs, cows, or other animals that are used as food, especially for cats and dogs, but also for humans. "Liver and lights" is a formulaic phrase, like "skin and bones" or "hide nor hair"; the three words come as a set.

The huntsman obeyed and led Snow White deep into the forest. When he pulled his hunting knife, she began to cry and said, "Dear Huntsman, let me live. I'll run far away into the wild woods and never come home again."

And because she was so beautiful, the huntsman took pity on her and said, "Run away, poor child." To himself he thought, "The wild beasts will eat you soon enough," but he felt as though a great stone had been rolled from his heart because he had not had to kill her. Instead, he killed a young wild boar that came crashing through a thicket, and took its liver and lights and brought them to the queen, who had them cooked with salt and ate them, thinking they were Snow White's.

Now the poor child was completely alone in the great forest and was so frightened that she saw danger in every trembling leaf. She began to run, over sharp stones and through thorny thickets, and wild animals ran past her but did her no harm.

She ran until her feet could carry her no farther. By then it was evening, and when she saw a small house among the trees, she knocked on the door and entered. Inside the house everything was small, but more dainty and clean than words can tell. There was a table with a white cloth set with seven little plates, seven little spoons and knives and forks, and seven little cups. Against the wall were seven little beds in a row, covered with the whitest linen.

Snow White was so hungry and thirsty that she ate a little bread and some greens from each plate and drank a drop of wine from each cup. Then she lay down on one of the small beds but found that it didn't fit her, so she tried each one in turn until she came to the seventh, which was just right, and there she fell fast asleep.

When it was dark, the masters of the house came home. These were seven dwarfs who dug for ore in the mountains. They lit their seven lamps, and by their light they saw that someone had been there, for things were not as they had left them. The first said, "Who sat on my chair?"

The second said, "Who ate from my plate?"

The third, "Who took some of my bread?"

The fourth, "Who ate some of my greens?"

The fifth, "Who used my fork?"

The sixth, "Who cut with my knife?"

The seventh, "Who drank from my cup?"

Then the first one looked around and saw that his bed had a hollow in the bedclothes. "Who lay on my bed?" he said.

The others came and looked, and five of them cried, "Someone has been on my bed, too!"

But the seventh dwarf, when he looked at his bed, saw Snow White sleeping in it. He called the others over, and all seven of them raised their lamps so that the light shone on her. "Good heavens!" they cried with astonishment. "What a beautiful child!" And they were so taken with her that they let her go on sleeping instead of waking her, and the seventh dwarf shared the beds of the others, one hour in each, until the night was over.

In the morning, Snow White woke up and was frightened when she saw the seven dwarfs. But they were friendly and asked, "What is your name?"

"My name is Snow White," she answered.

"How did you come to be in our house?" they asked further.

She told them that her stepmother had wanted her dead, that the huntsman had spared her life, and that she had run and run for a whole day before she had finally come to their house. The dwarfs then said to her, "If you will keep house for us, cook and make the beds and wash and sew and knit, and keep everything tidy and clean as we do, you may stay with us and you shall want for nothing." Snow White said that she would, and so she stayed with them.

Snow White kept house and the dwarfs went off into the mountains every morning to dig for gold and iron and copper ore, and when they came home in the evenings, their supper was ready for them. Snow White was alone all day, and so the good dwarfs warned her, "Watch out for your stepmother—she'll soon find out that you're here. Be careful not to let anyone into the house."

But the queen, after she had eaten what she thought were Snow White's liver and lights, was certain that she was once again the most beautiful woman in the land. She went to her mirror and said,

> *"Mirror, mirror on the wall,*
> *Who is the fairest one of all?"*

And the mirror answered,

> *"My Queen, you are the fairest here, it's true.*
> *But Snow White, with the seven dwarfs*
> *Across the seven mountains,*
> *Is a thousand times fairer than you."*

The queen was astounded. She realized that the huntsman must have betrayed her and that Snow White was still alive. So she schemed and planned for a long time, thinking of a way to kill Snow White, because her jealousy gave her no rest. When she had come up with a plan, she stained her face brown and dressed herself as an old peddler woman. In this disguise, she made her way across the seven mountains to the house of the seven dwarfs. There she knocked on the door and cried, "Fine, fancy goods for sale."

Snow White looked out the window and called to her, "Good day. What are you selling?"

"Pretty things," the peddler woman answered, "Laces of all colors," pulling one out of her pack that was made of bright silk.

"Surely I can let this honest woman in," thought Snow White. She unbarred the door and bought the silken lace.

"Child," said the old woman, "you look very untidy. Come, let me lace you up properly." Snow White stood willingly while the new lace was threaded into her bodice, but then the peddler pulled the lace so tight that all the breath was squeezed out of Snow White, and she fell to the ground as if she were dead. "There's an end to your beauty!" said the peddler woman, and hurried away.

Soon it was evening and the dwarfs came home. They were horrified to find their Snow White lying motionless on the floor. They lifted her up, and seeing at once what was wrong, they cut the new lace. Snow White began to breathe again, and little by little she came back to life. When she told the dwarfs what happened they said to her, "That old peddler woman was nobody but the queen. You must be more careful, and let no one in when we aren't with you."

The wicked queen meanwhile made her way home, and when she got there she went at once to stand in front of the mirror and said,

> "Mirror, mirror on the wall,
> Who is the fairest one of all?"

And the mirror answered,

> "My Queen, you are the fairest here, it's true.
> But Snow White, with the seven dwarfs
> Across the seven mountains,
> Is a thousand times fairer than you."

The queen went white with shock at these words. "Now I will devise something that will make Snow White's death certain!" she said. And she went to work and made a poisonous comb. Then she disguised herself again as a poor old peddler woman, a different one, and crossed the seven mountains to the house of the seven dwarfs where she knocked at the door and cried, "Fine goods for sale!" Snow White looked out the window and said, "You'll have to go elsewhere, old woman. I'm not supposed to let anyone into the house."

"Surely you can at least look," said the peddler and held up the poisonous comb. Snow White liked the look of the comb so much that she foolishly opened the door and bought it. Then the old woman said, "Now I'll comb your hair for you properly." As soon as she drew the comb through Snow White's hair, the poison began to work, and Snow White fell down dead. "This time you'll stay dead!" said the old woman as she left.

Luckily it was near evening, the time when the dwarfs came home. When they found Snow White lying there, they suspected the wicked queen at once and looked until they found the comb in Snow White's hair. As soon as they pulled it out Snow White came back to life and told them what had happened. Once more the dwarfs warned her to be careful and to open the door to no one.

When the queen got home she stood before her mirror and said,

> *"Mirror, mirror on the wall,*
> *Who is the fairest one of all?"*

And the mirror answered,

> *"My Queen, you are the fairest here, it's true.*
> *But Snow White, with the seven dwarfs*
> *Across the seven mountains,*
> *Is a thousand times fairer than you."*

The queen trembled with rage when she heard this. She said, "Snow White will die if it costs me my own life!" And she went off to a small, secret, hidden room and made a deadly poisonous apple. Outwardly the apple looked so delicious that anyone who saw it would want to taste it, but anyone who did take a bite would die instantly. When the apple was finished, the queen dyed her face and dressed herself like a peasant woman, and in this disguise she crossed the seven mountains to the house of the seven dwarfs and knocked at the door.

Snow White looked out of the window and said, "I'm not allowed to let anyone in, the seven dwarfs have forbidden it."

"That's all right," said the peasant woman. "I can sell my apples somewhere else. But I'll give you one as a present."

"Oh, no," said Snow White, "I'm not allowed to accept anything."

"Are you afraid it's poisoned?" asked the woman. "Look, I'll cut the apple in half. You can have the red half and I'll eat the white half." For the apple was so cleverly made that only the red half was poisoned.

Snow White looked at the apple with longing, and when she saw the apple seller eating half, she couldn't resist any longer. She reached out through the window and took the red half of the apple, but as soon as she had the first bite in her mouth, she fell down dead.

The queen looked at the lifeless girl and said, "This time no one will wake you." She went home across the seven mountains, and when she stood before the mirror and asked,

"Mirror, mirror on the wall,
Who is the fairest one of all?"

The mirror finally answered,

"My Queen, you are the fairest one of all."

And her jealous heart was finally satisfied, or as satisfied as a jealous heart can be.

The dwarfs, when they came home that night, found Snow White lying on the floor. There was no breath of life in her, and she was dead. They lifted her up and looked for anything poisonous, undid her laces, combed her hair, washed her with water and wine, but nothing helped. The dear child was dead—and stayed dead. They laid her on a bier and wept and watched over her for three days. But when the time came to bury her, she still looked so fresh and alive, her cheeks were still so red, that they could not bring themselves to hide her in the black earth. They had a coffin made of glass and laid her in it and wrote her name on it in gold letters saying that she was a king's daughter. They put the coffin out on the mountain, and one of them watched by it always. And the animals came and wept for Snow White, first an owl, then a raven, and finally a dove.

Snow White lay in the coffin for a long time and did not wither away. She looked as if she were only sleeping, for she was still as white as snow, as red as blood, and as black haired as ebony. One day a king's son turned up in the forest and came to the dwarfs' house to spend the night. He saw the coffin on the mountain, and lovely Snow White, and read the golden letters. He said to the dwarfs, "Let me have the coffin. I will give you anything you like for it."

The dwarfs answered, "We would not give it up for all the gold in the world."

"Then give it to me as a gift, because I cannot live without seeing Snow White. I will honor and cherish her as my very dearest."

When they heard these words, the good dwarfs took pity on him and gave him the coffin, and the prince had his servants carry it away on their shoulders. But they stumbled, and when the coffin jolted on their shoulders the piece of poisoned apple was jarred loose and shot out of Snow White's mouth, and she came back to life.

She sat up and said, "Where am I?" and the prince answered joyfully, "You are with me," and told her what had happened.

"I love you more than all the world," he said. "Come with me to my father's castle and marry me." Snow White was willing, and the wedding was celebrated with great splendor and magnificence.

Snow White's wicked stepmother was invited to the wedding, too. When she was dressed in her finest clothes, she stood in front of the mirror and said,

> *"Mirror, mirror on the wall,*
> *Who is the fairest one of all?"*

And the mirror answered,

> *"My Queen, you are the fairest here, it's true,*
> *But the young queen is a thousand times fairer than you!"*

When she heard that, the queen was frightened, so frightened that she didn't know what to do with herself. At first she didn't want to go to the wedding, but her jealousy drove her to go and see this young queen. When she stepped into the great hall of the palace and recognized Snow White, she stood as if rooted to the ground with horror. But a pair of iron shoes were already heating in the coals of the fire, and when they were red-hot she was made to put them on and had to dance in them until she was dead.

Source: Grimm KHM #53, 1819, 1837

Spindle, Shuttle, and Needle ❧ Spindel, Weberschiffchen und Nadel

Once there was a girl whose father and mother died when she was just a small child. But she had a godmother, who lived alone in a little house at the end of the village and earned her living by spinning, weaving, and sewing. This old woman took the child in, taught her how to work, and raised her properly.

When the girl was fifteen years old, her godmother fell ill. She called the girl to her bedside and said, "Dear daughter, I feel that I'm close to the end of my journey. I'm leaving you this little house so that you'll be sheltered from wind and weather, and the spindle, the shuttle, and the needle, so that you can earn your living." She laid her hands on the girl's head to bless her, and then died.

The girl lived on in the little house, spinning and weaving and sewing, and everything she did seemed touched by the old woman's blessing. Her supply of flax never seemed to get smaller and the cloth and carpets and shirts she made always sold for a good price as soon as she finished them, so she had enough for her own needs and some left over to give to others.

Around this time the king's son was traveling through the country looking for a wife. He wasn't supposed to pick a poor woman, but he didn't want a rich one, so he declared, "I'll marry the woman who is both the richest and the poorest at the same time."

When he came to the village where the girl lived he asked, as he did everywhere, who was the richest and who was the poorest woman there. The people told him the name of the rich one first. The poorest one, they said, was the girl who lived in the little house right at the end of the village.

The rich woman was sitting by her front door, all dressed up, and when the king's son rode up to her house, she went to meet him and greeted him with a deep curtsey. He looked at her without saying a word and rode on. When he came to the house of the poorest, the girl wasn't at the door. She was inside working. The king's son reined in his horse and looked in through the open window. There she was, spinning diligently. She glanced up, though, and when she saw the king's son she blushed a deep red. But she dropped her eyes again and kept on spinning. I don't know whether her thread was as even as it should have been, but she kept on spinning until the king's son had ridden off. Then she went to the window saying,

"It's so hot in here," and stood there watching him ride away until the white feathers on his hat vanished in the distance.

As she sat down to her work again, a verse that the old woman used to murmur when she was spinning came to her mind, and she sang it to herself:

> *"Spindle, spindle, go and see,*
> *Bring my suitor back to me."*

And what happened then? The spindle jumped out of her hand, hopped through the door, and danced out of sight, unspooling a long gleaming golden thread as it went. Since she couldn't spin any more, the girl sat down at her loom and began to weave. But the spindle danced down the road and reached the king's son just as it got to the end of its thread. "What's this?" cried the king's son, "Does this spindle want to show me the way?" He turned his horse and followed the golden thread back along the way he had come. In the meantime, the girl wove and sang to herself,

> *"Shuttle, shuttle weave some more,*
> *Lead my suitor through the door."*

The shuttle jumped out of her hand, hopped through the door, and began to weave the most beautiful carpet you've ever seen. Roses and lilies bloomed in the borders, green vines grew on a golden background in the center, rabbits and squirrels hopped among the vines, elk and deer poked their heads through the leaves, and bright birds sat in the upper branches looking so lifelike that you could almost hear them sing.

While the shuttle leapt to and fro just outside the door, the girl sat down to sew. As she made tiny, even stitches in the seam, she sang to the needle in her hand:

> *"Needle, needle, sharp and steady,*
> *Clean the house and make it ready."*

The needle jumped out of her hand and flew about the room as quick as lightning. Invisible ghosts seemed to be at work: the table and benches covered themselves with green linen, the chairs were suddenly upholstered with velvet, and silken curtains hung at the windows. Just as the needle took its last stitch, the girl looked out the window and saw white feathers on a hat.

The spindle with its golden thread had brought the king's son back. He climbed down from his horse and walked across the beautiful carpet into the little house. There stood the girl, dressed in shabby clothes but glowing like a rose blooming on a bush.

"You are both the poorest and the richest," said the king's son. "Come with me and marry me." The girl said nothing, but she gave him her hand. Then he kissed her and led her out of the house. He helped her mount his horse and they rode away to the royal palace, where the wedding was celebrated joyfully.

And the spindle, the shuttle, and the needle were kept in the palace treasury, always given great respect and honor.

Source: Grimm KHM #188, 1857

Table Set Yourself, Donkey Stretch Yourself, Stick Jump Out of the Sack ~ Tischchen deck dich, Goldesel, und Knüppel aus dem Sack

Long ago there was a tailor who had three sons and one goat. Because the goat fed all of them with her milk, she had to have good fodder, and the three sons took her out to graze by turns. One day the eldest son took her to the churchyard where the greenest grass grew and let her eat and frisk around as she liked. When evening came and it was time to go home, he asked her, "Goat, are you satisfied?" And the goat answered,

> *"I ate so much*
> *I couldn't touch*
> *Another leaf: meh! meh!"*

"Then let's go home," said the boy, and, taking her by the rope, he led her to her stall and tied her up.

"Well," said the old tailor when his son came to the supper table, "Has the goat been fed properly?"

"Oh," answered the son, "She ate so much, she couldn't touch another leaf."

But the tailor wanted to see for himself. He went downstairs to the stall, stroked his precious goat, and asked, "Goat, are you satisfied?" The goat answered,

> *"My stomach is hollow,*
> *I didn't swallow*
> *A single leaf: meh! meh!"*

"You poor creature!" cried the tailor. He ran upstairs and said to his son, "You liar, you said the goat was satisfied, but she's starving!" And in his rage he took his ell stick* from the wall and drove the boy out of the house.

---

*The traditional measure of length in Germany was the ell, and every tailor had an ell stick, the equivalent of our yard stick, with which to measure cloth. An ell was roughly the length of a forearm, and the word is related to the Latin *ulna*, the large, thinner bone of the forearm. The English word "elbow," the joint of the forearm, has the same root. The actual length of an ell was not standardized from place to place, and each market town had to display the ell measure in use there in a public place.

The next day, it was the second son's turn to take out the goat. He picked a place by the garden hedge where the tastiest wild herbs grew, and the goat ate them down to the roots. When evening came and it was time to go home, he asked her, "Goat, are you satisfied?" And the goat answered,

> *"I ate so much*
> *I couldn't touch*
> *Another leaf: meh! meh!"*

"Then let's go home," said the boy, and, taking her by the rope, he led her to her stall and tied her up.

"Well," said the old tailor, "Has the goat been fed properly?"

"Oh," answered the son, "She ate so much, she couldn't touch another leaf."

But the tailor wanted to make sure, so he went down to the stall and asked, "Goat, are you satisfied?" The goat answered,

> *"My stomach is hollow,*
> *I didn't swallow*
> *A single leaf: meh! meh!"*

"That wicked boy!" cried the tailor, "letting such good animal starve!" He ran back upstairs and drove the boy out of the house with blows from his ell stick.

The next day it was the third son's turn, and he wanted to make absolutely sure the goat had enough to eat. So he picked a place in the bushes where the juiciest leaves grew and let her browse. When evening came and it was time to go home, he asked her, "Goat, are you satisfied?" And the goat answered,

> *"I ate so much*
> *I couldn't touch*
> *Another leaf: meh! meh!"*

"Then let's go home," said the boy, and, taking her by the rope, he led her to her stall and tied her up.

"Well," said the old tailor, "Has the goat been fed properly?"

"Oh," answered the son, "She ate so much, she couldn't touch another leaf." But the tailor didn't trust him, so he went downstairs and asked, "Goat, are you satisfied?" The goat answered,

> *"My stomach is hollow,*
> *I didn't swallow*
> *A single leaf: meh! meh!"*

"Oh, that pack of liars!" cried the tailor. "Each one as wicked and neglectful as the others! They won't make a fool of me any longer!" Beside himself with rage, he leapt up the stairs and tanned the poor boy's back with his ell stick until he ran out of the house.

Now the old tailor was alone with his goat. The next morning, he went down to the stall, petted the goat, and said, "Come, my beautiful goat, I'll take you out to graze myself." He took her rope and led her to green hedges and patches of yarrow and all the other things goats like to eat. "For once you can eat to your heart's content," he said to her, and let her browse and graze until evening. Then he asked her, "Goat, are you satisfied?" And the goat answered,

> "I ate so much
> I couldn't touch
> Another leaf: meh! meh!"

"Then let's go home," said the tailor, and he took her to her stall and tied her up. "There!" he said. "For once you really are satisfied." But the goat bleated,

> "My stomach is hollow,
> I didn't swallow
> A single leaf: meh! meh!"

When the tailor heard this he stopped short. Suddenly he realized that he had driven his sons away for nothing.

"You, you ungrateful creature!" he cried. "Throwing you out isn't enough. I'll mark you so you won't dare show your face among honest tailors again!" He ran up the stairs, grabbed his razor, lathered the goat's head with soap, and shaved it as smooth as the palm of his hand. And then, because the ell stick would have been too good for her, he got the whip and hit her so hard that she shot out of the stable and leapt away.

The tailor, all alone in his house now, fell into a deep melancholy and wished he had his sons back. But no one knew where they had gone.

The eldest had apprenticed himself to a joiner. He learned cheerfully and well, and when he was made journeyman and had to set out on his years of travel, his master gave him a little table. This table didn't look like anything special, and it was made of ordinary wood, but it had one good quality. If you put it down and said, "Table, set yourself," it would suddenly be covered with a clean tablecloth, and there would be a plate with knife and fork on either side, and bowls full of food, stewed and roasted, as many as there was room for, and a big glass glowing with the red wine that makes the heart glad.

The young journeyman thought, "Here's riches enough for a lifetime," and cheerfully wandered through the world, never caring whether an inn was good or bad, or whether he could get something to eat there or not. When he felt like it, he didn't even go to an inn, but stopped in field, forest, or meadow—wherever he happened to be—and said to the table, "Set yourself." And there before him would be whatever food and drink his heart desired.

One day the thought came to him that he'd like to go home to his father. The old man's anger would have died down by now, and with the magic table the son could be certain his father would be happy to have him back. Now it happened that on the road home, he stopped one evening at an inn that was full of guests. They bade him welcome and invited him to sit and eat with them, because otherwise there was little chance that he would get food. "No," the young joiner answered, "I won't take that bit of food from your mouths. You should be my guests, instead." They laughed and thought he was joking. But he put his little wooden table in the middle of the room and said, "Table set yourself." In the blink of an eye the table was covered with food better than anything the innkeeper could have served, and the good smells filled the room.

"Help yourselves, my friends," said the joiner, and when they saw that he meant it, the guests didn't wait to be asked twice. They pulled up their chairs, took out their knives, and fell to. And what amazed them most was that whenever a dish was empty, a full one would immediately take its place.

The innkeeper stood in a corner and watched. He couldn't think of a word to say, but he thought to himself, "I could use a cook like that in my business."

The joiner and his company made merry late into the night, but they finally went to bed and the joiner lay down to sleep, too, after setting his table against the wall. But the innkeeper's thoughts kept him awake. It occurred to him that in his lumber room he had a little old table that looked just like the joiner's, so he brought it out very quietly and exchanged it for the magic table.

The next morning the joiner paid for his bed, took his table on his back without ever thinking that he might have the wrong one, and went on his way.

At midday he reached his father's house, and his father welcomed him home with great joy. "Now, my dear son, what trade have you learned?" he asked.

"I've become a joiner, father."

"A good craft," said the old man. "And what have you brought with you from your journey years?"

"Well, father, the best thing I've brought with me is this little table."

The tailor looked at it from all sides and said, "That's no masterpiece you made there. It's an old and ugly table."

"Ah, but it's a magic table, father. When I put it down and tell it to set itself, the most delicious food appears, and wine to gladden a man's heart. Invite all our relatives and friends to eat and drink with us. The table will provide more than enough."

When all the guests had gathered the joiner put his table in the middle of the room and said, "Table, set yourself." But nothing happened. The table stayed as bare as any other table that doesn't understand the words spoken to it. Then the poor young man realized that his table had been switched with another, and he was ashamed to be standing there like a foolish liar. The guests laughed at him and left as hungry and as thirsty as they had come. But his father got out his cloth and needle and went back to tailoring, while the son found work with a master joiner.

The second son had apprenticed himself to a miller. When his years were up and he was made journeyman, the miller said to him, "Because you've been such a good apprentice, I'm going to give you a very special donkey. He doesn't pull carts and he doesn't carry sacks."

"What's he good for, then?" asked the new young journeyman.

"He spits gold," said the miller. "If you put a cloth under him and say, 'Donkey, stretch yourself' he will stick out his head and lift his tail and produce gold coins fore and aft."

"That's a good present," said the journeyman, and set out on his journey years. When he needed money, he just said, "Donkey, stretch yourself" to his four-footed companion, and the gold coins fairly rained down. All he had to do was pick them up. Wherever he went, the best was good enough for him, and the more expensive the better, because he always had a full purse.

One day the thought came to him that he ought to look up his father. The old man's anger would have died down by now, and with the gold-donkey he was certain his father would be happy to have him back. Now it happened that on the road home, he stopped at the inn where his brother's table had been switched. He was leading his donkey, and the innkeeper wanted to take the animal and tie it up in the stable. But the young miller said to him, "Don't trouble yourself, I'll lead my old grey to a stall and tie him up myself. I need to know where he is."

The innkeeper found this odd, and thought to himself that a man who had to look after his donkey himself probably had very little money in his pockets. So when the stranger pulled out a couple of gold coins and told him to buy something good to cook for supper, he was astonished and ran off to get the best he could find.

After his meal, the guest asked what he owed. The innkeeper chalked up double the price and said he owed two more gold coins. The journeyman reached into his pocket and found it empty. "Just wait a moment," he said, "I'll go get my money," and he took the tablecloth with him. This made the innkeeper curious, so he stole after him, and when the guest shut and barred the stable door the innkeeper watched through a knothole. The young miller spread the tablecloth under the donkey, said, "Donkey, stretch yourself," and right away the animal began to spit out gold fore and aft so that it fairly rained down onto the cloth.

"Goodness gracious!" said the innkeeper, "What a way to mint ducats! I'd like a moneybag like that myself."

The guest paid his reckoning and went to bed, but during the night the innkeeper crept down to the stable, led the gold-donkey away, and tied another donkey in its place. Early the next morning the journeyman set off with the innkeeper's donkey, never noticing the difference.

At midday he reached his father's house, and his father welcomed him home with great joy. "Now, my dear son, what trade have you learned?" he asked.

"I'm a miller, father."

"And what have you brought back from your journeyman travels?"

"Just a donkey."

"We've got plenty of donkeys here," said his father. "I would have liked a good goat better."

"Yes," said the son, "but this is no ordinary donkey. It's a gold-donkey. When I say, 'Donkey, stretch yourself' he spits out a whole cloth-full of gold. Ask all our relatives over and I'll make them all rich."

"That sounds good to me," said the tailor. "I won't have to slave with my needle any more," and he ran off to invite his relatives.

When they were all there the miller told them to make room, spread out his cloth, and brought in the donkey.

"Now watch this," he said, and cried, "Donkey, stretch yourself!" But what dropped onto the cloth wasn't gold, and it became clear that this animal didn't know the art of coining money. And, in fact, few donkeys are successful at that. The poor miller made a long face when he realized that he had been cheated and apologized to his relatives, who left as penniless as they had come. So the old tailor had go back to his needle, and the young man went to work for a miller.

The third brother had apprenticed himself to a turner, and because that is a very skillful craft, his apprenticeship was the longest. But his brothers wrote him a letter about their misfortunes and how the innkeeper had tricked them out of the magic table and the gold-donkey. When the turner's apprenticeship was over and it was time for him to set off as a journeyman, his master gave him a reward for his good work. It was a sack, with a heavy stick inside.

"I can hang the sack over my shoulder and I'm sure I'll find it useful, but why the stick? It just makes the sack heavy."

"I'll tell you," said the master. "If someone has done you harm, you only have to say 'Stick, out of the sack,' and the stick will jump out and dance a such a fandango on his back that he'll be sorry he ever crossed you, and it won't stop until you say, 'Stick, into the sack.' "

The journeyman thanked his master and set off with the sack over his shoulder. Wherever he traveled, whenever someone threatened him he said, "Stick, out of the sack!" and the stick would dust the fellow's coat or jacket without waiting for him to take it off, and it would happen so quickly that if there were two of them, the second fellow was getting the treatment before he realized what had happened to the first one.

One evening the young turner arrived at the inn where his brothers had been cheated. He put his knapsack on the table and began to tell stories about all the unusual things he had seen in his travels.

"Oh, yes," he said, "there are magic tables that set themselves, and donkeys that spit gold, and other fine things like that. I wouldn't turn up my nose at any of them, but they're nothing compared to the treasure that I've got in my sack, here."

The innkeeper pricked up his ears, "What in the world could that be?" he wondered. "The sack must be full of jewels. I should be able to get it easily, because all good things come in threes."

When it was bedtime, the guest stretched out on a bench and put his sack under his head as a pillow. The innkeeper waited until he thought his guest was fast asleep. Then he went over, and very gently and carefully tugged at the sack to see if he could pull it out and put another in its place. That was exactly what the turner had been waiting for.

Just as the innkeeper was going to try a stronger tug, the turner cried, "Stick, out of the sack." The stick jumped out and was all over the innkeeper in an instant, whacking him like nobody's business. The innkeeper yelled, but the louder he yelled, the harder the stick beat time on his back, until he finally fell to the floor, exhausted. Then the turner said, "If you don't give back the magic table and the gold-donkey, the dance will start again."

"No, no!" said the innkeeper, quite subdued. "I'll gladly give everything back, only make that cursed goblin crawl back into the sack."

"I'll give mercy instead of justice this time," said the turner, "but don't let me catch you at such tricks again."

The next morning the turner took the magic table and the gold-donkey and went home to his father. The tailor was happy to see him again, and asked him, too, what trade he had learned. "Dear father, I've become a turner."

"A skillful craft," said the tailor. "What have you brought back from your journeyman travels?"

"A very precious thing," answered the son, "A stick in a sack."

"What?" cried the tailor, "A stick? Oh, that's worth a lot! You can cut one of those from any tree."

"Not one like this, dear father. If I say, 'Stick, out of the sack,' the stick jumps out and beats a lively tune on the back of anyone who means to harm me and won't stop until the fellow is lying on the ground begging for an end to the concert. See, with this stick I made that thieving innkeeper give back the magic table and the gold-donkey that he stole from my brothers. Send for them both, now, and invite all our relatives. I'll wine them and dine them and fill their pockets with gold."

The old tailor wasn't sure he wanted to try this again, but he did gather the relatives together. Then the turner spread a cloth on the floor, brought the gold-donkey in, and said to his brother, "Now, dear brother, talk to him." The miller said "Donkey, stretch yourself," and immediately gold coins came raining down on the cloth like a cloudburst. The donkey didn't stop until they all had as much as they could carry. (I can see by the look on your face that you wish you had been there!)

Then the turner brought the little table and said, "Dear brother, now talk to it." And before the joiner finished saying, "Table, set yourself," it was crowded with the finest dishes. Then they had a meal the likes of which the tailor had never had in his house before, and all the relatives stayed until late into the night feasting and making merry. The tailor locked his needle, thread, ell stick, and scissors up in a cupboard, and lived with his three sons in joy and splendor for the rest of his life.

But where is the goat whose fault it was that the tailor chased his three sons away? Well, I'll tell you. She was so ashamed of her bald head that she ran to a fox's den and crawled in. When the fox came home, a pair of big yellow eyes glittered at him out of the darkness and gave him such a fright that he ran out again.

The bear happened to meet him, and because the fox looked so panicked, the bear asked, "What's wrong, brother fox? Why are you making such a face?"

"Oh," answered the fox, "a ferocious beast is sitting in my den. It stared at me with fiery eyes."

"We'll soon drive it away," said the bear. He went along to the fox's den and looked in. But when he saw the fiery eyes. he was overcome by fright: he didn't want to mess with the ferocious beast either, and so he ran away.

The bee happened to meet him and because he looked so shaken, she said to him, "Bear, you're making a terribly miserable face. Where's your usual good humor?"

"Oh, bee," said the bear, "There's a ferocious beast with goggle-eyes in fox's den, and we can't drive it out."

The bee said, "I feel sorry for you, bear. I'm a poor, weak creature below your notice, but I think I can help you out." She flew into the fox's den, sat down on the goat's smooth-shaven head, and stung her so mightily that the goat jumped up, bleating, "Meh, meh!" and ran like crazy out into the world. And so far nobody knows where she ran to.

Source: Grimm KHM #36, 185

The Three Little Men in the Woods ❧ Die drei Männlein im Walde

Once there was a man whose wife died, and a woman whose husband died, and each of them had a daughter. The girls were acquainted with each other, and one day they went for a walk together. Afterward, they went to the woman's house. The woman said to the man's daughter, "Listen, tell your father I want to marry him. If we marry, you will wash yourself in milk every morning and have wine to drink, while my daughter will have water to wash in and water to drink"

The girl went home and told her father what the woman had said.

"What shall I do?" he asked himself. "Marriage has its pleasures but it also has its pains."

In the end, because he couldn't make up his mind, he took his boot off and said, "This boot has a hole in it. Take it to the attic, hang it up on the big nail, and fill it with water. If the boot holds water, I'll marry again, but if the water leaks out, I won't."

The girl did as she was told. But the water made the sole of the boot swell so that the hole closed up, and the boot held water right to its top. The girl told her father what had happened. He climbed up to the attic to see for himself, and then he went to the widow and proposed marriage to her. Soon they were wed.

The morning after the wedding, when the two girls got up, there was milk for the man's daughter to wash in and wine for her to drink, while the woman's daughter had water to wash in and water to drink. The morning after that, both girls had water to wash in and water to drink. And on the third morning the man's daughter had water for washing and drinking, while the woman's daughter had milk and wine, and that's the way it stayed. The woman hated her stepdaughter like poison and tried to make life harder for her with each passing day. She was jealous, too, because her stepdaughter was pleasing to look at and sweet-tempered, while her own daughter was sour-faced and cranky.

One day in winter, when the ground was frozen as hard as stone and the hills and valleys were deeply covered with snow, the woman made a dress out of paper and gave it to her stepdaughter with these words: "Put this dress on and go into the forest and pick me a basket of strawberries—I feel like eating some."

"Strawberries don't grow in winter," said the girl. "The earth is frozen, and everything is covered with snow. How can I go out in that paper dress? It's cold

The Three Little Men in the Woods / 181

enough to freeze your breath, and the wind will blow right through it and the thorns will rip it to shreds."

"Are you contradicting me?" asked the stepmother. "Get out of here, and don't come back until you've got a basketful of strawberries!" Then she gave the girl a small piece of stale bread and said, "Here's your food for the day." The girl obeyed her stepmother, put on the paper dress, and went out with the basket. There was nothing but snow as far as the eye could see, not a single blade of green. When she had gone into the woods a little way, she saw a small house with three little men looking out the window. She wished them good-day and knocked on the door, and they invited her in. Once inside, she went to the bench by the stove to warm up and eat her breakfast.

"Give us some, too," said the little men.

"Gladly," said the girl. She broke her bit of bread in two pieces and gave them half of it.

"What are you doing in the woods in winter wearing that thin paper dress?" asked the little men.

"Oh," she said, "I'm supposed to pick a basketful of strawberries, and I can't go home without them."

When she had eaten her bread, the little men gave her a broom and said, "Sweep the snow away from the back door."

And when she was outside they said to each other, "What shall we give her for being so polite and sharing her bread with us?"

The first said, "My gift is that she will be more beautiful with each passing day."

The second said, "My gift is that when she speaks golden coins will fall from her mouth." The third said, "My gift is that a king will come and take her as his wife."

Meanwhile the girl swept the snow away from the back door and found that under the snow the ground was red with ripe strawberries. She joyfully filled her basket, thanked the little men, and ran home to her stepmother. And when she stepped into the house and said good evening, a golden coin fell from her mouth. Then she told what had happened in the forest, and with each word another golden coin fell from her mouth until the floor was quite covered with them.

"Look at the show-off, throwing money around like that!" said her stepsister. But secretly she was jealous and asked her mother to send her out into the forest, too. Of course, her mother refused, saying, "No, my dear little daughter, it's far too cold, you might freeze." Still the girl badgered and pestered her until she finally gave in, but first she sewed a splendid fur coat that she made her daughter wear, and she gave her bread and butter and a cake to take with her.

The girl went into the forest and straight to the little house. The three little men were looking out as before, but she neither greeted them nor knocked at the door. Instead, she just walked in, sat on the bench next to the stove, and began to eat her bread and cake.

"Give us some, too," said the little men.

But she said, "There isn't even enough for me. Why should I give you any?"

When she had finished eating, they said to her, "Here's a broom, sweep the snow from the back door for us."

"Sweep it yourselves!" said she. "I'm not your servant." And when she saw that they weren't going to give her anything, she left.

Then the three little men said to each other, "What should we give her for being so rude, and for having a wicked, envious, ungenerous heart?"

The first one said, "My gift is that she will be uglier with each passing day."

The second said, "My gift is that when she speaks a toad will jump out of her mouth." The third said, "My gift is that she will come to a bad end."

Meanwhile the girl looked for strawberries outside, and finding none, she went home in a bad temper. When she started to tell her mother what had happened in the forest, a toad jumped out of her mouth with every word, so that in the end no one wanted to be near her.

Now the stepmother liked her stepdaughter even less, and kept thinking of new ways to make life hard for her. One day she took a kettle, set it on the fire, and boiled some skeins of linen yarn in it. And when the yarn had boiled enough, she gave it to her stepdaughter, together with an axe, and told her go out onto the ice of the frozen river, chop a hole in it, and rinse the yarn. The girl was obedient and went to the river. While she was chopping the hole in the ice, a splendid carriage drove by. It was the king's, and the king himself. He stopped the carriage and asked, "Who are you, and what are you doing?"

"I'm just a poor girl, and I'm rinsing yarn."

The king felt sorry for her, and when he saw how beautiful she was, he asked, "Will you drive with me?"

"Yes, with all my heart," she answered, glad at the prospect of getting away from her stepmother and her stepsister. So she climbed into the carriage and drove away with the king to his palace where they were married with great splendor, just as the little men had promised.

A year later, she give birth to a son, and when her stepmother heard of this great joy, she came with her daughter as if to pay the young queen a visit. But in a moment when the king had left the room and no one else was present, the wicked woman grabbed her stepdaughter by the head, and her daughter took her feet, and the two of them threw her out the window into the river below. Then the step-mother put her own daughter into the queen's bed and drew the covers up over her head.

When the king came back and wanted to speak with his wife, the stepmother cried, "Quiet, quiet! You can't talk to her right now. She's in a fever. She must have complete rest." The king didn't suspect anything and stayed away until the next morning. But the next day the trick didn't serve. The king wanted to speak to his wife, and when he spoke, she had to answer him. What a shock it was to see toads jump out from under the bedcovers with each word she said! The king was horrified. What had happened to the gold coins that usually fell from his wife's lips? The stepmother told him the change was a result of the fever and would soon pass, but the king went away sorely troubled.

That night the kitchen boy saw a duck swimming up the channel in the stone floor through which the washing water ran out of the great kitchen. The duck spoke,

> *"King, do you smile or are you weeping?*
> *Do you wake, or are you sleeping?"*

And when the boy didn't answer she said,

> *"How are my guests keeping?"*

At that the kitchen boy answered,

> *"They're soundly sleeping."*

The duck asked further,

> *"Is my child safe from harm?"*

And he answered,

> *"It sleeps in its cradle soft and warm."*

Then the queen took on her own shape again, went to her child and nursed it, tucked it back into the cradle, and swam away as a duck down the water channel.

The same thing happened the second night, but on the third night, the duck said to the kitchen boy, "Go and tell the king to bring his sword and swing it three times over my head on the doorstep." The kitchen boy ran to tell the king, and the king came with his sword and swung it three times over the head of the duck. After the third swing, his wife stood before him, alive and healthy as she had been before.

The king was overjoyed and hid the queen away until the Sunday came on which the baby was to be baptized. At the feast after the baptism, he asked all the guests, "What should be done to a person who has taken someone from her bed and thrown her into the river?"

"He should be put into a barrel that has had nails driven into it and rolled down the hill into the water," said the stepmother. So the king had a barrel brought, had nails driven through the sides, and stuffed in the stepmother and her daughter. Then he rolled the barrel down the hill into the river. And that was the bad end that the three little men in the woods had prophesied.

Source: Grimm KHM #13, 1857

The Brave Little Tailor ❧ Das tapfere Schneiderlein

One summer morning a little tailor sat on his table at the window and sewed. A peasant woman came down the street calling, "Good jam for sale, good jam for sale!" The little tailor liked the sound of that.

He stuck his head out the window and called, "Up here, dear lady, I'll buy some jam."

When the woman had climbed up the stairs, he had her unpack every jar in her basket. He looked at them all and finally bought only the smallest jar of jam, which made the woman angry and she went away grumbling.

Then the tailor got his loaf of bread from the cupboard, cut off a thick slice, and spread it with the jam. "You'll taste good," he said, "but I want to finish off that waistcoat before I eat."

He put the slice of bread and jam down next to him and started sewing again, taking bigger and bigger stitches as he thought of the treat waiting for him. Meanwhile, the smell of the jam spread in the warm air and attracted a crowd of flies that all settled down on the bread slice. The tailor, who couldn't help looking at his piece of bread now and then, soon noticed them.

"Hey, who invited you!" he said and chased them away. But the flies didn't speak German. They just came back and brought even more flies with them. The tailor lost his temper. He reached down under his table for a big scrap of cloth, and saying, "Just wait, I'll fix you!" he snapped it down on the flies. When he picked it up again and counted, there lay seven flies, dead as doornails.

"What a fellow you are!" he said to himself, full of admiration. "The whole city ought to know about this."

And he quickly cut out a belt, sewed it, and embroidered on it in big letters: "Seven with one blow!" Then he said to himself, "Not just the city! The whole world ought to know!"

So the tailor put on his new belt and looked around his house for anything that might be useful on a journey, for he was going to set out to see and be seen by the world. All he could find was an old cheese, so he put that in his pocket. Just at the gate he got lucky and caught a bird, so he put that in with the cheese. Then he took to the road and climbed up a high mountain. When he got to the top, he saw a giant sitting on the peak.

"Hey, friend," he said to the giant, "Are you just sitting up here and watching the world go by? I'm going traveling, would you like to come with me?"

The giant looked at the little tailor and said, "With you, you puny little fellow?"

"As if!" said the tailor, unbuttoning his coat, and he showed the giant his belt. "There you have it in writing. That's the kind of man I am!"

The giant read "Seven with one blow," and thinking that the tailor had killed seven men, he was prepared to give him some respect. But he thought he would test the little man first. He picked up a stone and squeezed it in his fist so hard that water dripped out of it. "Let's see you do that if you're so strong."

"Nothing to it," said the tailor. He reached into his pocket, took out the rotten cheese, and squeezed it until the juice ran out of it. "Better than you, eh?" he said.

The giant couldn't believe his eyes. He picked up another stone and threw it so high in the air that it was almost out of sight. "Beat that, little man!" he said.

"No problem," answered the tailor. "Your throw was good, but the stone fell back down to the ground. I'll throw one so high that it never comes down again." He reached into his pocket, took out the bird, and threw it into the air. The bird, happy to be free again, flew high into the sky and out of sight. "Now, my friend," said the tailor, "How do you like that?"

"You certainly can throw," said the giant, "but now we'll see if you can carry a decent weight." And he led the little tailor to a huge oak tree that had been cut down and was lying on the ground. "We'll carry that out of the forest together," he said.

"Fine," said the tailor, "you lift the thick end at the bottom on your shoulder, and then I'll pick up the top with all its branches, which is even heavier." The giant picked up the trunk of the tree and put it on his shoulder, but the little tailor, instead of lifting his end, sat on one of the branches and the giant had to carry the whole tree and the tailor, too. And all the while the tailor whistled and sang as if carrying half of a huge tree was child's play.

After the giant had gone a fair way with his enormous load, he simply couldn't carry it any farther and said, "Listen, I have to let my end of the tree drop." The tailor jumped down to the ground, put his arms around the tree as if he were carrying it, and said, "Such a big fellow you are, and you can't even carry half of this tree!"

Leaving the tree on the ground, the giant and the tailor went on and soon came to a cherry tree. The giant pulled down the crown of the tree where the ripest cherries were and put it into the tailor's hand so that he could eat some, too. But the little tailor was so light and weak that he couldn't hold it down: the tree sprang back up, and up went the tailor with it. "What's the matter?" asked the giant. "Can't you hang on to a weak little twig like this one?"

"Holding the tree down is easy," answered the tailor, "especially for a man like me who killed seven with one blow! But I heard hunters shooting down there in the bushes so I jumped over the tree to get safely out of their way. Let's see you do the same!"

The giant tried to jump over the cherry tree, but every time he jumped he got caught in the branches, so the little tailor won this contest, too.

"Well, come along and spend the night with me and my family in our cave," said the giant, and the tailor willingly went with him. The giant gave him a bed to sleep in, but the tailor didn't get into it. Instead, he crept into a corner and hid. At midnight the giant came with an iron bar and gave the bed where he thought the tailor was sleeping such a blow that he broke it in two.

"That's the end of the little grasshopper," he thought, "he won't bother me again."

The next day the giant, now traveling with another giant, went off into the forest and forgot all about the dead tailor, until he came walking along as bold and cheery as ever. The giants were shocked and terrified that he would kill them all, so they ran away as fast and as far as they could.

So the tailor went on alone, always following his nose, until he came to the castle of a king. And because he was tired, he lay down on the grass and went to sleep. As he was lying there, some courtiers came and looked at him from all sides.

"Seven with one blow" they read on his belt and wondered what such a mighty warrior was doing here during peacetime.

"He must be a great fighter," they thought. They went and told the king and suggested that if war broke out, this would be a useful man to have around. The king thought that was good advice and sent a man to offer the stranger a job in the army when he woke up.

"Yes," answered the tailor, when the offer was made, "that's why I've come here, to offer my services to the king."

So he was made welcome and given a very comfortable room. But the officers of the king's army, who were completely fooled by the little tailor, wished him to the devil.

"What's going to happen if we get into an argument with him?" they asked each other. "He'd start hitting and kill seven of us with each blow." They went to the king and, saying they felt unequal to serving with such a strong man, asked to leave his service. The king was sorry to lose all of his best men for the sake of a stranger and began to wish he had never laid eyes on the little trailor. But he didn't dare send him packing because he feared the man would kill them all and take the throne for himself.

The king thought long and hard, and finally came up with a plan. He sent for the tailor and told him, "Because I know what a heroic fighter you are, I am going to make you a proposal. In one of my forests live two giants who terrorize the surrounding countryside, robbing and murdering people and burning houses and barns. No one has been able to stop them. But if you kill them, you may marry my daughter and have half the kingdom as her dowry. And you can take a hundred armed men on horseback to help you fight the giants."

The tailor thought to himself, "That's certainly a job for a fellow like me, and a beautiful princess and half a kingdom are nothing to sneeze at." So he told the king, "I'll get rid of the giants for you, but I won't need the hundred horsemen—a man who can kill seven with one blow needn't fear two."

So the little tailor set out for the forest, and when he got there he said to the horsemen, "You wait out here, I'll deal with the giants myself."

He walked into the forest and looked for the giants. Finally he found them sleeping under a tree, snoring so heavily that the branches waved up and down to the rhythm of their breathing.

"Piece of cake!" said the tailor to himself.

He filled his pockets with stones and climbed up into the tree. Then he threw one stone after another at the chest of the first giant until he woke up. The first giant punched the second giant and asked, "Why did you hit me?"

"You're dreaming," said the second giant, "I didn't hit you." Both giants went back to sleep again, and the tailor threw a stone that struck the second giant on the chest.

The second giant sat up and said, "Hey, why are you throwing things at me?"

"I'm not throwing anything," answered the first giant. They squabbled for a while, but because they were tired, they agreed to forget it and went back to sleep. The little tailor picked out his biggest stone and threw it as hard as he could at the first giant.

The giant shouted, "That's too much!" He jumped up and hit the second giant, who hit him right back. In a fury, they uprooted trees and beat and bashed each other until both of them were dead.

The little tailor said, "It's a good thing they didn't pull up my tree, or I would have had to make a very long jump." He climbed down and went back to the horsemen.

"There are two dead giants in there," he told them. "Only a man who kills seven with one blow could have finished them off, though. They ripped out whole trees to fight me."

Are you wounded?" asked the horsemen.

"Not a bit," answered the tailor. "They didn't touch a hair on my head."

The horsemen didn't believe him and rode into the forest to see for themselves. There they found the giants lying dead, with uprooted trees scattered around them. The men were amazed, but even more frightened of the little tailor—and even more certain that he would kill them all if they got on the wrong side of him.

They rode home and told the king what they had seen. The little tailor came, too, and asked for his promised reward: the king's daughter and half the kingdom. But the king regretted his promise and tried to think of another way to get rid of this mighty warrior. He said to the tailor, "There's a unicorn in the forest that has killed a lot of animals and people. Catch it first if you want to marry my daughter."

That was all right with the tailor. He took a short length of rope, went to the edge of the forest, and told the men who had been sent with him to wait there. Then he went into the forest himself and looked for the unicorn. He found it soon enough: it came galloping straight at him, its head down to spear him with its horn. "Gently, gently," said the tailor, and stood his ground in front of an oak tree until the unicorn was very close. Then he jumped nimbly behind the tree.

The unicorn was moving too fast to stop or turn. It ran its horn so deeply into the oak that it couldn't pull free. The tailor came out from behind the tree, tied the rope around the unicorn's neck, led it out of the forest to the king, and asked again for his reward.

The king was really alarmed now, but he thought of a third excuse that might rid him of this hero. He told the tailor that the wedding couldn't take place until he had caught a very dangerous wild boar that lived in the forest. The king's hunters would go with him to help.

"Fine," said the tailor, "That's the least of the tasks." So he went back to the forest but left the hunters outside, where they were happy to stay because they had met the beast before. When the wild boar saw the tailor, it ran at him, foaming at the mouth and gnashing its teeth. But the little tailor was standing next to a small chapel, and he ducked inside and then jumped lightly out the window. The boar followed him in, by which time the tailor had come around to the front again and could slam the door shut. The beast was caught.

The tailor called the hunters as witnesses, and then he went back to the king and said, "I've caught the pig, and therefore the princess, too." The king wasn't happy, but he had run out of excuses and had to give the tailor his daughter as he had promised. The wedding was held with great splendor but not much happiness, and the little tailor became a king.

After a few days the young queen heard the tailor talking in his sleep at night. "Boy, make that waistcoat and mend those trousers or I'll wrap my tape measure around your ears!" Then she knew what street her new husband had been born in, and in the morning she complained to her father the king and asked him to help her get rid of this husband who was only a tailor.

The king comforted her saying, "Tonight, after your husband is asleep, open your chamber door. I'll have some men waiting there who will go in and overpower him while he is sleeping."

The young queen agreed, but the king's swordbearer had heard it all, and because he liked the new king and was loyal to him, he ran and told him everything.

The little tailor was not in the least disturbed. That night he went to bed with his wife at the usual hour and soon pretended that he was asleep. When he started snoring, his wife got up, opened the door, and lay back down in bed. Then the little tailor began to speak in a loud voice as if he were talking in his sleep, "Boy, make that waistcoat and mend those trousers or I'll wrap my tape measure around your ears! I've killed seven with one blow, I've slain two giants, I've caught a unicorn and a wild boar, and I'm supposed to be afraid of the men standing by the door?"

When the men waiting outside heard these words, they fled as though a thousand devils were after them. So the little tailor was and remained a king for the rest of his life.

Source: Grimm KHM #20, 1819

Starsilver ❧ Die Sterntaler

There once was a little girl whose father and mother had died. She was so poor that she had no place to live, no bed to sleep in, and nothing at all of her own except the clothes she was wearing and a bit of bread some kind soul had given her. But she was a good child, and clever and capable, and so she went out into the world that had abandoned her, trusting in God.

Soon she met a poor man who said to her, "Oh, please, give me something to eat. I am so very hungry!" So she gave him her bit of bread and was happy that she had it to give. Next she met a boy who complained bitterly that his head was freezing and asked her for something to cover it with. So she took off her cap and gave it to him. Farther along the way, she met another child shivering with cold, and to this one she gave her bodice. Then came another, who asked for a skirt, and so she gave her skirt away, too. Finally, at the end of the day when darkness was falling, she came to a forest. There she met yet another child who was cold, and this one begged for a shift.

The little girl thought to herself, "It's night, no one can see me in the dark anyway, I can do without my shift." So she took her shift off and gave it to the child.

As she stood there, wearing nothing, having nothing, the stars began to fall from the sky, and as they fell around her they turned into shining silver coins. She had given her shift away, but she found she was wearing a new one of the finest linen. So she caught the shining star coins in the skirt of her shift and was rich for as long as she lived.

Source: Grimm KHM #153, 1837

Sagen

(Local Legends)

HCS '03

The Little Woodwife on the Cart Shaft ❧ Das Waldweibchen auf der Wagendeichsel

In Wöhlsdorf there was a shepherd who usually pastured his sheep by the woods near Ranis, and next to the sheepfold stood the little hut on wheels in which he slept. A little woodwife, which is a kind of forest spirit, sometimes came to visit him and would tell him how she and her relatives were persecuted by the Wild Hunter. She also told him that the only safeguard and ward against the Wild Hunter was a piece of wood on which three crosses had been carved together to form triangle.

Out of pity, the shepherd cut three deep crosses into the shaft of his cart with his pocketknife so that the little woodwife could take refuge there. The safeguard worked. As soon as the noise of the Wild Hunt rose from the forest nearby the little woodwife fled to the protection of the cart shaft and was safe there from pursuit. As a thank you for this protection, she gave the shepherd, who was always knitting, a ball of yarn that she told him would never come to an end, even if he knitted his whole life long.

The folk in that neighborhood enjoyed seeing the little woodwife swinging on the cart shaft and chatting happily with the shepherd, who sat beside her knitting industriously with the ball of yarn. But one night the Wild Hunter came with the whole Wild Hunt roaring behind him and followed the little woodwife as she fled to the three crosses on the cart shaft. The Hunter couldn't touch her there, but he broke off the whole cart shaft and took the shaft and woodwife away with him.

The shepherd went on knitting with the ball of yarn for many years and told everyone the story of how it came to him and what was special about it. One day he got into an argument about it with a fellow who refused to believe the shepherd's story. The shepherd told him, "Go on, start unwinding it and keep as much of the yarn as you want. I know, and I'll prove it to you, that the ball has no end." But when the other man started unwinding the yarn, the ball did soon come to an end.

(Thüringen) Source: Petzoldt, *Deutsche Volkssagen* #249

How a Poor Old Woman Got a Lot of Linen and Lost It Again ❧ Wie ein armes Mütterchen zu vieler Wäsche kam und dieselbe wieder verlor

In a lonely village on a high mountain lived a very poor old woman. One day she took her stick and set out for the valley to beg for alms. On her way through the pinewoods, she passed a cliff in which the forest spirits called woodwives lived and smelled the good smell of freshly baked bread. It made her feel faint with hunger, and she thought, "Oh, if only I had one piece of bread!" Suddenly a little woodwife stood before her with a whole loaf of bread and said, "This is for you, you hungry thing." The astonished old woman wanted to thank her, but the woodwife instantly vanished into the cliff again.

So the old woman satisfied her hunger and went on down into the valley. But the people who lived there were stingy and proud. They only mocked and mistreated her and gave her nothing. At the end of the wearisome day, when it was too dark to find her way home up the mountain, she had nowhere to lie down except the fields, where she was so cold that she couldn't sleep all night.

The next morning, she started back up the mountain. It was still very cold, and the old woman shivered in her torn and ragged clothing. Only the loaf of bread kept her going. It gave her new strength and never grew less, no matter how much she ate. When she came to the cliff in the pinewoods she saw long lengths of linen cloth spread out on the grass to bleach. "Oh, if only I had a piece of linen like that!" she thought, "I could make good underclothes to keep me warm." She had scarcely finished the thought when the woodwife stood before her again with a big skein of spun linen. "Here's linen for you, poor naked thing. It will never come to an end unless you wish it yourself." With these words, the woodwife vanished again, and the old woman happily went the rest of the way home

At home, she sat down and began to wind the skein of yarn into balls, and no matter how much she wound, the yarn never came to an end. She took yarn to the weaver, paid him at first with some of the cloth he wove for her, and made herself shifts and petticoats and dresses. The rest of the cloth she sold. The weaver had all the work he could do from the little old woman alone, and she made so much money from selling the fine linen cloth that she was able to live happily and without a care.

Things went on like this for a long time, and the little old woman became richer and richer. People wondered where she was getting so much yarn and so much money, but they could find nothing to hold against her. Then one day, the little old woman got into a quarrel with one of her neighbors, and both of them became angry. The neighbor said, "Shut up, you old witch! We all know there's some black magic going on with that yarn of yours!"

They went on quarrelling and saying bitter things for a long time. By the time the old woman finally turned away and went back to her house, she was very unhappy. She sat down to wind yarn, but the hurtful things her neighbor had said kept running through her mind, until, without thinking, she said, "You cursed yarn, if only you would come to an end!" The words were hardly out of her mouth before the wish was granted: the yarn, all the linen cloth, and all her money vanished. Even the clothes she wore, which had been woven from the magic yarn, disappeared into thin air, and she sat there stark naked, poorer than she had been before.

(Tirol) Source: Zaunert

The Ratcatcher of Hameln ❧
Der Rattenfänger von Hameln

Background: Rats, mice, and other vermin were ubiquitous in medieval towns and cities, and there are "ratcatcher" stories about many places in Germany. The Ratcatcher of Hameln is the most famous of German legendary figures and is known all over the world. The best-known English version is Robert Browning's narrative poem, "The Pied Piper of Hamelin: A Child's Story," but the name "Pied Piper" first occurs in the earliest English version of this legend, published in 1605 in Richard Verstegan's book A Restitution of Decayed Intelligence.

Scholars have tried and so far failed to identify an event or set of circumstances in the history of the city Hameln that might have given rise to this legend. The theory that is given the most credit claims that the root of the story is the departure of a group of citizens who went as settlers to Olmütz, a region that is now part of the Czech Republic. The "Ratcatcher" would have been the agent of the Bishop of Olmütz who recruited the settlers and led them to the new territory. Research has discovered family names from Hameln in Olmütz, and in the thirteenth century the inhabitants of a town were often referred to as "children of the town."

In Hameln the story itself was treated as historical fact long ago. In the medieval register of town statutes, there is an entry made by the town clerk in which the date "in the year of the Lord 1351 on St. Ambrosius day" was given a curious addition: "after the departure of the children in the year 1283." There are also sixteenth-century references to a colored glass window in the market church that seems to be the oldest source for the story. The window was made around 1300 and restored by order of the mayor in 1572. According to a description published in 1654, it showed a man in colorful clothing surrounded by a troupe of children. The inscription was no longer readable. Unfortunately, the window was taken out in 1652 to be replaced with another and it disappeared forever. The inscription on it probably said much the same as the inscription on the west wall of the so-called Ratcatcher House built in 1602–3:

> A.D. *1284—on the 26th of June—the day of St. John*
> *and St. Paul—130 children—born in Hameln—*
> *were led out of the town by a piper*
> *wearing multicolored clothes.*
> *After passing the Calvary near the Poppenberg*
> *they disappeared forever.*

The story has long since defined the city: it is the "Rattenfängerstadt," the Ratcatcher Town, and the Pied Piper appears everywhere. He walks daily in costume along the main streets; there are statues of him in squares and fountains; and his image and name appear on street signs, hotels and restaurants, posters, books, and countless souvenirs. There is an extensive Ratcatcher collection in the Hameln Museum, and open-air performances of a Ratcatcher play are held every summer.

In the year 1284, a strange man appeared in Hameln. He wore a coat of many bright colors, and it is said that because of this coat, he was called the Pied Piper. He claimed he was a ratcatcher, and he promised that for a certain sum of money, he would rid the town of all its mice and rats. The citizens came to an agreement with him and guaranteed a specified payment.

The ratcatcher then took out a small fife and began to play on it. At the first notes rats and mice came creeping out of all the houses and gathered around him. When he reckoned that none remained hidden, he walked out of the town and the hundreds and thousands of rats and mice followed him. He led them down to the bank of the river Weser. There he tucked up his clothes and walked into the water. The creatures all followed him into the river and drowned.

After the citizens were rid of their plague of rodents, they regretted the payment they had promised. Using all kinds of excuses, they refused to give the man his money, so he left angry and embittered.

On June 26, the feast of Saint John and Saint Paul, at seven in the morning (though some say it was noon), the ratcatcher came to the town again, this time as a hunter with a frightening face and a strange red hat. Once again he played his fife in the streets, and out of the houses came running not rats and mice, but children—boys and girls of four years and up—in great numbers. Among them was the daughter of the mayor, who was almost grown up. The whole swarm followed after him, and he led them out of the town and vanished with them into a mountain. A nursemaid carrying a child had followed them at a distance, but when they disappeared, she turned back to the town and told what she had seen. Messengers were sent out immediately in all directions by water and by land to ask whether anyone had seen the children, but no one had.

One hundred and thirty children were lost altogether. Some say that two who had lagged behind the others came back. One of them was blind and the other was mute. The blind child couldn't point out the place, but he could tell how they had followed the piper. The mute child could show the place where the others had vanished, although he could say nothing. One little boy, who had run out in his shirt, had turned back to get his coat and so escaped the tragedy. For when he returned to follow the piper, the others had already disappeared into a cave in the hillside, which people still point out to this day.

In the middle of the eighteenth century, and still today, the street the children traveled to reach the gate out of the town was called the Silent Street because no dancing was allowed and no stringed instruments could be played there. Even when a wedding procession came that way, the musicians had to be silent as they crossed that street. The mountain where the children vanished is called the Poppenberg. Two stone crosses were erected there to mark the place. Some people say the children were led into a cave and came out again in Siebenbürgen.

The citizens of Hameln recorded the event in the town register. From then on, they dated their official announcements by the number of years and days that had passed since their children were lost. The following lines were carved on the Town Hall:

> *In the year of our Lord 1284*
> *In Hameln were led out*
> *A hundred and thirty children born here*
> *Lost by a piper under the mountain.*

And on a commemorative stone that stood by the New Gate the following Latin inscription was carved under the date 1556:

> *Centum ter denos cum magus ab urbe puellos*
> *duxerat ante annos CCLXXII condita porta fuit.*

"This gate was built 272 years after a magician led 130 children out of the city."

In 1572, the mayor had the story depicted in the church windows together with an explanatory inscription. A coin was also struck to commemorate the event.

(Niedersachsen, Westfalen) Source: Rölleke, *Große deutsche Sagenbuch* #246, "Die Kinder zu Hameln"; Petzoldt, *Deutsche Volkssagen* #80, notes p. 364. Donald Ward's note on this legend in his translation of Grimm's *Deutsche Sagen* gives a summary of the research into the possible origins of this legend (Grimm, *The German Legends* #245).

The Mouse Lake ❧ Maussee

Between Inning and Seefeld lies the Wörthsee, which is also called Maussee ("Mouse Lake"). There was a time of great famine, and people were begging for bread. In one village the graf, or count, of Seefeld shut all the starving people up together. As he listened to their pitiful cries, he laughed and asked his companions if they could hear the mice squeaking. At that a numberless horde of mice appeared, and they followed him everywhere. Day and night they ran all over him and bit him. Nothing he did could keep them away.

Finally the graf fled to the island in the Wörthsee, but even this offered him no relief. Thousands of mice followed. They nipped and nibbled constantly. The man couldn't sleep a wink. He even had his bed hung up with iron chains to no avail. Nipping and nibbling, biting and gnawing, the mice slowly ate him up.

(Bayern) Source: Petzoldt, *Deutsche Volkssagen* #296. An almost identical story is told about a tower in the middle of the Rhine, near Bingen, in Thüringen with Bishop Hatto of Mainz as the villain (Grimm, *Deutsche Sagen* #241; #242 in Ward's translation). Petzoldt has a similar story from Posen about a Polish king called Popiel (*Deutsche Volkssagen* #295).

The Golem

Background: This legend is a famous Jewish tale, well known in Germany. At the time it in which it is set, Posen and Prague were within the extended territory of the German Empire, and Prague had a large Jewish community. The Jews were a vital part of German culture for centuries and should be represented in this collection. Tragically and inevitably, most German folktales about Jews reflect the centuries of anti-Semitism they suffered in Europe, and most Jewish folktales from the German Jewish tradition are set in the distant past and in another place. However, the legend of the Golem is strong enough to stand alone. The golem is a figure so powerful that it has entered the imaginative vocabulary of European culture.

In Worms there lived a righteous man named Bezalel to whom a son was born on the night of Passover. It was the year 5273* after the creation of the world, and the Jews were suffering terrible persecution. From the moment of his birth, it was shown that the son of Rabbi Bezalel was a blessing to his people. When his mother's labor pains began, the others living in the house ran out to fetch the midwife. They surprised a man with a burden on his back and prevented him from carrying out a wicked plan: the man had a dead baby in a sack and intended to throw it into the street where the Jews lived, so that the Jews would be accused of murder, for the people among whom the Jews lived accused them of using human blood to make the Passover bread.

Then Rabbi Bezalel prophesied about his son, saying, "This one will console us and free us from the plague. His name in Israel will be Juda Arje, according to the verse in the blessing of Jacob that says, 'Juda is a young lion. When my children were being torn apart, he rose.' " And the boy grew up to be a scholar and a wiseman, acquainted with all branches of knowledge and with a command of all languages. He became rabbi of the city of Posen, and soon after that he was called to Prague to be the highest judge in the community there.

All the thoughts and endeavors of Rabbi Löw** were aimed at helping his afflicted people and freeing them from the blood-libel. He asked heaven to tell him in a dream how he might defend his people against the priests who spread the dreadful lie. And in the night he was given this advice: "Make a man out of clay and you will confound the intentions of the evildoers."

---

*The date of 5273 is from the Jewish calendar, counting from the Jewish date for the creation of the world. All versions of the tale give this date without translating it into the Christian system of dating years.

** The rabbi's Hebrew name, *Juda*, means lion. *Löw* means lion in German

---

So the Rabbi Löw called his son-in-law and his oldest student to him and told them this answer. He also asked for their help in carrying out the work. All four elements were necessary to create the Golem: earth, water, fire, and air. The rabbi said that he held the power of the wind; his son-in-law was an embodiment of fire; the student was the symbol of water; and so he hoped that the three of them might succeed in making a man out of earth. He made them promise to tell no one what they were doing and to prepare themselves for their task for the next seven days.

When the seven days had passed, on the twentieth day of the month of Adar in the year 5340, at the fourth hour after midnight, the three men went to a clay pit on the bank of the river that ran outside the town. Here they kneaded the soft clay into the shape of a human being. They made it three ells* high, gave it a face and hands and feet, and laid it on the ground on its back. Then all three of them stood at the feet of the image and the rabbi ordered his son-in-law to walk seven times around it reciting a certain formula that he had devised. When this had been done, the clay figure glowed red like a hot coal.

Then the rabbi bade his student also to circle the image seven times while reciting a different formula. When this had been done, the clay figure cooled down, became damp, and began to steam. Its fingers grew nails, its head grew hair, and the body and face looked like those of a thirty-year-old man. Then the rabbi circled the image seven times and the three men together recited the sentence from the creation story that said, "And God blew living breath into his nostrils, and the man became a living soul."

When this sentence was completed, the eyes of the Golem opened and looked at the rabbi and his disciples with a gaze that expressed astonishment. Rabbi Löw said to the image, "Arise!" And the Golem raised itself up and stood on its feet. Then the men dressed the image in clothing and shoes like those worn by servants of the synagogue and the rabbi spoke to it: "Know that we have created you from the dust of the earth that you may guard our people from the evil that our enemies put upon us. I name you Joseph; you will live in the room where I sit in judgment and will do the work of a servant. You must obey my orders in all things, even if I were to command you to walk through fire or jump into the water or throw yourself from the highest tower." The Golem nodded its head in agreement, for it heard and understood what was said but was denied the power of speech. And so it happened on that remarkable night that three men left the house of the rabbi, but four returned to it.

To others in his house the rabbi said that he had met a beggar on the way to the bath who seemed to be a simple and blameless man, and so he had brought him home to employ as a servant in his study but that they were forbidden to use him for housework.

* An ell (German *Elle*) was the standard measure of length in Germany. It was roughly the length of a forearm.

And the Golem sat always in a corner of the room, his head propped on his hands, as motionless as a creature who had lost both spirit and wits and cared nothing for the world around it. The rabbi said of him that neither fire nor water could harm him and no sword could wound him. For he had named him Joseph in memory of the Joseph Scheda mentioned in the Talmud who had been half spirit and half man and had served scholars and often saved them from great affliction.

The High Rabbi Löw used the Golem only to fight against the blood-libel, which was the greatest cause of suffering for the Jews of Prague. When the rabbi sent him out to places where he should not be seen, an amulet written on deerskin made the Golem invisible to others although he himself could see everything. In the time before Passover, the Golem was sent to roam through the city every night to stop anyone carrying a burden. If the burden was a dead child that was to be thrown into the street of the Jews, then the Golem tied up the man and corpse with a rope and led them to the town hall. There he gave them over to the officials. The power of the Golem was supernatural, and he did many deeds.

The Death of the Golem

After a decree had been issued that declared the blood-libel baseless and forbade any accusation of this kind, Rabbi Löw decided to take the breath of life away from the Golem. He had the Golem laid down on a bed and ordered his brother-in-law and his oldest student to circle him seven times again and to say again the words they had spoken at the creation of the Golem, but to say them backward this time. When the seven circles were completed, the Golem was nothing more than a lump of clay. They took off its clothing, wrapped it in two old prayer shawls, and threw the image on a heap of damaged old books in the rabbi's attic.

Rabbi Löw told the following story about the making of the Golem. When he was preparing to give the Golem the breath of life, two spirits came to him: the spirit of Joseph Scheda and the spirit of Jonathan Scheda. The Rabbi chose the spirit of Joseph because he had been a savior of the Talmudic scholars. The power of speech could not be given to the Golem because, although animated by a sort of life force, he had no soul. The Golem had the power of discernment to some extent, but was denied matters of wisdom and higher insight.

Although the Golem had no soul, some said that they noticed something different about him on Shabbat, in particular, that his face looked friendlier than it did on weekdays. But others said that during the preparations for Shabbat, the rabbi always removed from the Golem's mouth the little tablet bearing the holy name of God. On other days, the Golem carried this tablet under his tongue, but

Rabbi Löw was afraid that Shabbat might make the Golem immortal and that the people might worship him as an idol.

The Golem himself was inclined neither to good nor to evil. He acted only under compulsion and from fear of being returned to nothingness. He could easily reach anything from ten ells above ground to ten ells below ground, and nothing could stop him from completing any task he was bidden to do.

He was made without a drive to procreate because otherwise no woman would have been safe from him and what had happened once at the beginning of time when the angels desired the daughters of men would happen again. Because he had no urges, he was immune to all illnesses. He was also aware of the changing hours, both night and day. For at the beginning of every hour, a fresh wind blows from the Garden of Eden to cleanse the air on earth, and the Golem knew each time it came because he had a very fine sense of smell.

Rabbi Löw said the Golem would share in eternal life because he had protected Israel at a time of great need and that he would awake with the dead. Then, however, he would not have the form of Joseph Scheda but would appear in a new shape of his own.

(Böhmen) Source: Rölleke, *Das große deutsche Sagenbuch* #860 and 861

The Little Old Woman ❧ Das alte Mütterchen

In a large city a little old woman sat alone in her room one evening. She was thinking about all the people death had taken from her: first her husband, then both children, then all her relatives one by one, and today her very last friend. She felt herself completely forsaken by everyone she had loved, but her sorrow was greatest for the loss of her sons, which was so hard to bear that she even blamed God for it.

She sat lost in her sad thoughts until she heard the church bells ringing for the early morning service. Then, surprised to find that she had grieved the whole night through, she lit her lantern and went to the church. When she got there, she found that it was already lighted inside, not by a few candles as usual, but by a dim twilight glow. It was also full of people, although usually only a handful of pious folk came this early in the morning. Every seat was taken, and the pew where she usually sat was crowded with strangers. But when she looked at them more closely, she saw that they were not strangers, but all her dead relatives, sitting there with pale faces and dressed in old-fashioned clothing. They didn't speak and they didn't sing, but a quiet humming and fluttering moved through the church.

Then an aunt of hers stood up, came over to the old woman, and spoke to her: "Look there, to the altar, and you will see your sons."

The old woman looked and saw her two children, one hanging from the gallows and the other broken on the wheel. Her aunt said, "You see, that's what would have happened to them if they had stayed alive and if God had not taken them to him as innocent children." The old woman went home trembling and thanked God on her knees for a goodness that had been beyond her understanding. Three days later she lay down and died.

Source: Grimm KHM, "Kinderlegenden" #8, 1857

The Twelve Apostles ❧ Die zwölf Apostel

Three hundred years before the birth of Christ, there lived a mother who had twelve sons but who was so very poor that she no longer knew how to find enough food to keep them among the living. She prayed to God every day that all her sons might live on earth together with the savior whose coming had been foretold. As her poverty grew greater and greater, she sent her sons out one after the other to seek bread for themselves.

The eldest, Peter, traveled for a whole day before he lost himself in a large forest. He looked for a way out but only found his way deeper and deeper into the wood, growing so hungry that he could hardly stay on his feet. Finally, he could go no farther and sat down on the ground, certain that he was about to die. But suddenly there stood beside him a shining little boy who was as beautiful and friendly as an angel. The child clapped his hands to get Peter's attention and asked, "Why do you sit there so sadly?"

"Oh," answered Peter, "I'm wandering in search of bread so that I might live long enough to see the savior whose coming has been prophesied to us. That is my greatest wish."

The child said, "Come with me and your wish will be fulfilled." He took poor Peter by the hand and led him between steep crags to a large cave. Everything in the cave glittered with gold and silver and crystal, and in the middle stood twelve golden cradles in a row. "Lie down in the first one," said the little angel, "and sleep for a while; I'll rock you."

Peter lay down, and the angel rocked him and sang to him until he fell asleep. And as he slept, a guardian angel led his second brother into the cave and rocked him to sleep in the second cradle, and so the rest of his brothers came, one after the other, until all twelve lay in the golden cradles and slept. They slept for three hundred years into the night when the savior was born. Then they woke up and were together with the savior on earth and were called the twelve apostles.

Source: Grimm KHM, "Kinderlegenden" #2, 1857

The Two Mothers ❧ Die zwei Mütter

Mary was wandering sorrowfully across a field lamenting the death of her son Jesus when she met a little field mouse. The field mouse asked Mary, "Why are you so sad?"

"Why should I not be sad? I have lost my only son," answered Mary.

The field mouse said, "I lost my nine sons all at the same time when a cow stepped on my nest."

Mary smiled at the little mouse. And people say that if Mary had not smiled then, the whole world would have been lost.

Source: Kuhlmann and Röhrich

Frau Holle

Background: A holle *is a spirit, and in Germany, Frau Holle is a very well-known one. The German word "Frau" can mean "woman" or "wife" and is also the title of respect used to address women, the equivalent of "Mrs." or "Mistress." Some English translations of the Frau Holle stories use "Mother Holle" for "Frau Holle," but that sounds cozier than Frau Holle truly is. If you compare the following three legends with the fairy tale called "Frau Holle," the difference between the two genres of folktale becomes quite clear.*

Frau Holle's Pond 🦢
Frau Hollen Teich

In Hessen there is a range of hills called the Meissner Gebirg, and in these hills there are a number of places associated with old magic. Among them is a small, spring-fed pond called the Frau Hollenteich, Frau Holle's pond, no more than forty or fifty feet across. It lies at the corner of a marsh that is surrounded by a half-submerged stone dike. The marsh is dangerous: horses that wander into it vanish, sunken without a trace.

The people who live in the Meissner Hills tell a number of stories about this holle, or spirit—some good, some bad. They say that Frau Holle makes women who climb down to her at the bottom of her spring healthy and able to bear children. New babies are said to come from her spring: Frau Holle brings them out of the water into the world. She has a wonderful garden at the bottom of her pond, and she gives flowers and fruit from it, as well as cake and pastries, to people she meets who know how to please her.

She is extremely tidy and a demanding housekeeper. When it snows, people say that Frau Holle is shaking out her featherbeds. She punishes lazy spinners by dirtying the wool on their distaffs, and snarls their thread or sets fire to their flax. On the other hand, she gives diligent spinsters new spindles and sometimes does their spinning for them overnight so that when they wake up, they find their spools filled. Lazybones may wake up to find Frau Holle has stripped off their blankets or laid them naked on the cold stone floor, while a diligent woman who gets up early in the morning to carry water to the kitchen in freshly scrubbed pails may find a silver penny at the bottom when she empties them.

Frau Holle also likes to pull children into her pond. To the good ones she gives good fortune for the rest of their lives. But the bad ones, she turns into changelings. Every year she walks through the fields and meadows and makes them fruitful. But she can also be terrifying when she rides through the forest leading the Wild Hunt. Sometimes she shows herself as a beautiful, white woman in the middle of her pond. At other times she is invisible, and the only signs of her are a sinister rushing noise and the sound of a bell ringing deep down in the water.

Holle's Eve ❧
Der Holleabend

In a town named Rehe lived a woman who was a most diligent spinner, working busily at her wheel all day long and late into the night. One evening, it was the last Thursday before Christmas, a holle, or spirit, came to her. The holle brought twelve empty spools with her and sternly told the woman that she was to spin them full of thread before midnight. If she failed to finish the task, the holle would twist her head around on her neck, back to front. Then the holle smiled and left the room. The terrified woman ran to her neighbor's house and told what had happened. Since she couldn't possibly spin twelve spools full before midnight, the neighbor advised her to spin only one layer of thread onto each spool. So that's what she did. As the clock struck twelve, the holle appeared again and asked for the twelve spools. The woman, trembling, handed them over. When the holle saw the single layer of thread, she was furious. "Who taught you this?" she demanded fiercely. And when the frightened woman didn't answer, the holle said, "The devil must have told you!" Then the holle vanished, although the door was closed.

That's the reason the evening of the last Thursday before Christmas is called Holle's Eve and why many old women were careful not to spin on that night, for fear of the holle.

Frau Holle's House ❧
Die Wohnung der Frau Holle

In Hilgershausen, near Bad Sooden, there is a steep cliff. It is completely hidden by trees, and very few people know where to find it. High up in the rock is a cave, the largest cave in all Hessen. Mossy old stones lead up to it like a giant staircase, and in front of the entrance stands a massive offering-stone. The top-most branches of two beech trees meet over the stone in an arch. Inside the cave, huge, dusty boulders are piled up like the steps to a temple, reaching right up to the vaulted roof of the cave. One can hear invisible drops of water hitting stone somewhere. This is Frau Holle's house, and this is where the fairy tale about Goldmarie and Pitchmarie takes place.

(Hessen) Source: Röllecke, *Das große deutsche Sagenbuch* # 516, #517, #518

The Devil's Chapel ❧ Des Teufels Kapelle

In the year 1250, a fire destroyed the Marienkirche, the Church of Saint Mary, in Lübeck. The town council of Lübeck voted to build a grand new church to replace it. In 1251, shortly after the foundation stone for the new Marienkirche had been laid, the master builder gathered all his journeymen to tell them the ground rules for the job. They were to work hard, stay sober, refrain from singing profane songs on the building site, and remember at all times that this building was to be a holy church raised to the glory of God. The journeymen solemnly swore that they would keep to these rules and started work on the project.

Now it happened that a few days later the Devil came by and thought the new foundations must be for a wine bar or tavern, so he stopped and asked what the men were building. When he heard that it was to be a great church, he began to curse it, but the master builder held out a cross in front of him just in time and the Devil had to fly away. He flew in a rage straight to the Brokken, a mountain in the Harz region, which is traditionally a meeting place for witches and devils of all sorts. There he picked up one of the enormous granite boulders that are strewn about the mountain's dome and flew back to Lübeck to smash the new church. But the bricklayers and masons saw him coming, and a young journeyman stepped forward and called out to him:

> Mr. Devil, Sir, don't throw that stone,
> You'd be better off to leave the church alone.
> We surely can agree to a compromise,
> Much easier than heaving a rock that size.

The Devil agreed not to throw the stone, on the condition that the workmen build his kind of chapel for him—a wine bar! Then he threw the rock away. It landed not far from the church, and its impact made a huge hole in the ground. The workmen building the church covered the hole with a vaulted ceiling, and it became the Ratsweinkeller, the wine bar under the town hall. The Devil made good use of it. Sad to say, its sooty rooms attracted larger congregations than the soaring church did.

There's a bronze statue of a small, impish looking devil outside the Marienkirche sitting on a big block of stone. So many people touch his horns for luck that they are as shiny as gold.

(Lübeck) Source: Röllecke, *Das große deutsche Sagenbuch* #86

The Little Stone Man ❧ Das steinerne Männlein

High on the roof of the Marienkirche stands a strange little stone figure, the statue of a small man, wizened and hunched into himself. The story told about the statue goes like this.

Long ago in Lübeck lived a very old man. Death had come for him a number of times, but each time the old man had refused stubbornly to go with him, so in the end Death simply gave up and left him alone. The old man grew amazingly old—horribly old. All his friends and all his family died, but he lived on.

Eventually, after many, many years, people broke into his house because it had stood seemingly empty for such a long time and no one knew who the owner was any more. They found the old man on the floor. He had shrunk to the size of a two-year-old and was so shriveled that his head looked like a skull. Instead of dying he had withered away into stone. It didn't make sense to bury a man of stone, so he was put on the roof of the Marienkirche. And there he stands today.

(Lübeck) Source: Told by Anne Welcker Altmann

Another version of the story about the little stone man appears on the following page.

Mr. Stone-Old ❧ Herr Steinalt

A little stone man sits on the roof of the Marienkirche by the Briefkappelle (the Letter Chapel). He was once a rich merchant who could buy everything he wanted. For this reason, he loved his life, and every time Death came for him, he sent him away. So he grew older and older. For a while there were still one or two people in the city who knew him. But soon all the friends he had had were dead.

Because he became stranger as well as older, the children in the streets mocked him and called him Stone-Old. So he finally looked for Death because his life was no longer a pleasure to him. But Death had forgotten all about him, and the merchant couldn't find him. Then he remembered a legend, which said that at midnight Death stepped out of the wall painting by Bernt Notke in the Marienkirche to dance. The merchant went to the church that night to speak to Death. But the church was already locked. He looked here, and he looked there. Finally, he found a ladder and meant to climb up on the roof to see if any of the windows were open. But because he was old and weak, he only managed to get as far as the first level of the roof next to the Briefkappelle. There he sat down to rest for a moment, and while he was resting, he fell asleep. The next morning people saw him up there, but they couldn't wake him. He had turned to stone.

Source: This version is given in the guidebook to the Marienkirche. *The Dance of Death* was painted in the Marienkirche by Bernt Notke in 1463.

The Casting of Two Great Bells at Breslau ❧ Der Glockenguß zu Breslau

Background: The Church of Saint Mary Magdalena in Breslau was built in the fourteenth century with two great towers joined by a bridge. In each of these towers hangs a great bell. It takes three or four men to ring one of these bells, and they are so heavy that after they have been rung fifty times, they ring on by themselves for another fifty with only a little help. The bells are rung for church services, for vespers, and for a death. They never toll for people of good standing in the city, but they do ring a death knell for every poor sinner who is brought to judgment at the Rathaus and condemned. The story behind this curious custom goes like this.

The bell-founder who was commissioned to make the bells had everything prepared for the casting. The clay mold had been made, the copper and tin had been melted together and heated until the metal boiled, and all was ready to run the molten bronze into the mold. But first the bell-founder went to eat his dinner. He had ordered his apprentice not to touch the tap on the huge melting-kettle if he valued his life.

The apprentice was a terribly nosy fellow, though; he couldn't resist opening the tap just a little to see what the molten bronze would look like. But the tap came off in his hand and all the metal ran into the mold until the kettle was empty and the mold was full. The boy went crying to his master and confessed what he had done, asking for forgiveness, but the master was so angry that he stabbed the boy on the spot. Once the bell had cooled, the master broke the mold open and saw that the bell was perfect. In the meantime, though, the apprentice had died of his wound.

The bell-founder was taken away to prison and eventually sentenced to beheading. By then the bells had been hung in their towers. The bell-founder asked that he be allowed to hear their resonance before he died. So the bells were rung for him, as they have been rung ever since for every criminal condemned to die.

(Schlesian) Source: Petzoldt, *Historische Sagen* #31

The Buried Bell ❧ Glocke Vergraben

A long time ago a gräfin, or countess, gave the little church at Berndsweiler a bell that had a lot of silver in it. She named it after herself, Anne Susanne. (In those days church bells were given names and baptized, just like people.) During the war with Sweden, the bell was taken down for safekeeping, and buried in the forest where the "White House" now stands. It lay there for a hundred years or more before wild pigs dug it out of the ground. No one knew where it belonged, so it was hung in the church tower in the nearby village of Sinbron. But whenever the bell was rung there, its tone was muffled and rang faintly:

> *"Anne Susanne*
> *In Berndsweiler*
> *I want to hang."*

When people finally understood what the bell was saying, they took it to Berndsweiler, and the very first time it was rung there its tone was clear and strong again.

(Baden) Source: Petzoldt, *Deutsche Volkssagen* #543

The Poor Folks' Bell ❧ Die Armenglocke

The church in Dambeck is ages old. In fact, it is so old that it was built before the Great Flood. The walls are still standing, but the tower with its three bells sank into the sea long ago. In the old days, people often saw the bells come out of the sea at noon on Saint John's Day to sun themselves on the sand. Once some children took the noon meal out to their parents in the fields and then went down to the shore. There they washed out the cloths in which the food was wrapped, and then they saw the bells on the sand.

One little girl hung her cloth on one of the bells to dry. After a while, two of the bells climbed back down into the sea, but the third couldn't move from the spot. The children ran to the town and told what they had seen, and everyone in Röbel came out to have a look. The rich people, who wanted it for themselves, hitched eight, sixteen, and even more horses to the bell, but they couldn't budge it an inch. Then a poor man came down the road driving two oxen and saw what was going on. He hitched his two oxen to the bell and said:

> "With God, for all,
> Great and small!"

And he took the bell to Röbel without the least effort. There they hung it in the Newtown church, and when poor people die who can't pay to have the other bells rung for them, then this bell is rung, and it says "Dambeck, Dambeck."

(Mecklenburg) Source: Petzoldt, *Deutsche Volkssagen* #547

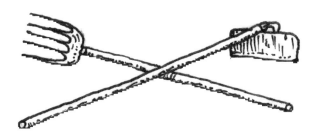

Doctor Faust ✤ Doktor Faust

The famous magician Johannes Faust was born in a little town in Württemberg called Knittlingen, about an hour's walk from Maulbronn. There are many stories told about Dr. Faust. He was a very learned man, and because he wanted to become a master of the magic arts, he sold his soul to the Devil. After that, the Devil had to do anything he asked.

For example, the Devil had to bring him strawberries in the middle of winter, and then cover a road with snow in the middle of summer so that Dr. Faust could use his sleigh. When he drove through a town in his coach, Dr. Faust often made the Devil rip up the bumpy cobblestone paving in front of his wheels and lay it down again behind him, and—mind you—he drove pretty quickly. Sometimes he demanded just the opposite: the Devil would have to pave a country lane for him and then rip up the paving as soon as he had passed over it.

When Dr. Faust wanted to choose a servant, he commanded all the devils in hell to come to his room. The legion appeared and lined up in a long row. He asked the first how fast he was. "As fast as water," was the answer. He asked the second, who said, "As quick as a bird." The third answered, "As fast as lightning." The fourth said, "Quicker than thought." That's the one Faust chose.

Once Dr. Faust came to an inn where four men were trying to carry a huge barrel up from the cellar. "You fools," called Faust, "I can bring that up for you all by myself!" The innkeeper told his men to stand aside and then challenged the doctor to try it. Without making a lot of fuss, Faust sat down on the barrel and rode it up the stairs.

Another time a farmer bought a horse from Dr. Faust at the market. It looked to be a fine, healthy horse, but Faust warned the farmer not to ride it through running water because it would buck him off if he did. The farmer didn't believe Faust, and on the way home he rode the horse through a river. Halfway across he found that instead of a horse, he had a wisp of straw between his legs. You see, magic can't cross running water.

Dr. Faust played a similar trick on another farmer who bought a horse from him at the market. Faust had doctored up that animal as well as the cleverest horse trader could have done. On his way home, the farmer got caught in a heavy rainstorm that drastically changed the appearance of the horse: it turned out to be a miserable nag not fit even for the knacker's yard. The farmer went to the doctor's house to ask for his money back. When he got there, he saw Faust sleeping on a bench outside the door. He shook him by the feet to wake him up, and when that didn't work, shook and pulled harder until one foot came off in his hand. The farmer was so frightened that he forgot all about his money and ran away.

The death of the great magician was very sad. Because they couldn't get at him in any other way, his enemies tried to poison him with a diamond. But Dr. Faust got a frog, shut himself up in his room, lay down on his back, and set the frog on his mouth to draw out the diamond he had swallowed. Faust could already feel the diamond at the top of his throat when someone came into the room and interrupted the process. So the Devil won the game, and Faust had to die.

This happened in Maulbronn. You can climb out of the cloister there through a window and go across several roofs to a room that's been walled in. That's where Faust died, and on the wall there's a big bloodstain. That's where the Devil smashed his head before he took Faust away with him.

(Schwaben, Kärnten, and Oberpfalz) Source: Petzoldt, *Deutsche Volkssagen* #61

The Wartburg: Five Legends

Background: In the region of Thüringen lies a town called Eisenach. This is the place where Martin Luther went to choir school as a boy and where Johann Sebastian Bach was born. From whatever direction travelers approach Eisenach, the first landmark they see is the Wartburg, an eleventh-century castle high on a mountain overlooking the broad valley.

An important center of culture and political power for its first five hundred years, the Wartburg fell into neglect in the seventeenth and eighteenth centuries. But the German Romantic movement of the nineteenth century, fascinated as it was with the Middle Ages, drew attention back to the Wartburg and made it arguably the most famous and best-loved castle in Germany. Wagner's opera Tannhäuser *is based on the third of the Wartburg legends told here.*

The first two Wartburg legends are about Graf Ludwig, the count who first built the castle. The folk etymology of the castle's name plays with the two syllables of its name: Wart *is a slightly abbreviated form of* warte, *"wait"; and* Burg, *"castle," sounds like* Berg, *"mountain." There is no historical evidence that the event described in the third story, "The Singers' War," actually happened. But there are historical documents about contests like this Sängerkrieg, and two of the Meistersänger (master singers), Walther von der Vogelweide and Wolfram von Eschenbach, did spend time at the Wartburg. Heinrich von Ofterdingen and the magician Klingsor are fictitious characters, but they appear in other legends, too.*

The Origin of the Wartburg

Graf Ludwig, called the Springer, was a mighty lord in Thüringen. Once, when he was hunting in the mountains, he followed a deer to the little river Hörsel and Lower Eisenach and up onto the mountain where the Wartburg stands today. There he stopped, and while he waited for his followers to catch up with him, he admired the beautiful countryside, the steep cliff of the mountain rising almost straight up from the valley, and the flat top where there was room to build. He thought to himself, "Wart' Berg, du sollst mir eine Burg werden!" ("Just wait, mountain, you'll become a castle for me!")

But however much he wanted it, the mountain wasn't his to build on. It belonged to the lords of Frankenstein, who owned a castle nearby called Mittelstein, which in the time before the Wartburg was the best castle in Thüringen. Ludwig had twelve knights with him, brave free men, and when they caught up with him, he took secret council with them and devised a cunning trick that would make the mountain his. He gathered a large number of his people at the Schauenberg nearby, which belonged to him, and in one night had enough earth carried in baskets from his own land to cover the top of the Wartberg. Then he hastily threw up a perimeter wall behind which he could defend himself and began to build his castle.

The lords of Mittelstein and Frankenstein soon came to challenge him, but they couldn't get at him in his stronghold at the top of the steep cliff. So they went to the emperor and the imperial court and accused Ludwig of illegally taking by force what was theirs. In response to an imperial inquiry, Ludwig answered that he had built the castle on his own ground and that therefore it was rightfully his. The court ruled that if twelve honest men were willing to swear an oath that the land he built on was his, he could keep it. Then Ludwig called his twelve knights to testify for him, and they went with him to the top of the mountain. There they drew their swords, stuck them into the earth that had been carried up there, and swore that their lord, Graf Ludwig, stood on his own land and that this ground (the top layer of earth) had of old been part of the territory of the lords of Thüringen.

So the mountain became his and the present town of Eisenach was founded and fortified with walls. This happened in the year 1067.

Why Graf Ludwig Was Called the Springer

Ludwig fell in love with Adelheid, the wife of Margrave Friedrich, and the two of them conspired to give Ludwig the opportunity to kill the margrave. After he had killed her husband, Ludwig took Adelheid to his castle Schauenburg and married her. But Friedrich's brothers and friends accused him of murder, and he was imprisoned for more than two years in a house on the Gibichenstein high above the River Saale. When he saw that he was likely to be executed, he asked that he be allowed to arrange for masses to be said for his soul after his death and alms distributed in his name. To that end one of his most trusted servants was sent for, and Ludwig made a secret plan with him: after the servant left with the instructions concerning the money to be spent on masses and alms, he was to come back the next day with two horses and wait at the bottom of the cliff below the house.

Ludwig wasn't held in chains, but there were always six reliable men to guard him in the stone room where he was imprisoned. As the hour for his escape drew near, Ludwig complained that he was very cold and used that as an excuse to put on several layers of clothing. Then he walked quietly up and down the room. Meanwhile, the six guards were playing checkers to pass the time and didn't pay much attention to his pacing. When he saw that his servant had arrived with the two horses he ran to the window and jumped out. It was a long, long drop to the river, but the wind caught his cloak, slowing his fall so that he landed safely in the water. The waiting servant swam to meet him with the horses. Ludwig mounted his white stallion, which he called the Swan. He cast off some of his wet clothing and galloped all the way to Sangerhausen.

This leap earned him his byname, the Springer.

The Singers' War

In the year 1206, six gifted poets met at the Wartburg by Eisenach. They wrote and sang their songs in a competition that was later called the War at the Wartburg, and later still, the Singers' War. The names of these six master singers were Heinrich Schreiber, Walter von der Vogelweide, Reimar Zweter, Wolfram von Eschenbach, Biterolf, and Heinrich von Ofterdingen. Their chosen topics were the sun and the day, and the masters had agreed among themselves that the loser of the singing war would forfeit his life. Stempfel the Executioner was standing by with his rope in hand. Five of the singers compared their host, Hermann, landgrave of Thüringen and Hessen (the family had grown more powerful since Ludwig the Springer's time), with the day, and set him above all other princes.

Only Heinrich von Ofterdingen praised his own lord, Leopold, duke of Austria, even higher, and compared him to the sun. Ofterdingen sang with wit and skill, but in the end the others had the advantage over him and trapped him with cunning words, for they were envious and wanted him gone from the Thüringian court.

Ofterdingen complained that they had made him play with loaded dice and that the competition was rigged, but the five others called to Stempfel that he should hang Heinrich from a tree. Then Heinrich fled to the landgrave's wife, the Lady Sophia, and took shelter under her cloak. They couldn't touch him there, and he proposed a compromise: he would have a year's reprieve, and in that year he would go to Siebenbürgen in Hungary and bring back Master Klingsor to be the final judge of their quarrel. This Klingsor was at that time the most famous of the German mastersingers, and also a magician. Because the landgravine had chosen to protect Heinrich, the others let themselves be persuaded.

Heinrich von Ofterdingen left the Wartburg and went first to the Duke Leopold in Austria, who gave him letters of recommendation. Then he went to Siebenbürgen in Hungary. There he told Master Klingsor the reason for his journey and he sang his songs for him.

Klingsor praised Heinrich's songs and promised to go to Thuringen with him to settle the singers' dispute. But time passed, and Klingsor made no preparations for the journey. When Heinrich's year of grace was almost over, he became frighten and said, "Master, I'm afraid you are going to let me down, and I will have to travel back alone and unhappy. And if I do not return to my death, then I will be dishonored and can never go Thuringen again."

But Klingsor answered, "Don't worry! We have strong horses and a light wagon, and we'll get there in no time."

The night before they were to leave, Heinrich was too restless to sleep, so the Master gave him a drink that sent him into a deep slumber. Then he wrapped a leather coverlet around both of them and commanded his spirits to convey him quickly to Eisenach in Thuringen and to set him down at the best inn.

It all happened as he ordered, and they brought him to the Helgreven Inn before daybreak. Still in his sleep, Heinrich heard familiar bells ringing and said, "It seems to me that I have heard those bells before, and that I am in Eisenach."

"You must be dreaming," said Master Klingsor.

But Heinrich got up, looked around, and realized that he really was in Thüringen. "Praise be to God that we are here. This is the Helgreven Inn, and there's Saint George's Gate, and I can see people standing in front of it waiting to leave the town once it's opened."

The arrival of the two guests was soon known at the Wartburg. The landgrave had gifts sent to the foreign master and commanded that he be received with full honors. When someone asked Ofterdingen how things had gone for him and where he had been, he answered, "Last night I went to bed in Siebenbürgen, and this morning I went to the early mass in Eisenach. How that happened is a mystery to me."

Several days passed before the masters would sing and Klingsor would judge them. On one of those days, Klingsor was sitting after dark in the inn's garden, looking up with great concentration at the stars. The men sitting with him asked what he saw in the heavens. Klingsor said, "Know that tonight a daughter will be born to the king of Hungary. She will be beautiful, virtuous, and saintly, and she will be married to the son of the landgrave."

When the landgrave was secretly informed of this prophecy, he was delighted and summoned Klingsor to the Wartburg, showed him great honor and had him sit at the high table. After the meal Klingsor went to the Knights' Hall, where the singers sat, to free Ofterdingen from the death sentence. Then Klingsor and Wolfram von Eschenbach sang against each other, but Wolfram was so thoughtful and nimble that the master couldn't best him. So Klingsor called one of his spirits, who came in the form of a youth. "I'm tired from talking," said Klingsor. "This is my squire, let him contend with you for a while, Wolfram." The spirit began to sing, and his subject was the time from the beginning of the world to the age of the Graces. But Wolfram chose to sing about the divine birth of the eternal Word, and when he came to the holy transformation of bread and wine, the spirit fell silent and vanished.

Klingsor had listened as Wolfram sang with learned words about the divine mystery and thought that Wolfram might also be an adept of the magic arts. Wolfram was staying in Titzel Gottschalk's house, opposite the bread market, in the center of the town. That night while he slept, Klingsor sent his spirit again to test whether Wolfram was learned in magic. But Wolfram, a simple man and without knowledge of arts other than music, was learned only in the word of God. The demon sang to him about the stars in the sky and asked him impossible questions that even Master Klingsor could not solve. Finally the demon laughed loudly and wrote with his finger on the stone wall as if it were soft dough: "Wolfram, you are a greenhorn snippety-snap!" Then the demon vanished, but the writing stayed on the wall. It would still be there today, but so many people came to see the wonder that the master of the house had the stone broken out of the wall and thrown into the river Horsel.

Klingsor, once he had tested Wolfram, took his leave of the landgrave, and, loaded with presents and gifts, he returned home in the leather blanket, just as he had come. Heinrich von Ofterdingen left Eisenach with his honor intact and lived to sing for many a year.

The Roses

As Klingsor prophesied, Elisabeth, daughter of the king of Hungary, was betrothed to Landgrave Hermann's eldest son, Hermann. She was sent to the Wartburg in 1211 when she was four years old. Young Hermann died when she was ten, and the engagement was transferred to the second son, Ludwig, whom she married at the age of fourteen.

Elisabeth was extraordinarily pious, even as a young child, and devoted herself to helping the poor and the sick. She established a hospice at the foot of the mountain below the Wartburg for the destitute who were incurably ill, and not only supplied it with food and firewood, but nursed the sufferers herself. After her husband died on a Crusade when she was only twenty, Elisabeth and her three children left the Wartburg, and a year later she dedicated herself to a religious life. She died when she was only twenty-four years old and was canonized a saint in 1235.

This version of the legend is probably unfair to Ludwig, who the biographers say loved his wife and encouraged her boundless alms giving. But it is true that the Thuringian court was not as wealthy as it had been under Ludwig's father, and some of the family resented Elisabeth's extreme generosity.

There was a famine in Germany and Elisabeth exhausted the treasury to feed the poor and distributed the whole crop of wheat and barley to those who were the hungriest. Her husband warned her harshly that she must give no more away. But she couldn't bear to see the poor, and especially the sick, starve. So she smuggled food as often as she could down to the hospital she had established at the foot of the mountain below the Wartburg.

One day she and one of her ladies were carrying baskets full of bread down to the valley when her husband came riding up from the town to the castle. The two women hid the baskets under their cloaks, but the landgrave had seen them and angrily demanded to know what was in the baskets. Elisabeth, in a panic, hoping to prevent discovery, said, "Roses." Her husband didn't believe her and told them to show him the baskets. And when Elisabeth and her lady brought the baskets out from under their cloaks, the bread had vanished and they were indeed full of roses.

Doctor Luther at the Wartburg

Martin Luther, the great reformer of the Catholic Church, nailed his ninety-five theses to the door of the castle church in Wittenberg in 1517. He was excommunicated by the pope, and the Edict of Worms made him an outlaw in May 1521. Luther started home from Worms under a temporary safe-conduct, but clearly his life was at risk. On his way home on May 4, some of Luther's supporters staged a fake kidnapping in the Thüringian forest near Altenstein and whisked Luther away to the Wartburg, which was pretty much abandoned at that time. There they hid him as Junker Georg, Knight George—he had to grow a beard, let his monk's tonsure grow out, and trade his monk's robe for a knight's gear. He stayed in the bailey at the Wartburg for ten months, writing and, as he wrote his friends, fighting ten thousand battles with Satan. It was at the Wartburg that he translated the New Testament from Greek into German in only ten weeks, working at a white heat. His translation, poetic, flowing, eminently readable and clear, was the most important factor in the development of a standard written form of the German language, an enormous cultural influence.

Doctor Luther sat in the Wartburg and translated the Bible. The Devil didn't like that and wanted to disrupt Luther's holy work. But when the Devil tried to tempt him, Luther grabbed the inkwell and threw it at the Devil's head. The Devil vanished and the inkwell hit the wall, making a big black ink spot. People say that the ink spot has been scrubbed off the wall many times, but it always reappears. If you go to the Wartburg today, you can see the room Luther worked in, the chair he sat on, and the ink spot.

(Thüringen) Sources: Rölleke, *Das Große deutsche Sagenbuch* #579–583; Wartburg-Stiftung; Petzoldt, *Historische Sagen* #183, #245

Hitler and Mussolini ❧ Hitler und Mussolini

Legends grow around famous people of all kinds and in all times, not just heroes and villains in the distant past.

Hitler went to Heaven and asked Saint Peter at the gate to let him in. Peter said, "But you don't have a horse," and sent him away until he could come back with a horse. On the way back down, Hitler ran into Mussolini and told him what had happened. Mussolini said, "Oh, come on back up with me. He wouldn't throw both of us out." So they both went to Heaven and Peter said, "I told you to come with a horse, not with a horse's ass."

Mussolini once had an accident with his car and fell into a river. A farmhand who saw the accident ran and pulled him out. Then Mussolini said, "What can I do for you in return for saving my life? I'll give you whatever you ask."

"Nothing," answered the farmhand, "it's just human decency."

"Now, you know who I am, don't you? I'm Mussolini, il Duce."

"Oh, well then, I guess I will ask for something: don't tell anybody that I rescued you. If people knew, I'd get beaten up or maybe even killed."

(Südtirol) Source: Petzoldt, *Historische Sagen* #208, #209

The Waterman as the Keeper of Souls ❧ Der Wassermann als Seelenhüter

The waterman looks like a human being, except that his teeth are green. He also wears a green hat. He shows himself to girls when they go by the pond he lives in, and he measures out lengths of ribbon and throws it to them.

Once the waterman had a good neighborly relationship with a farmer who lived near the lake. The waterman would visit the farmer sometimes and one day asked the farmer to visit him in his house under the water in return. The farmer agreed and went with him. The waterman's house was like a splendid palace on land, with sitting rooms and halls and bedrooms full of beautiful things. The waterman led his guest through all the rooms and showed him everything. Finally they came to a small room full of shelves, and the shelves were full of new pots, all standing upside down with their open side on the shelf. The farmer asked what the room was for.

"This is where I keep the souls of people who drown. I keep them under the pots so that they can't escape," said the waterman.

The farmer said nothing and soon after was back up on land. But the thought of the souls under the pots nagged at him, and he kept watch to see when the waterman went out.

One day he saw the waterman crossing a field and went straight to the lake. He had been careful to remember the way under the water so he found the water-house easily enough and also found the little room with the pots. He went in and turned over the pots, one after another, until they were all right-side up. The souls of the people who had drowned rose up out of the water, high into the open air, and were free again.

(Böhmen) Source: Petzoldt, *Deutsche Volkssagen* #338

The Nix and the Midwife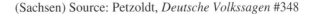
Der Nix holt die Wehmutter

A nix, which is a water-elf, lived with his wife in the River Saale by Giebichenstein. One night the nix came to the local midwife and asked her to come with him. She didn't want to go, but he threatened to kill her on the spot if she didn't, so she followed him, shaking in her shoes. When they reached the Saale, the nix struck the water with a rod. The waves parted, and the nix and the midwife went down a fine wide staircase to the nixhouse, which was a large palace glittering with gold and silver and jewels.

The midwife found the nixwife in labor and helped her through the birth. When it was over and the nix left the room to get the midwife's payment, the nixwife whispered to her, "When my husband comes back and offers you great treasure, don't take more than your usual fee or something dreadful might happen to you." The nix came back with a big basin full of gold and silver coins and said to the midwife, "Here, take as much as you want in payment for your work." And running his hand through the coins to make them clink and jingle he held the basin out. But she took only one four-penny piece.

"You're lucky, old woman," said the nix. "If you had taken more, I would have wrung your neck." Then he led the midwife back to the stairs, and she climbed up in fear and trembling and heard the rushing of the water closing up behind her, but she didn't dare look back until she was safely on her own doorstep again.

(Sachsen) Source: Petzoldt, *Deutsche Volkssagen* #348

The Klabautermann

When a new ship is finished and its first crew is aboard, a little spirit moves in. The sailors call it the *Kalfater* (caulker) or *Klabautermann* (hobgoblin). He's a good spirit for both the ship and the crew. Very few people have actually set eyes on a Klabautermann, because it's supposed to be unlucky for the person who sees him. Those who have seen one say that he is scarcely two feet tall, and that he wears a red jacket, wide sailor's pants, and a round hat. But others say that he's quite naked. The less you see of him, the more you hear him in the ship, because he looks after it day and night and in all weathers. He keeps the cargo securely stowed in the hold when the seas are rough and caulks leaks in places no human being could reach. If the captain is asleep in the cabin when the ship is in danger, he'll be nudged awake by the Klabautermann so that he can quickly do what is needed to keep the ship safe. The sailors know that this is all the Klabautermann's work, but all they say is, "Listen, there he is again!" when they hear him puttering around down in the hold or inside the walls.

Many believe that only a few ships, not all of them, have a little caulker. They think the ships' Klabautermen are the souls of children who were born dead or died before they were baptized. When such children are buried under a tree outside the churchyard, and when the wood of that tree is used to build a ship, the soul of the child goes into that ship with the wood as the ship's Klabautermann. And they say that a ship with a little caulker will never sink.

When ships are moored in a harbor, the Klabautermen get together and talk about their voyages. One conversation between two Klabautermen went like this:

"Yes," said the one, "My last trip was a hard one. One of the side planks tore loose and I had to hold it in place for the rest of the voyage to keep the water from rushing into the hold."

"Oh," countered the other one, "I had harder work than that. Shortly after we sailed, a storm blew up and the mainmast broke off at its foot. I had to hold it up for the whole trip."

The first one wouldn't concede that the second one had worked harder, so they got into an argument that finally ended in blows.

Once a ship sailed into harbor after a long voyage. That evening a sailor on the deck suddenly heard a high little voice talking to someone on a ship that was moored nearby. "Did you have a successful trip?" a similar voice from the other ship called back. "Yes, but what a lot of work I had! Without me, the ship would have sunk. But I don't like it here any more—the captain and the sailors take all the credit for our quick and successful voyage and forget about me. Tonight I'm leaving the ship."

The sailor realized that he had heard two ship's Klabautermen talking and that the luck was about to leave his ship. The next morning he went ashore and looked for a new berth. The ship eventually sailed again, but it never reached its destination.

(Pommern, Rügen, Schleswig-Holstein)
Source: Petzoldt, *Deutsche Volkssagen* #425, #426

The Elves ❧ Die Wichtelmänner

There once was a poor servant girl who was hardworking and clean. She swept the house every day and dumped the sweepings on a big rubbish heap outside the door. One morning, as she was about to start work, she found a letter on the rubbish heap. She couldn't read, so she put her broom in the corner and took the letter to her mistress. It turned out to be an invitation from the elves, who were asking the girl to be godmother at a baptism. The girl didn't know whether or not to go, but after much persuading, and because her mistress told her such an invitation could not be refused, she agreed.

Three elves came and led her to a hollow mountain where the little folk lived. Everything was small, but dainty and splendid beyond words. The baby's mother lay in a bed of black ebony with pearls as bed knobs, the blankets were embroidered with gold, the cradle was made of ivory, and the bathtub was made of gold.

After the girl stood godmother at the baptism, she wanted to go home. But the elves begged her earnestly to stay with them for three days. So she stayed, and spent the time agreeably and happily, and the little folk did everything they could to please her. At last the three days were past. When the girl was ready to leave, the elves stuffed her pockets full of gold and led her back out of the mountain. When she came home, she wanted to start her work, picked up the broom that was still standing in the corner, and started to sweep.

As she swept, people who were strangers to her came out of the house and asked her who she was and what she was doing there. It turned out she had spent not three days but seven years with the little folk in the mountain, and her previous employers had died in that time.

The elves once stole a child right out of its cradle and left in its place a changeling with a big head and glassy eyes that would do nothing but eat and drink. In her distress, the mother went to her neighbor for advice. The neighbor told her to carry the changeling into the kitchen, set him on the hearth, make a fire, and boil water in two eggshells. That would make the changeling laugh, and when he laughed, that would be the end of him. The woman did everything as her neighbor had said. When she put the eggshells full of water on the fire to boil, the blockhead said:

> *"I'm as old*
> *As the Westerwold,*
> *But I've never seen anyone cook in eggshells."*

And then he started to laugh. As he laughed, a crowd of elves came, brought the right child in, set it on the hearth, and took the changeling away with them.

Source: Grimm KHM #39, 1857. The Grimms put three stories about elves together as number 39 of the KHM. The first, widely known as "The Shoemaker and the Elves," is in the "Zaubermärchen" section of this book. The second and third, given here, are legends. The third story was one of the sources for Maurice Sendak's *Outside Over There*.

The Haalghost ❧ Der Haalgeist

There is a ghost in Schwäbisch Hall who is called the Haalghost after the salt spring, or "Haal," where he can be heard splashing around. He is an old salt boiler, and he always appears three days before a flood. He comes up from the Kocher River with a lantern in his hand and walks into the lower town crying "Clear out! Clear out!" He stops and turns back at the highest point the flood will reach. Whenever he appears, people clear out their cellars and rooms on the ground floor to avoid flood damage. And he has been right every time about how high the water would come.

The Haalghost does no harm as long as he is left alone. But if people tease him, he appears as something dreadful—a huge black hound or a shaggy calf with fiery eyes, and folks who see

The Henkersbrücke at Schwäbisch Hall.

him become terrified and get sick. Once a night watchman tried to make a fool of the Haalghost, but the ghost saw what he was up to and threw him off the Executioner's Bridge (Henkersbrücke) into the Kocher, where he drowned.

(Baden-Württemberg) Source: Rölleke, *Das Große Deutsche Sagenbuch* #944

The Egg-layers ❧ Die Eierleger

There was farmer's wife from Jartheim who kept only a few hens but always brought a large number of eggs to the market at Crailsheim. Finally, her neighbor got suspicious that something funny was going on and asked the woman's hired man to keep an eye on her. He was happy to do that, because he had already noticed that the woman always baked two kinds of bread, half-white for herself and black for the rest of the people in the house.

The next time the woman went to the market, the hired man jimmied open the bread cupboard. He cut himself a big slice of the half-white loaf. The last bite had hardly gone down his throat when he started clucking like a hen. He ran to the henhouse, sat down on a nest, and started laying eggs. While he was sitting there, he heard the farmer calling for him, but he couldn't leave the nest, so he yelled for the farmer to come to the henhouse and told him the whole story. The farmer went straight to the kitchen and ate some of the half-white bread himself. He started clucking, too, ran to the henhouse, sat down next to the hired man, and they laid two big piles of eggs. Now they knew where the farmer's wife, who only ever ate half-white bread, got all those eggs. As the story got around, nobody at the market wanted to buy her eggs any more. The folks in Jartheim were nicknamed "egg-layers" and they're still called that today.

(Baden-Württemberg) Source: Rölleke, *Das große deutsche Sagenbuch* #945

The Buttermaiden in Zerbst ✺
Die Butterjungfer in Zerbst

In Zerbst, in front of the town hall, stands a tall wooden column, and on the column there's a statue of a girl with long, flowing hair. Her left hand lies on her breast, and in her right hand she carries a full purse. Her skirt is red. She represents freedom from tolls. In earlier days, she was replaced with a new version a number of times. Sometimes she held a rose, sometimes an apple. The city pays for the renewal. The wooden column was replaced roughly every forty years; but it had to be done in the summer, between twelve and one o'clock, and the new column had to be standing before the old one could be taken down.

The story goes that in earlier times the butter women wouldn't come to Zerbst to sell their wares. Instead, they set up on the so-called butterdam, about half an hour outside the town, because they couldn't pay the high tolls charged at the town gate. So the housewives of Zerbst had to go out of town to buy their butter. To save them the trouble, a rich young woman offered to buy freedom from tolls for the town. She achieved this by paving the road from the butterdam to the market place with talers.*

In the fourteenth century, the statue of the buttermaiden was erected in her honor by the grateful people of Zerbst. Many people say that on a fine summer night the buttermaiden goes for a walk with the statue of Roland, which also stands in the market square.

(Niedersachsen) Source: Petzoldt, *Deutsche Volkssagen* # 59

*A taler is a silver coin that was the official currency in German territories in the eighteenth century. The English word "dollar" is derived from "taler."

The Donkey with the Bagpipe
Der Esel als Dudelsackpfeifer

In the old cathedral in Hamburg, which was demolished long ago, there was a very odd gravestone. It had a donkey carved on it, and the remarkable thing about this donkey was that it stood on its hind legs and held a bagpipe in fore hooves and seemed to playing the instrument with vigor. The story of the donkey goes like this.

Around the time of the Thirty Years War, a rich Hamburg merchant boasted that he would never be poor: it was more likely that a donkey could play the bagpipes than that the merchant could lose his money and possessions. But man proposes, and God disposes. All of a sudden he became a very poor man, and he died in dire want. So when they buried him, his acquaintances put the piping donkey on his gravestone.

Other people claim to know better. They say that the stone marks the grave of Gesche van Holten, who was once the richest woman in Hamburg. When a poor relation came to her one day to ask for help, she turned him down flat. He reminded her that fortune is fickle, but she answered, "A donkey could learn to play the bagpipes sooner than I could become poor!"

Later she was reduced to such poverty that she would creep into her former garden and eat the bread that was thrown to the hens in the chicken coop. One day as she was stealing down the alley from the garden after such a sad meal, she encountered an itinerant jester who had a dancing, bagpipe-playing donkey as his companion. She remembered the insolent words she had spoken when she was rich and was frightened to her very soul. Soon afterward, she died. Her family had the donkey carved on her gravestone as a warning to those who luxuriate in their good fortune.

(Hamburg) Source: Petzoldt, *Historische Sagen* #23

The Tailor and the Flood ❧ Der Schneider und die Sündflut

When God commanded Noah to build a big ship and bring on board a pair of every kind of animal, he also ordered that one master of every craft should be taken into the ship, except for tailors. Tailors were a wicked species from the beginning and were supposed to be exterminated.

Noah was very careful, but somehow a tailor snuck onto the ship and hid himself so well that no one knew he was there. As the rains came down and the waters rose, the tailor became bored. He hated staying so still and not being able to play tricks on people to plague them.

Finally he caught a pair of fleas and made sharp little stings for them out of his needles. He also gave the bees and the hornets their stings, which they've kept ever since. And soon there was a great hullabaloo in Noah's ark. The fleas stung Mother Noah, and the bees and hornets tormented the rest of the people and all the animals. No one knew who had given these little creatures their needles, but the suspicion soon arose that there must be a tailor in the ark.

The whole ship was searched, and sure enough, they found the tailor, and they threw him overboard without a thought for mercy. The tailor would have drowned, and we would be without tailors today, forced to make our own clothes, if there hadn't been a water spider close by. The tailor quickly climbed on her back and rode around until the great flood had drained away and the earth was dry again.

(Schwaben) Source: Meier #34

The Origin of the Pretzel / Brezel

Bakers are very strong because they knead dough so much. Once a young journeyman baker got into an argument in a tavern. In the heat of the argument he hit the other man—just a slap, really, but the man fell down dead. The baker was taken off to prison. He sat and wept. He was exceptionally strong, even for a baker, and he knew he could bend the bars over the window and escape, but he was an honest young man and believed justice must be done, even though he hadn't meant to kill the man. Still, he didn't want to die, so he sat and wept.

When the local magistrate came to have a word with him, he saw how young and well intentioned the baker was and concluded that the death was an accident rather than murder. So he offered the young baker a chance: if he could bend an iron bar, in one movement, so that the sun would shine through the resulting figure in three places at once, then he could go free. The baker thought for a moment, took hold of the ends of the bar, and slowly bent them up and around and in so that they crossed each other. When he got back to his bakery, he made the same shape out of dough, a hundred times, and when they were baked, he gave them away to celebrate his freedom. Bakers have been making *brezel,* or pretzels, ever since. But why are they called *brezel*? Because they look like crossed arms.

Source: Told by Artur Bohnet. The German word *brezel* dates back to the twelfth century and has the Latin *brachia* ("arms") as its root, through the Italian diminutive *bracciatello* (Kluge).

Pumpernickel

The black bread made of coarsely ground rye that is common in Westfalia is called pumpernickel. Some people say that a traveling Frenchman who was served the bread didn't like it and fed it to his horse with the words: "Bon pour Nickel," which means good for Nickel, Nickel being his horse. Other people say that Nickel wasn't a horse but a servant, for whom the Frenchman thought the dark, sour bread would be good enough. Still others say it got its name from the baker Nickel Pumper, who first baked it in Osnabrück in the sixteenth century.

(Westfalen) Source: Petzoldt, *Historische Sagen* #50. According to Kluge, there's a ruder etymology. Before the word was transferred to the bread, it was used as a term of derision: a boor or loutish fellow might be called a pumpernickel. Nickel is a short form of Nikolaus, and pumper a dialect word for fart, breaking wind (Kluge).

The Pear Tree in the Churchyard in Ribbeck ❧ Der Birnbaum auf dem Kirchhofe zu Ribbeck

An enormous wild pear tree stands in the churchyard in Ribbeck, on the southeast side of the church. The people in the Mark call this kind of pear tree a dumpling tree. It grew out of a grave, and this is the story that's told about it.

The old squire of Ribbeck who lies in that grave liked children and always had a treat for them in his pocket. He particularly loved pears, and when the pears on his trees ripened, he gave them away to every child he met. Soon after he died, a little pear tree shoot grew up out of his grave. It quickly grew into a stately tree that was heavy with fruit every summer. People believe that when the old gentleman was buried, he must have had one of his beloved pears in his pocket, and one of the seeds of the pear must have sprouted and grown such amazing roots to make sure that none of the village children would lack for pears after the squire's death.

(Mark Brandenburg) Source: Petzoldt, *Historische Sagen*, #57

Closing Tale

The Narrow Bridge ❧ Die schmale Brücke

Once there was a shepherd who had a very big flock of sheep, and he wandered with them over hill and dale, far out into the world. One day he came to a deep river. There was a bridge across it, but the bridge was so very small and narrow that only one sheep could cross it at a time. And it was so rickety that the next sheep had to wait until the first one was all the way across, because the bridge might have broken under the weight of two sheep. You can imagine how long it would take before all of those many, many sheep could get across the river. So now we'll just have to be patient until all of the sheep and the shepherd are on the other side. That will probably take quite a while yet. And then I'll go on with the story of the shepherd and his very big flock of sheep.

Source: Meier #90

Recipes

German folk cooking is plain cooking. The common ingredients are those that are locally grown and easily preserved or kept over winter—potatoes, onions, cabbage, heavily smoked bacon, lard, butter, apples, fresh herbs in season, and not much by way of spices beyond salt and pepper. The bacon is often a seasoning rather than meat content. The most popular vegetable is the potato, and cabbage in its many varieties comes a close second. Sauerkraut was made to preserve cabbage through the winter, and the same simple pickling process, which requires no sterilizing or sealing, was also used for cucumbers, beans, kohlrabi, celeriac, and mushrooms. Sausages and rye bread were and are staples of the country kitchen, although I've included no recipes for them here: bread making takes experience and a feel for the local flour, and a variety of sausages is available in German butcher shops or delicatessens in most North American cities.

Traditional recipes are by their nature inexact. They are learned by experience, not from books; when they are written down, either by hand or in older cookbooks, they give directions that call on experience, such as "add enough flour to make a medium-thick dough," "add some salt," or "bake at low heat." So the following recipes come with a warning: it may take some trial-and-error to get them right.

Dumplings (Knödel or Klöße)

The German dumpling has many, many variations, all of them pretty much guaranteed to stick to your ribs. They are served with roasts, sauerkraut, gravies, or other sauces. You can buy dumpling mixes at German grocery stores, but it's worth trying them from scratch at least once. Dumplings must be round, smooth, and evenly shaped. They are cooked in a wide, flat pot so that they have plenty of room. Bring salted water to a rolling boil, carefully put in the dumplings, and then turn the heat down to simmer. When the dumplings rise to the surface and begin to roll, they are done. Take them out with a slotted spoon and drain well. Leftover dumplings make great breakfast food—sliced thick and fried in a little butter. The following recipes are traditional. Rombauer and Becker's *The Joy of Cooking* has two potato dumpling recipes that North American cooks of today may prefer.

Potato Dumplings (Cooked Potatoes)

- 2 1/4 lb. starchy potatoes (large white or baking potatoes)
- 4 oz. potato flour (available in health food stores or specialty food shops)
- 1 cup milk
- 1 tablespoon salt
- 1/8 teaspoon nutmeg

Boil the potatoes in their skins until they are tender (about 1 hour); peel when cool, grate. Mix in potato flour, salt, and nutmeg. Bring milk to a boil and pour over the potato mixture. Knead well. With floured hands make 10 to 12 round dumplings the size of a small fist (2 1/2 to 3 inches in diameter). Cook uncovered in a large pot of boiling salted water for approximately 10 minutes, then remove with a slotted spoon and serve hot. Serve with roasts, meat cooked with gravy, or stewed fruit.

Potato Dumplings (Raw and Cooked Potatoes)

- 1 1/2 lb. starchy white potatoes, boiled with skins on 1 lb. large red potatoes, raw
- 1 large egg
- 1/2 cup flour
- 1 teaspoon salt

The day before making the dumplings, boil the potatoes in their skins, peel them while they are still warm, mash them or press them through a potato ricer, and refrigerate over night. Then press them through a fine sieve. Peel the raw red potatoes, grate them finely, gather them in a tea towel, and press out the water so the mass is as dry as possible. Add them to the cooked potatoes, and knead in the egg, flour, and salt. With floured hands make round dumplings the size of a small fist. Place them in boiling salted water and cook uncovered at just above a simmer for 20 minutes. Remove with slotted spoon and serve hot.

Thüringer Dumplings

- 3 lb. peeled, raw starchy potatoes
- 1 cup milk
- 1 teaspoon salt
- 4 tablespoons butter
- 3/4 cup plus 1 tablespoon semolina flour
- 1 thick slice of stale white bread cut into cubes and browned with a little butter in a frying pan to make croutons

Grate the raw potatoes into a bowl filled with water. Drain and press in a cloth to squeeze out as much liquid as possible. In a small pot bring the milk, salt, and butter to a boil. Add the semolina all at once, stir until it forms a lump, and cook for 1 more minute. Add the semolina mixture to the grated potatoes and mix in thoroughly. With floured hands, make dumplings the size of a small fist. Before rounding them, press several croutons into the middle of each dumpling. Place them in boiling salted water and cook uncovered for 12–15 minutes. Remove with a slotted spoon and serve hot.

Bavarian Plum Dumplings (Bayerische Zwetschenknödel)

- 2 1/4 lb. cooked, grated, starchy potatoes
- 2/3 cup flour
- 1/3 cup plus 1 tablespoon semolina flour
- 2 eggs
- 16–20 pitted fresh prune plums
- 1/2 cup toasted breadcrumbs
- 2 tablespoons butter
- Sugar and cinnamon

Fry the breadcrumbs in the butter. Mix the grated potato, flour, semolina, and egg and knead to make a fairly firm, smooth dough. Mold the dough into a sausage shape and cut it into pieces large enough to encase a plum. With floured hands, form the dough around the plum into a round dumpling. Cook the dumplings uncovered in a large kettle of salted water for 5 to 10 minutes. Remove with a slotted spoon. Drain them well and roll them in the breadcrumbs. Serve with sugar and cinnamon, or with a plum sauce.

Liver Dumpling Soup (Leberknödel Suppe)

- 8 stale bread rolls, cut into slices
- 1 teaspoon salt
- 1 cup lukewarm milk
- 1/2 lb. (250 g) pork or beef liver, cut into cubes
- 1 small onion
- 1/2 clove garlic
- 1 sprig parsley
- 2 eggs, beaten
- 1 tablespoon finely chopped fresh marjoram
- 4 cups (1 liter) strong beef stock

Place the bread roll slices and salt in the milk and soak for 5 minutes. Squeeze out all the liquid and mix together the bread rolls, liver, onion, garlic, and parsley. Put this mixture through a meat grinder or food processor. Add the eggs and marjoram and, using floured hands, make small dumplings. Heat the beef stock, place the dumplings into it and simmer uncovered for approximately 20 minutes. Season to taste and serve hot.

Spaetzle (Spätzle, which means "little sparrows")

Spätzle, or Swabian noodles, are almost dumplings and almost pasta. They are served with meat dishes that have gravy, with sauerkraut, or in soup. The recipes vary primarily in the stiffness of the dough, from soft enough to drop small amounts from a spoon to stiff enough that you can roll it out and cut it into small strips. One of my aunts-by-marriage is said to make the best spätzle in Schwaben, and this recipe approximates hers. You can leave out the nutmeg, but I think it makes all the difference. You can buy a spätzle maker, like a coarse grater, in specialty kitchen shops.

- 2 1/2 cups flour
- 2 eggs, beaten
- 1/2 teaspoon salt
- (a little grated nutmeg)
- 1/2 cup water or milk

Put the flour in a bowl and make a depression in the middle. Beat the eggs with the salt and nutmeg and pour them into the hollow in the flour. Stirring outward from the center, mix the eggs into the flour, adding the water gradually and being careful that no lumps are forming. You should have a relatively soft dough. Beat it with a wooden spoon until it begins to form bubbles. In the meantime, bring a large pot of water to a rolling boil. Either push the dough through a spätzle maker into boiling salted water or spread the dough on a cutting board and quickly scrape small pieces of it into the boiling water with a big knife. Do not put too many spätzle in the pot at one time because they will stick. Cook them over medium heat for about 5 minutes, until they rise to the surface. Drain well and add some browned butter before serving. Leftover spätzle can be fried in butter until the edges are brown and crispy. As a child, I loved them with sugar sprinkled on them hot from the pan.

Pancakes

German egg pancakes are heavier than crepes, but they're not like North American pancakes, either. In the two pancake recipes below you can substitute milk for the water if you want a richer batter. Germans don't eat pancakes for breakfast, although my mother made them for us on desperately cold winter mornings in Canada to fortify us for the walk to school. They're served as dessert, especially if the main dish is soup. They're ideal for the North American brunch.

 ## Egg pancakes (Pfannkuchen)

- 4 large eggs
- 1/2 cup water
- 1/2 teaspoon salt
- 1 cup flour
- Butter for frying

Beat together eggs, water, and salt. Beat in the flour until the batter is smooth. Heat butter in a frying pan over high heat. Fry thin pancakes (6 to 7 inches across) over high heat on the first side, turn heat down to medium for the second side. Cook until lightly browned on both sides. The pancakes can be served individually with syrup or spread with jam and rolled up. They can also be piled into a stack, with a little lemon juice and sugar sprinkled on each pancake before the next one is put on top. Or spread each pancake with a little jam instead. The stack is cut like a cake and served in wedges.

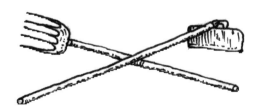

Cherry Pancakes (Kirschpfannkuchen)

- Pancake batter (recipe above) made a little thicker by using only 2/3 cup water
- 1 cup pitted sliced sweet cherries
- Butter for frying

Mix the cherries into the batter and make pancakes roughly 6 inches across, distributing the cherries fairly evenly. Fry over medium-high heat until browned on both sides. Stack the pancakes as they are cooked, sprinkling each pancake with sugar before the next one is put on top. Cut into wedges and serve warm.

Instead of cherries you can use thinly sliced pitted plums or thinly sliced apples. Although not traditionally German, maple syrup is delicious with apple pancakes, which are not as juicy as cherry or plum pancakes. Or serve the apple pancakes with cinnamon and sugar.

Potato Pancakes (Kartoffelpuffer)

These pancakes also appear in traditional Jewish cooking as latkes.

- 2 1/4 lb. starchy potatoes
- 1 teaspoon salt
- 1 small onion (optional)
- 2 eggs
- 3 tablespoons flour
- Vegetable oil or shortening for frying

Peel the potatoes, grate them, and mix them with the salt, onion, eggs, and flour. Heat the oil or shortening, make small pancakes of the potato mixture, and fry over high heat until browned and crisp on both sides. Serve with applesauce, sour cream, or stewed fruit as the main course.

The flour can be omitted if the potatoes are well drained in a sieve after they are grated. Mix the potato starch that settles out in the drained liquid back into the potato mixture.

Farmer's Breakfast (Hoppel-Poppel, oder Bauernfrühstück)

This egg-and-potato dish can, of course, be eaten for breakfast, but it is usually served with a salad or pickles as a light supper.

- 1 1/2 lb. (750 g) waxy potatoes
- 1/4 lb. side bacon diced
- 3 large eggs
- 3 tablespoon milk
- 6 oz. ham, diced
- 1/4 cup chopped chives or green onions

Cook the potatoes in their skins until they are just tender (40 minutes to an hour, depending on the size of the potatoes), peel while warm; allow to cool, cut into thick slices. Fry the bacon, add the potatoes, and brown them. Beat the eggs and milk together lightly and add the ham and chives. Pour the mixture over the potatoes and cook, stirring occasionally, until the eggs are set but not dry. Serve immediately.

Game: Hare (Rabbit), Venison, and Wild Boar

Hunting is a venerable and highly ritualized tradition in Germany. Game—from pigeons and ducks to wild boar and deer—is common on the family table and in restaurants. Hunters supply their grateful friends and family with this treat. The restaurant at the Bach Haus in Eisenach is regularly supplied with game by the owner's brother. If you don't like the strong taste of wild meat, soak it overnight in milk or buttermilk.

Karlsbader Hare Stew (Hasen-Ragout)

This delicious dish came from Bohemia. Rabbit (a smaller, domesticated animal) may be used instead of hare.

- 2 lb. hare or rabbit meat removed from the bone and cut into cubes
- 4 tablespoons butter
- 1 large onion, chopped
- 2 cups beef stock
- 2 tablespoons tomato puree
- 2 bay leaves

- 8 juniper berries, crushed
- 1/2 teaspoon crushed caraway seeds
- 1/2 teaspoon dried thyme
- 2 tablespoons paprika
- Salt
- Freshly ground black pepper
- 1 cup sour cream

In a heavy lidded casserole, brown the meat in the butter. Add the onion and fry until it is soft and transparent. Add the stock, tomato puree, bay leaves, juniper berries, caraway seeds, thyme, paprika, salt, and pepper. Cover and simmer over low heat for 50 minutes. Add the cream, mix well, and gently simmer for a further 5 minutes. If necessary, adjust seasoning. This is traditionally served with potato dumplings, lettuce salad, and apple and cranberry compote.

Hasenpfeffer (Braised Hare in Red Wine)

The German name has to be kept for this dish: it is so distinctive and so much fun to say. Literally, it means "hare pepper." Hare is traditionally used in this recipe, but it is equally good with rabbit, which is usually easier to get; the quantities have been shown for both. The same recipe works well for venison.

- 3 cups red wine
- 1/4 cup red wine vinegar
- 1 onion, chopped
- Salt
- Freshly ground black pepper
- 4 whole cloves
- 6 juniper berries, crushed
- 6 bay leaves
- 1 baron (saddle and back legs) of hare or 2 barons of rabbit
- 1/2 cup flour
- 4 tablespoons butter

Make a marinade by combining the wine, vinegar, onion, salt, pepper, cloves, juniper berries, and bay leaves. Joint the meat by cutting off the back legs and cutting the saddle into two. Place the meat in the marinade and refrigerate for 24 hours. Remove the meat, dry it, and dust it with the flour.

In a heavy-bottomed saucepan, melt the butter and fry the meat until brown. Pour the marinade over the meat, cover the saucepan, and simmer covered over low heat for approximately 1 hour or until the meat is tender. Remove the meat from the saucepan and keep it warm. Strain the cooking juice and return it to the pan. Cook it uncovered until it reduces by approximately half. If the resulting sauce is not thick enough, it may be thickened with a little flour. Arrange the meat on a serving platter and pour the sauce over it. Serve with spätzle, potato dumplings, or mashed potatoes.

 ## Roasted Wild Boar

- 1 wild boar ham
- 1 tablespoon salt
- 1 tablespoon marjoram
- 3 tablespoons vegetable oil
- 1 cup red wine
- 5 juniper berries
- 2 bay leaves
- 1 medium-sized onion stuck with 6 whole cloves
- 1/4 teaspoon grated nutmeg
- 2 tablespoons blackberry jelly, or to taste

Bone and skin the ham, rub it with salt and marjoram, and brush it with oil. Chop the bones into pieces. Preheat oven to 450 degrees. Put the roast and bones in the oven and turn the heat down to 350 degrees. Pour a little of the red wine over it frequently. When juices begin to build up: in the pan, add the juniper berries, bay leaves, and onion. Total roasting time: approximately 90 minutes.

When the meat is cooked, drain off the juices and sieve them. Make a flour-and-butter roux to thicken the gravy, add red wine to taste, add nutmeg and blackberry jelly. Sprinkle the roast with grated cheese and breadcrumbs, and return to the oven at high heat for a few minutes until the cheese and crumbs are brown and crisp.

Serve with potato dumplings and red cabbage or with cranberries and applesauce.

Roast Venison

- 2–3 lb. venison (loin, round, shoulder, or rump roast)
- 1/4 lb. thinly sliced bacon
- 2 teaspoons salt
- 1/4–1/2 lb. butter
- 1 cup stock or water
- 1 cup sour cream
- 2 tablespoons flour

Rub the meat with salt, cover it with bacon slices, and put it in a roasting pan that has been rinsed with water but not dried. Preheat oven to 500 degrees. Melt butter and pour it over the roast. Put in the center of the hot oven and turn the heat down to 350 degrees. Baste frequently with pan juices. To prevent the juices from getting too dark, you may add 1/4 cup water if necessary. Roasting time: 45 minutes to 1 hour.

Drain the pan juices, stir in the flour, cook over low heat, stirring, for 5 minutes. Add the sour cream and correct seasoning. Serve with red cabbage, mashed potatoes, potato dumplings or spätzle, red currant jelly, or cranberries.

Goose Fat (Gänseschmalz)

Schmalz is rendered animal fat or lard, usually pork, used for frying and baking. The dripping from fat roasts or bacon is schmalz with flavor. Goose schmalz is a delicacy that you can buy in German delicatessens. If you are roasting a goose, render the fat from the stomach cavity in the following way: remove the fat from the goose before roasting; wash the fat in cold water, soak overnight in water or milk, dice it, and fry it over low heat in an open pan until the solid bits remaining after the fat has melted turn yellow. Sieve the fat and pour it into a small stone crock (or equivalent). You can add the dripping from the roast—there will be lots, and the stuffing will have flavored it. You can flavor the goose fat further by frying finely diced onion and apple in the fat over low heat until they are brown. The apple and onion bits may be strained out, but if the schmalz is to be used on bread, they add a pleasant texture. Goose schmalz is used in cooking, especially for sauerkraut and cabbage. It is also delicious spread on rye bread and lightly salted. Try a cheese sandwich made with rye bread and lightly salted schmalz instead of butter. Goose fat is runny at room temperature, so pork fat is sometimes added to solidify it if it is to be used as a spread.

Cabbage and Sauerkraut

Sauerkraut is a staple of German cooking. It is high in vitamin C and an easy way to preserve cabbage for the winter. The following recipe is Swabian and can be served with spätzle.

Cooked Sauerkraut

- 2 lb. sauerkraut
- 4 tablespoons schmalz (rendered pork or goose fat, or bacon drippings; see p. 257)
- 1 onion, sliced
- 4 tart apples, peeled and diced
- 1 tablespoon sugar
- 1/2 teaspoon crushed juniper berries
- 2 tablespoons flour
- 2 cups dry white wine
- 1/2 teaspoon salt
- Black pepper to taste

Fry the onions and apples in the schmalz until light brown. Add the juniper berries and sugar. Rinse and drain the sauerkraut well and add to the apples and onions with a little water, cover tightly, and simmer over low heat for 1 hour. Sprinkle the flour over the sauerkraut, mix well, add the wine, salt, and pepper, and simmer for another half hour.

Sauerkraut Salad

- 1 1/2 lb. raw sauerkraut
- 3 apples
- A pinch of salt
- A pinch of sugar
- 1 cup sour cream or 1/2 cup oil
- 1 tablespoon grated horseradish or 1 tablespoon chopped parsley

Rinse the sauerkraut with hot water, drain well, and chop finely. Core and grate the apples. Mix the apples, sauerkraut, and all remaining ingredients.

Red Cabbage (Rotkohl)

- 2 lb. red cabbage
- 4 tablespoons butter or lard or bacon dripping, goose schmalz preferred
- 1 large onion, chopped
- 1 bay leaf
- 2 whole cloves
- 1 teaspoon salt or to taste
- 3 tablespoons vinegar
- 1 cup water
- 3–4 tart apples, cored and diced
- 1 teaspoon sugar or to taste
- 1 tablespoon potato flour or 1 teaspoon cornstarch

Remove the large outer leaves of the cabbage, quarter and core it, wash it, and cut into fine shreds. Fry the onion in the butter or dripping until it just begins to brown. Add the cabbage and cook, stirring, for 3 minutes. Add the bay leaf, cloves, salt, vinegar, water, and apples. Cover and simmer over low heat for 2 hours. Remove pot from heat. Mix sugar with potato flour or cornstarch, stir with a little cold water, mix into the cabbage, cook 2 or 3 minutes longer, stirring. The cabbage should looked glazed, but there should be no sauce. Especially good with roast goose or roast pork.

Red Cabbage and Apples (Rotkohl II)

A lighter, crunchier version.

- 3 tablespoons butter
- 1 to 1 1/2 lb. red cabbage, shredded
- Juice of 1 lemon
- 2 apples, peeled and diced
- 2 tablespoons red currant jelly
- 2 cloves
- 2 tablespoons beef stock

Remove the outer leaves of the cabbage, quarter and core it, wash it, and cut it into fine shreds. In a heavy-bottomed casserole, melt the butter. Add the cabbage and pour over the lemon juice (this will help to preserve the color). Add the apples, red currant jelly, cloves, and beef stock. Mix all the ingredients together and simmer, covered, for 10 to 20 minutes. The cabbage should not be overcooked.

Hunter's Cabbage or Bavarian Kraut (Jägerkohl)

- 2 lb. cabbage
- 1/4 lb. bacon, diced
- 1 medium onion, diced
- 1 cup white wine
- 1 teaspoon caraway seed
- Pepper, sugar, salt, to taste
- 2 tablespoons vinegar (or more, to taste)
- 2 tablespoons flour

Remove the damaged outer leaves of the cabbage, cut into quarters, remove the core, wash it, and cut into fine shreds. Fry the bacon and onion until they are browned, add the cabbage and caraway, and cook, stirring, for a few minutes. Add the wine, cover the pot, and simmer on low heat until the cabbage is cooked (traditionally for a good hour, but 10–20 minutes for a fresher, crunchier texture). Dust the flour over the cabbage, cook, stirring, for another 5 minutes. Add the vinegar and pepper, salt, and sugar to taste. Very good served with roasted game.

Other Favorites

Beans, Bacon, and Pears (Birnen, Bohnen und Speck)

This particular version of the dish comes from the north coast of Germany, Mecklenburg and Schleswig-Holstein. In Westfalia it's made without the cream. Instead, the pears are cooked with a little grated lemon rind and water, and the sugar, vinegar, and salt are added to the bacon fat with a teaspoon of lemon juice to make the sauce.

- 6 firm pears peeled and sliced. (If you are using soft pears such as Bartletts or Comices, choose ones that are not yet ripe.)
- 3/4 cup water
- 2 tablespoons sugar
- 2 tablespoons vinegar
- 1 lb. green beans cut into 1-inch lengths
- 3 large sprigs of summer savory (or 1/2 teaspoon dried)
- 6 thick slices bacon or heavy smoked speck, diced
- 1 tablespoon flour
- 1/4 cup heavy cream
- 1 teaspoon salt
- Black pepper to taste

In a covered saucepan simmer the pear slices in the vinegar, sugar, and water for 10 minutes. Lift out the pears with a slotted spoon and reserve the cooking liquid. Cook the beans with the summer savory for 7–10 minutes and drain. (If you cannot get fresh summer savory, add 1/2 teaspoon of the dried herb to the bacon fat with the flour or just leave it out.) Meanwhile, chop the bacon and fry until crisp. Remove it from the pan but leave the fat. Stir the flour into the bacon fat and cook over low heat, stirring, for 5 minutes. Remove from heat and gradually add the cooking liquid and the cream. Cook for another 10 minutes over low heat, stirring constantly.

Add the beans and salt to the pears and pour this sauce over them. Cook until the beans and pears are heated through. Just before serving, add the crisp pieces of bacon to the beans and pears. Serve with boiled potatoes alone or add smoked pork loin chops, or *Kasseler* in German.

Heaven and Earth (Himmel und Erde)

This is very much a peasant dish—real folk food. About the name: the apples are from the sky (German has only one word for both "sky" and "heaven"), and the potatoes and onions are from the earth.

- 1 1/2 lb. starchy potatoes, peeled
- 1 1/2 lb. tart apples
- 2 tablespoons sugar
- 1/3 lb. bacon, diced
- 1 onion, chopped
- Salt and pepper to taste

Boil the potatoes until they are cooked. Peel the apples, core and cut them into pieces, put them in pot with the sugar and a little bit of water, cover tightly, and cook over low heat until they are soft. Add pepper. Meanwhile, fry the bacon, and then brown the onions in the bacon fat. Mash the potatoes and apples separately, then mix them together, add salt to taste, and beat with a wooden spoon until light and fluffy. Distribute the bacon and fried onions in the bacon fat over the top of the combined mash. Serve as a main dish.

Eggs in Green Sauce (Eier in Grüner Soße)

A specialty of Frankfurt served in late spring when fresh green herbs are finally available after the winter.

- 1/2 cup sour cream
- 1/2 cup mayonnaise
- 1/2 cup yogurt
- 1 tablespoon dill
- 1 tablespoon parsley (other fresh green herbs may be used)
- 1/4 cup chives
- Juice of 1 lemon
- 1 egg, hard-boiled and finely chopped
- Salt and pepper to taste
- 1/2 teaspoon sugar
- 8 eggs, hard-boiled, cooled, peeled, and cut in half lengthwise
- Finely chopped dill for garnish

Combine sour cream, yogurt, and mayonnaise. Finely chop the herbs and add to the sauce. Add lemon juice, chopped egg, salt, pepper, and sugar. Arrange the egg halves on lettuce leaves on a serving plate. Pour the sauce over them, and garnish with more dill. Serve immediately. The sauce may be made ahead of time and kept chilled, but the eggs have better texture and flavor at room temperature.

Boiled Potatoes with Cottage Cheese (Pellkartofflen mit Quark)

Triggered by the season like the eggs in green sauce, and even simpler than heaven and earth, this is a midsummer meal when the first little new potatoes can be dug in the garden.

- 2 lb. new potatoes
- 1/2 cup finely chopped chives
- 1/4 cup finely chopped parsley
- 2 cups cottage cheese

Boil (or even better, steam) new potatoes. Mix the chives and parsley into the cottage cheese. Eat them together, with a little salt on the potatoes if you like. Pickled herring goes well with this dish.

Herring Salad (Heringsalat)

There are many variations on herring salad. This recipe was brought into my mother's family by her mother's mother, for whom I am named. That Anna was born to a German-speaking family in Posen, then one of Germany's eastern territories, which was returned to Poland after the First World War. This dish was only made for supper on Christmas Eve, and the family speculation is that this tradition comes from the Catholic culture in which Great-Grandmother Anna grew up: it's the last meal within the Advent fast, and therefore meatless. The rest of my mother's family, on both sides, was Lutheran for many generations back, and that's probably why the meat crept in. The quantities of the thirteen ingredients have never been written down, and when as many hands as possible are gathered together on the evening of December 23 to make light the work of all the chopping and dicing, there's always doubt and guesswork about amount and number. Happily, the approximation mostly works out. Part of the tradition is that my mother always thinks we've made too much—"a bathtub full!"—and that this year it's a failure—"No one will eat it, and we'll have to throw most of it out!" But on the morning of the twenty-fourth, after another stir, it tastes just as it should, and family and friends who wouldn't touch it otherwise eat it because it's part of Christmas. I've done my best to give quantities and amounts here. The taste can always be corrected by adding a bit more of this or that—apple to make it sweeter, beets and potatoes to make it milder, more herring if it's not strong enough, more vinegar or pickle juice if it needs more zest. (Rombauer and Becker's The Joy of Cooking *has a herring salad recipe that's a not-too-distant relation of this one. You might want to try it as well, or instead.)*

- 3 matjes herring (or 2 small jars of pickled herring)
- 1 small onion
- 2 large cooked beets (or the equivalent canned or pickled)
- 4 hard-boiled eggs
- 3 tart apples
- 3 large waxy potatoes boiled in their skins
- (1/2 lb. of boiled beef shank, or dark meat from chicken or turkey, optional)
- 4 large dill pickles
- 1/2 cup vegetable oil
- 1/4 cup vinegar or 1/2 cup of the pickle juice
- Large pinch of sugar
- 1 teaspoon of salt (you can always add more)
- Generous grinding of black pepper

If you're using matjes herring, soak them for 12–24 hours in water, rinse them thoroughly, skin them, take out the bones, and cut them into very small pieces. Peel and chop the onion very finely. Peel and dice (1/4-inch cubes) the beets, eggs, and potatoes. Peel, core, and dice the apples. Dice the meat (optional) and pickles. Mix the oil, vinegar, sugar, salt, and pepper and pour over the other ingredients. Mix well, cover, and chill overnight. Stir again before correcting the seasonings. Kept refrigerated, the salad will last 3 or 4 days. It makes a refreshing change from Christmas baking and turkey.

Fairy-tale Mushrooms (Fliegenpilze)

The Fliegenpilz ("fly mushroom," a toadstool called "fly agaric" in English) has a slender white stem and a red cap with white spots. This pretty fungus is often included in illustrations of fairy tales. It is the subject of a widely known children's riddle song. Miniature replicas of it are made as decorations, and giant ones as garden ornaments. I recently saw some of the latter labeled as "fairy-tale mushrooms." The Fliegenpilz is hallucinogenic and poisonous. It combines a charming appearance with a deadly effect, and it grows in the wild, dark forest: these are certainly fairy-tale qualities. In my family, the edible Fliegenpilze described in the following recipe were made for parties.

- 6 round tomatoes
- 6 hardboiled eggs

Shell the eggs and stand them on end on lettuce leaves. Cut off the stem end of the tomatoes, hollow them out by removing the seeds and pulp, and cap the eggs with them. Make white dots on the tomatoes with mayonnaise, butter, or bits of cooked egg white.

Red Fruit Pudding (Rote Grütze)

Variations on this thick fruit soup or soft pudding appear all over Germany. Most restaurants, plain or fancy, have it on their dessert menu, and at home it makes its appearance in midsummer when the fruits in the garden ripen. Raspberries and red currants are the usual base, and sweet or sour cherries, strawberries, or black currants may be added according to taste and availability. The basic recipe calls for fruit juice: the fruit is cooked with a little water until it is soft. Then the fruit and cooking liquid are passed through a sieve. The skins and seeds left in the sieve are discarded, and enough water is added to the fruit juice to make 4 cups. For example, to get 4 cups of juice, cook 1 pound of red currants, a half pound of raspberries, and a half pound of strawberries until soft and put them through a sieve. Add enough water to make 4 cups of juice. Experiment with different combinations of fruit until you find your favorite.

Fresh crushed raspberries, black currants, or pitted cherries stirred into the pudding right after it is cooked, while it is still hot, intensify flavor and add texture. If you are using bottled juice, the best combination is 1 cup each of red currant, raspberry, and cherry juice, and 1 cup water. Instead of the tapioca, you can use 2/3 cup semolina.

- 4 cups fruit juice
- Sugar to taste (start with 1/3 cup and add in small increments)
- 1/8 teaspoon salt
- 5 to 6 tablespoons minute tapioca
- 1 cup crushed fresh berries or cherries (optional)
- Heavy cream or vanilla custard sauce

Bring the juice to a boil. Sweeten with sugar. Add the salt. Stir in the tapioca. Cook the mixture over hot water or on very low heat for about 20 minutes. Stir in the fresh fruit (optional). Chill and serve with cream or vanilla custard sauce.

Apples in Nightgowns (Äpfel in Schlafrock)

- 4 medium-sized apples
- Jam
- Almonds
- 1 recipe of short crust (see below)
- 2 egg yolks

Peel and core the apples, then fill the hole with jam and almonds. Roll out the short crust and cut into 4 approximately 8-inch squares. Flour each apple lightly, put it on a square of dough, bring the four corners together at the top of the apple, brush the edges with egg yolk, and pinch them shut tightly. Brush the "nightgown" with egg yolk, and press an almond on top where the four corners meet as a fastener to keep the nightgown from slipping down as it bakes. Bake at 350 degrees until the crust is golden brown.

Short Crust

- 2 cups flour
- 2/3 cup sugar
- 1/2 cup plus 1 tablespoon cold butter
- Grated zest of 1/2 a lemon
- 1 egg, lightly beaten

Mix the flour and sugar. Cut in the butter into small pieces and cut it into the flour mixture with a pastry cutter or rub it in with your fingertips until the mixture has the texture of cornmeal. Stir the lemon zest in lightly with a fork. Push the mixture into a heap, make a hollow in the middle, and pour the beaten egg into it. Stir the egg in lightly with a fork, and with your hands quickly work the mixture into a smooth dough, handling it as little as possible. Refrigerate at least a half hour before using.

Old German Pot Cake (Altdeutscher Napfkuchen)

There is Napfkuchen, and there is Altdeutscher (Old German) Napfkuchen. This one goes back a long, long way.

- 11 tablespoons (3/4 cup minus 1 tablespoon) butter at room temperature
- 1 1/2 cup sugar
- 8 large egg yolks
- 4 cups flour
- 3 teaspoon baking powder
- Grated zest of 1 lemon
- 8 large egg whites
- 14 oz. dried currants

Cream the butter with the sugar until it is very fluffy. Beat in the egg yolks one at a time, thoroughly. Mix the baking powder with the flour and beat into the egg mixture a little at a time. Stir in the lemon zest. In a separate bowl, beat the egg whites with a pinch of salt until they are stiff but not dry. Fold them carefully into the dough. Lightly fold in the currants. Transfer the dough carefully (you're trying not to lose the air from the egg whites) into a buttered fluted tube pan. Bake for 60–90 minutes in a preheated 350-degree oven. The cake is done when a toothpick inserted into the middle comes out clean.

Filled Honey Cake (Gefülter Honigkuchen)

This is one of the cakes traditionally baked at Christmas time, and it improves with age. There are two ingredients in it that are not normally found in North American grocery stores: the baker's salt or hartshorn salt (Hirschhornsalz), which is carbonate of ammonia, and the potash (Pottasche), which is potassium carbonate. If you have a local German grocery store or specialty cooking store, you should be able to find them there; you might also try Internet resources. This is a recipe from my mother's family that she has translated into "Canadian" after a good deal of experimentation. She suggests baking the two layers of the cake separately and then filling them afterward, although the recipe calls for baking the cake complete with filling.

Dough

- 1 1/2 cups liquid honey or syrup
- 1/2 cup fat: lard, butter, or margarine
- 7 cups flour
- 1 cup plus 2 tablespoons sugar
- 2 teaspoons cinnamon
- 1 teaspoon ground cloves
- 2 teaspoons baker's salt
- 2 teaspoons potash
- 8 tablespoons water
- 1 tablespoon rum or 1 teaspoon rum flavoring
- 1 lightly beaten egg

Heat the honey and fat over low heat until the fat is melted. Cool to lukewarm before adding to the other ingredients. Dissolve the potash in the 8 table-spoons of water. Mix the dry ingredients in a big bowl. (The baker's salt tends to become lumpy even in dry places. Grind it back to powder before measur-ing and using.) Add the potash, the egg, and the rum. Mix them in a little and then pour the honey-fat mixture over everything. Mix it in as much as possible and then start kneading with both hands. Knead until you have a smooth dough—it takes a long time, half an hour or more. If the dough stays very stiff and so dry that it cracks, carefully add a little more water by sprinkling it on the dough as you turn it. The dough should be pliable. Split the dough into equal parts and let it rest for an hour. Roll out half the dough to approximately 1/4 inch thickness; it should cover a 12 x 18–inch cookie sheet or the equivalent area. Roll up the dough loosely and transfer it to the cookie sheet. Cut off any dough that hangs over the edge and save it. Spread the filling (see below) evenly over the dough on the cookie sheet, reserving 2–3 tablespoons. Roll out the second half of the dough and cover the first half with filling with the second half. Cut off any dough hanging over the edge and save. Pinch the edges of the two layers together firmly to seal them so that the filling won't ooze out. Make a small extra cake with the saved scraps and reserved filling; you can use it for a taste test and it prevents waste. Bake the cake in a preheated oven at 275 de-grees for 1 to 1 1/2 hours. Cut to desired size while still warm (squares or smaller cakes to fit into cake tins). Let cool and cover with icing (see recipe that follows). The cake will keep for weeks in a tightly sealed tin.

Filling

- 2 2/3 cups thick strawberry jam or marmalade
- 1/2 cup ground almonds, toasted
- 1 cup candied citrus peel cut into very small pieces

Mix together all ingredients.

Icing

- 2 whole eggs
- 1/2 cup melted butter
- 1 cup cocoa powder
- 4 cups icing sugar
- Instant coffee, rum, or liquid coffee or evaporated milk

Beat the ingredients together. The rum, coffee, or evaporated milk must be added in small amounts until the mixture is spreadable but not runny.

Warm Beer (Warmbier)

Beer is taken seriously in Germany, and it is very good. It seems appropriate to end a collection of recipes with a festive drink.

- 2 cups milk
- 2–4 beaten egg yolks
- 1/8 teaspoon cinnamon
- 6–7 tablespoons sugar
- 2 cups dark beer

Bring the milk to a boil. Add it little by little to the egg yolks, stirring constantly. Heat the beer with the cinnamon and sugar. Add it to the milk, beating vigorously with a whisk. Serve hot and foamy.

Sayings

There are many books full of German folk sayings and proverbs. The ones here were in common use in my family, and my mother painted some of them on the kitchen walls as decorative guides to daily living. To this day, I think of the first one every time I thread a needle and of the second every time I pin up a hem with a safety pin.

Langes Fädchen, faules Mädchen.
Long thread, lazy girl.
(If you thread a needle with a long length of thread to save yourself the trouble of rethreading it frequently, the thread is likely to tangle and knot.)

Wer sein Kleid am Leibe flickt,
Hat den Ganzen Tag kein Glück.
If you mend your clothes while you have them on,
Your luck for the whole day is gone.

Ein Mädchen ohne Schürze ist wie ein Katze ohne Schwanz.
A girl without an apron is like a cat without a tail.
(One of my grandmother's sayings.)

Wer sich nicht zu helfen weiss ist gar nicht wert daß er in Verlegenheit kommt.
If you don't know how to help yourself, you're not worth the bother of getting into trouble in the first place.

Morgen, morgen, nur nicht heute
sagen all faulen Leute.
Tomorrow, tomorrow, just not today
That's what lazy people say.

Reden ist silber, Schweigen ist gold.
Speaking is silver, silence is gold.

Wenn einer nicht will können zwei nicht streiten
If one doesn't want to, two can't quarrel.

Wo man singt da laß dich ruhig nieder;
Böse Menschen haben keine Lieder.
Where people sing you'll be safe and sound;
Bad people have no songs, I've found.

Man soll dem Oxen der da drischt nicht das Maul verbinden.
It's not fair to muzzle the ox that's threshing.

Man soll den Teufel nicht an die Wand malen.
Don't paint the Devil on the wall.
(Which means don't expect the worst, or don't looking for things to go wrong.)

Lieber ein Ende mit Schrecken als ein Schrecken ohne Ende.
Better an end with horror than a horror without end.

Wer einmal lügt, dem glaubt man nicht,
Und wenn er auch die Wahrheit spricht.
One lie, and folks will doubt your word,
Even when it's the truth they've heard.

Lügen haben kurze Beine.
Lies have short legs.

Wie der Herr, So's Gescherr.
You can judge a man by his tools.

Sag mir mit wem du umgehst, und ich sag dir wer du bist.
Tell me whom you spend your time with, and I'll tell you who you are.

Wie man in den Wald ruft, schallt es heraus.
What you shout into the forest is what will echo back to you.

Man sucht nie jemanden hinter einem Busch hinter dem man nicht schon selbst gesessen hat.
You never look for someone behind a bush that you haven't already sat behind yourself.

Kalter Kaffee macht schön.
Cold coffee makes you beautiful.
(Another of my grandmother's favorite sayings: an incentive to drink the rest of the coffee in your cup rather than throw it out and get a hot refill.)

Scherben bringen Glück.
Shards (broken glass or china) bring good luck.

Mit einem Tropfen Honig fängt man mehr Fliegen als mit einem ganzen Liter Galle.
You'll catch more flies with a drop of (sweet) honey than with a quart of (bitter) gall.

Wer den Pfennig nicht ehrt,
Ist des Thaler's nicht wert.
If you don't honor pennies, you're not worthy to have dollars.
(The opposite of penny wise, pound foolish, similar to "If you look after the pennies, the pounds will look after themselves.")

Lieber den Spatzen in der Hand als die Taube auf dem Dach.
Better a sparrow in the hand than a pigeon on the roof.

Hier fliegen einem die gebratenen Tauben nicht in den Mund.
Roasted pigeons won't fly into your mouth here.
(You have to work for what you get.)

Den Vogel, der am Morgen singt, den holt am Abend die Katz.
The bird that sings in the morning will be eaten by the cat in the evening.

Man soll den Tag nicht vor dem Abend loben.
Don't praise the day until evening comes.

Der Apfel fällt nicht weit vom Baum.
The apple doesn't fall far from the tree.

Ein Kuß ohne Schnurrbart ist wie ein Ei ohne Salz.
A kiss without a moustache is like an egg without salt.
(Another of my grandmother's favorite sayings.)

Eulen nach Athen bringen.
Bringing owls to Athens.
(The German equivalent of "coals to Newcastle." The owl was the bird of Athena and therefore a very common image in Athens, especially on the coinage: Athens didn't need more owls.)

Gott hüte uns vor Wetter und Wind,
Und vor Deutschen die im Ausland sind.
From weather and wind protect us dear God,
And from Germans who are traveling abroad.
(Often quoted by my father, who loved to travel!)

Pronunciations

-ch- is pronounced as in the Scottish *loch* and *ach* (-kh- is the closest substitute)

-sch- at the beginning of a word is always -sh- as in *show*

-g- is always hard as in *give*

-th- is always t as in *time*

-s- is always -z- as in *zoo* except at the end of a word, when it is -s- as in *set*

-v- is always -f-

-w- is always -v-

-z- is always -ts-

-a- is -ah- before a single consonant and -uh- (as in *up*) before a double consonant

-e- at the end of a word is always short as in *get*

-ei- is always -i- as in *slide*

-ie- is always -ee- as in *sleep*

-i- is always short as in *kid*

-u- is -oo- as in *goose,* or -uh- as in *put* when it is followed by two consonants

The umlaut ä is either -ay- as in *may* or e as in *get*

ö and ü have no English equivalents, but ö in some dialects becomes -ay- (as in *may*) or -e- (as in *let),* and ü becomes -ee- (as in *sheep*) or -i- (as in *it),* and those are the pronunciations I've given here.

Note that in German, all nouns are capitalized.

Aschenputtel: AH-shen-put-tel—the German Cinderella

Celle: TSELL-le (as in let)—a town in Germany where Till Eulenspiegel played some of his tricks (this -ts- for -c- is uncommon)

Else: ELL-ze—a common girl's name

Frau Holle: FROW (as in *cow*) HOL-le hol- (as in *hot*), -le (as in *get*)—a spirit with many stories about her

Graf: grahf—a nobleman, equivalent to the English count

Gräfin: GRAY-fin—a noblewoman, equivalent to the English countess

Hans im Glück: HUNSS-im-GLICK—Hans in Luck

Märchen: MAYR-khen—folktale

Sage: ZAH-ge (as in *get*)—legend

Sagen: ZAH-gen—legends

Schwaben: SHVAH-ben—Swabia, a region in southwestern Germany; also Swabians, the people of Swabia

Schwank: SHWUNK (as in *skunk*)—a funny story

Schwänke: SHVEN-ke (as in *get*)—funny stories

Taler: TAH-ler—a silver coin, standard currency

Tiergeschichten: TEER-ge-shich-ten—animal stories

Till Eulenspiegel: Till OY-len-shpee-gel—the most famous folk hero in Germany, Till Owlglass

Volksbuch: FOLLKS-bookh (-oo- as in *goose*)—folk book, popular literature of the sixteenth and seventeenth centuries

Volksbucher: FOLLKS-beekher—the plural of Volksbuch

Zaubermärchen: TSOW-ber-mayr-khen—fairy tale, folktale with magic in it

Zaunkönig: ZOWN (as in *clown*) -kay-nik—winter wren

List of Works Cited

Bechstein, Ludwig. *Sämtliche Märchen*. Darmstadt: Wissenschaftliche Buchgesellschaft, 1967.

"Bechstein, Ludwig." *The Oxford Companion to Fairytales*. Ed. Jack Zipes. Oxford: Oxford University Press, 2000.

Bolte, Johannes, and Georg Polívka. *Anmerkungen zu den Kinder- u. Hausmärchen der Brüder Grimm, neu bearb.* 2 unverän. Aufl. Hildesheim, Georg Olms, 1963.

Dégh, Linda. "Folk Narrative." *Folklore and Folklife: An Introduction*. Richard M. Dorson, ed. Chicago: University of Chicago Press, 1972. pp. 53–84.

Enzyklopädie des Märchens: Handwörterbuch zur historischen und vergleichenden Erzählforschung. Begründet von Kurt Ranke. Berlin: Walter de Guyter, 1975–.

Grimm, Jakob, and Wilhelm Grimm. *Deutsche Sagen*. Lutz Röhrich, Hg. München: Goldmann, 1998.

Grimm, Jakob, and Wilhelm Grimm. *Die ursprünglichen Märchen der Brüder Grimm: Handschriften, Urfassung und Texte zur Kulturgeschichte*. Kurt Derungs, Hg. Bern: Edition Amalia, 1999.

Grimm, Jakob, and Wilhelm Grimm. *The German Legends of the Brothers Grimm*. Edited and translated by Donald Ward. 2 vol. Philadelphia, PA: Institute for the Study of Human Issues, 1981.

Grimm, Jakob, and Wilhelm Grimm. *Grimms Märchen*. Ausgewählt und mit einem Kommentar versehen von Heinz Rölleke. Frankfurt a.M.: Suhrkamp, 1998.

Grimm, Jakob, and Wilhelm Grimm. *Grimms' Tales for Young and Old*. Translated by Ralph Manheim. Garden City: Anchor Press/Doubleday, 1983.

Grimm, Jakob, and Wilhelm Grimm. *Kinder- und Hausmärchen.* [1857 ed.] Düsseldorf: Artemis & Winkler, 1999.

Grimm, Jakob, and Wilhelm Grimm. *Kinder- und Hausmärchen gesammelt durch die Brüder Grimm: Vollständige Ausg. auf der Grundlage der dritten Aufl. (1837).* Hrsg. v. Heinz Rölleke. Frankfurt a.M.: Deutscher Klassiker Verlag, 1985.

Grimm, Jakob, and Wilhelm Grimm. *Kinder- und Hausmärchen: Nach der zweiten vermehrten und verbesserten Aufl. v. 1819, textkritisch revid. u. m. e. Biographie der Grimmschen Märchen versehen.* Hrsg. v. Heinz Rölleke. Köln: Eugen Diedrichs, 1982.

Humburg, Norbert. *Der Rattenfänger von Hameln: die berühmte Sagengestalt in Geschichte und Literatur, Malerei und Musik, auf der Bühne und im Film.* 2. überarb. Aufl. Hameln: Niemeyer, 1990.

Jahn, Ulrich. *Volksmärchen aus Pommern und Rügen.* Bd. 1 Leipzig: Norden, 1891.

Keller, Albrecht. *Die Schwaben in der Geschichte des Volkshumors.* Freiburg (Baden): J. Bielefelds, 1907.

Kluge, Friedrich. *Etymologisches Wörterbuch der deutschen Sprache.* Bearb. von Elmar Seebold. 23. erw. Aufl. Berlin: de Gruyter, 1999.

Kuhlmann, Wolfgang, and Lutz Röhrich. *Witz, Humor und Komik im Volksmärchen.* Regensburg: Erich Röth, 1993.

Lappenberg, J. M., ed. *Dr. Thomas Murners Ulenspiegel.* Leipzig: T. O. Weigel, 1854. [Facsim. ed. Leipzig: Zentralantiquariat der Deutschen Demokratischen Republic, 1975.]

Meier, Ernst. *Deutsche Volksmärchen aus Schwaben: Aus dem Munde des Volkes gesammelt.* Stuttgart: S. P. Scheitlin, 1852. [Facsim. ed. Hildesheim: Georg Olms, 1971.]

Neumann, Siegfried. "Traditional Storytelling Today in the East of Northern Germany." *Traditional Storytelling Today: An International Sourcebook.* Ed. Margaret Read MacDonald. Chicago: Fitzroy Dearborn, 1999. pp. 234–238.

Oppenheimer, Paul. *Till Eulenspiegel: His Adventures.* Translated with introduction and notes by Paul Oppenheimer. New York: Garland, 1991.

Petzoldt, Leander. *Deutsche Volkssagen.* München: C. H. Beck, 1970.

Petzoldt, Leander. *Historische Sagen.* München, C. H. Beck, 1976.

Rölleke, Heinz. *Das große deutsche Sagenbuch*. Düsseldorf: Artemis und Winkler, 1996.

Rölleke, Heinz. "Kinder- und Hausmärchen." *Enzyklopädie des Märchens*, Bd. 7. Berlin: Walter de Guyter, 1975–.

Rölleke, Heinz. *Die Märchen der Brüder Grimm*. München: Artemis, 1985.

Scherf, Walter. *Lexikon der Zaubermärchen*. Stuttgart: Alfred Kröner, 1982.

Uther, Hans-Jörg. *Märchen vor Grimm*. Hrsg. v. Hans-Jörg Uther. München: Eugen Diederichs, 1990.

Wartburg-Stiftung. *Welterbe Wartburg: Portrait einer Tausendjährigen*. Hrsg. von der Wartburg-Stiftung; Text Jutta Krauß, Fotographien Ulrich Kneise. Regensburg: Schnell und Steiner, 2000.

Welcker, Rudolph. *Erinnerungen*. Hrsg. v. Klaus Schöning. Lübeck: Klaus Schöning, 2000.

Wienker-Piepho, Sabine. "Märchen 2000: Taking Care of the Fairy Tale in Germany." *Traditional Storytelling Today: An International Sourcebook*. Ed. Margaret Read MacDonald. Chicago: Fitzroy Dearborn, 1999. pp. 239–246.

Zaunert, Paul. *Deutsche Märchen aus dem Donauland*. Düsseldorf: Eugen Diederichs, 1958.

Zipes, Jack, ed. *The Oxford Companion to Fairy Tales*. Oxford: Oxford University Press, 2000.

Index

About the Author

The author and Till Eulenspiegel.

ANNA E. ALTMANN was born in Lčhbeck, Germany, and emigrated to Canada with her family when she was five years old. She is the Director of the School of Library and Information Studies at the University of Alberta in Edmonton, Alberta. Her primary teaching area is literature for children and young adults, and her research focuses on contemporary reworkings of folktales. Her two previous books, *New Tales for Old: Folktales as Literary Fictions for Young Adults* (1999) and *Tales Then and Now: More Folktales as Literary Fictions for Young Adults* (2001), written with Gail de Vos and published by Libraries Unlimited, won Storytelling World awards.